ADHD and Teens

A Parent's Guide to
Making It through the Tough Years

Colleen Alexander-Roberts

TAYLOR TRADE PUBLISHING

Lanham • New York • Oxford

TAYLOR TRADE PUBLISHING
An Imprint of the Rowman & Littlefield Publishing Group
4501 Forbes Boulevard, Suite 200
Lanham, MD 20706
Distributed by National Book Network

Designed by Hespenheide Design

Note: This book is not intended to serve in the place of a physician. Always consult your child's pediatrician before altering childcare practices.

Library of Congress Cataloging-in-Publication Data
Alexander-Roberts, Colleen.
    ADHD and teens : a parent's guide to making it through the tough
years / by Colleen Alexander-Roberts.
      p. cm.
    Includes bibliographical references (p.   ) and index.
    ISBN 0-87833-899-3
    1. Attention-deficit disorder in adolescence—Public works.
  I. Title.
  RJ506.H9A575 1995   95-23078
  616.85'89'00835--dc20   CIP

Printed in the United States of America

CONTENTS

v   Foreword by Paul T. Elliott, MD

ix   Acknowledgements

xi   Introduction by Louis B. Cady, MD

1   ONE   Pay Attention: Hyperactivity Is Not Just for Youngsters

13   TWO   Medical Management of ADHD in Adolescents, by Paul T. Elliott, MD

29   THREE   ADHD in the Teen Years

39   FOUR   Your Teen's Evolving Identity

49   FIVE   Guiding Teens' Behavior

65   SIX   Positive Discipline

85   SEVEN   Developing Social Skills

91   EIGHT   Comorbidity: The Many Faces of ADHD

97   NINE   Family Dynamics

109   TEN   School and the Student

131   ELEVEN   ADHD and Substance Abuse

139   TWELVE   Sexuality and Dating

149   THIRTEEN   The Suicidal Teen

155   FOURTEEN   Oppositional Defiant Disorder and Conduct Disorder

169   FIFTEEN   Breaking the Cycle

179   Afterword

181   Recommended Reading

183   Bibliography

191   Index

FOREWORD

Individuals with attention deficit hyperactivity disorder often live lives filled with contradictions and struggles. For some, simple survival requires a supreme effort on a daily basis.

This book, the natural and essential sequel to Ms. Colleen Alexander-Roberts's *The ADHD Parenting Handbook*, is replete with insights, tools, and techniques for properly rearing and training teens as they develop, producing far more functional and productive adults who will greatly benefit themselves, their families, and our entire society.

ADHD may first become apparent in the teenage years, particularly in those who are less hyperactive. There are several reasons for this, but certainly the onset of puberty has an amplifying effect on the underlying brain function. For this reason, parents often believe that it has simply begun out of nowhere. Careful questioning and reviewing the past behavior and performance of the patient, however, usually produces evidence of its pre-existence. This is especially true in girls, since they have a tendency to exhibit less hyperactivity when they are affected by ADHD.

Ms. Alexander-Roberts also emphasizes that ADHD is a life-long condition. The previously held opinion that most patients outgrew ADHD has recently been proven incorrect. In fact, this would be like saying that a patient outgrows her brain. ADHD does, however, change in different stages of life—often dramatically. Ms. Alexander-Roberts has correctly identified ADHD as a biological disorder, as is generally supported by current research. She has also correctly affirmed the position that we should remove ADHD and its accompanying stigma from the realm of "psychiatric" or "mental" disorders, viewing it instead as a neurological condition with psychological manifestations.

In the case of younger children, ADHD can be frustrating to parents and others who live around the affected child. However, living with and raising an ADHD person who is undergoing the "teenage experience" is a monumental task at best. This is an extremely trying time for everyone involved and usually involves not only to immediate family members but also the extended family, as well as friends and the school, with ramifications in extracurricular activities and every other aspect of the ADHD individual's life.

Living with and parenting such a child requires well-educated, highly experienced, infinitely patient, and doggedly determined parents. Obviously, this is a rare combination for any parent. Furthermore, by the time parents finally feel well qualified, they have all the family's teenagers launched into adulthood. These highly qualified people are then left with no one to assist. Therefore the majority of society's best qualified and most highly experienced people are underemployed as the next generation of teens arrive on the scene to be greeted by the next generation of parental naiveté, inexperience, and inadequacy.

A child development specialist once said, "Each year society is invaded by another generation of barbarians who must be civilized." It seems that some ADHD teens are often inaccurately described as barbarians. Many parents, grandparents, teachers, and family friends will testify that the language often completely fails an adequate description of the behavior of the ADHD teen.

Momentarily setting aside humor, it is an increasing theory that many conditions, previously otherwise defined, may actually be a part of ADHD. Whether or not this is the case, they certainly occur more frequently with ADHD. As Ms. Alexander-Roberts points out, these are most often referred to as comorbidities. Comorbidities may include, among other things, sleep disturbance, learning disabilities, oppositional behavior, or oppositional defiant disorder, speech pathology, depression, obsessive-compulsive disorder (OCD), panic attacks, anxiety, bipolar disorder (manic-depressive disorder), and many other behavior disorders. Whether these may often exist as a part of ADHD as well as existing as separate conditions present with ADHD, as is now thought, remains to be determined through more extensive research. As Ms. Alexander-Roberts appropriately points out, these are frequently more manageable, or perhaps become nonexistent, with proper medication.

A concept inadequately considered is that many suicides by teens and young adults may, in fact, be partially contributed to by the impulsive nature of the teen with ADHD, including the patient's tendency to have a poor recollection of past experiences and a short-term, dim, and narrow view of the future. This concept has not been adequately addressed before this book. This deserves far greater attention and much more study than it has received in the past. As our social structure deteriorates, providing a less supportive, less structured environment for the teen with ADHD, we must seriously consider that inadequate medical management and supportive techniques may contribute to an increasing teen-suicide rate.

Unfortunately, many in our society will continue to label ADHD as simply an excuse for poor self-discipline and a desire on the patient's part to avoid taking responsibility for his own actions. This distressingly superficial disposal of the patient with ADHD does not improve any situation. It frequently serves only to increase the sense of anger, frustration, and despair that the teen and parents experience. However, it should be clearly understood that ADHD is not an "excuse" for anything.

Ms. Alexander-Roberts effectively points out that the successful learning of these behaviors is much less likely if the teen is not adequately medicated first. She emphasizes that it is rather futile to attempt cognitive therapy and other training methods without adequate initial medication control.

While the majority of inmates in the criminal justice system have ADHD, it does not cause criminal behavior. However, criminal behavior, like suicide, may be a consequence of the ADHD patient's tendency to live for the moment. In the teenage years, fraught with a genuine dearth of experience, these impulsive tendencies may not be restrained by family or community social mores. It has been said that poor judgment is untreatable. However, poor judgment can be replaced by better judgment derived from proper training and education of the teen in the development process, but this is very difficult without proper medication at the outset.

It should be also understood that ADHD patients do not always want to do the things that they find themselves engaging in. Their own struggling efforts are frequently met with inadequate results without proper treatment.

As Thom Hartmann pointed out in his book, *Attention Deficit Disorder: A Different Perception,* ADHD may be a completely normal condition. While this must be emphasized, it must also be acknowledged that it can produce very abnormal behavior and situations that are difficult to resolve. While it may appear that the majority of the ADHD patients' difficulties are those imposed by a social structure with certain expectations of behavior, the ADHD patients must continue to live and function in the society in which they find themselves, learning to manage those social constraints and restrictions.

In this book, Ms. Alexander-Roberts addresses the truly superior abilities the person with the ADHD brain possesses, pointing out such things as their ability to handle change, deal with intense situations, think creatively, as well as their increased sensory awareness and their sensitive feelings for others. This is a great benefit to all concerned, since the emphasis in years past has been almost completely on the negative aspects of the ADHD brain and its performance. Of course, these abilities need to be properly educated and trained.

It may not be amazing to learn that, with appropriate medical therapy, management in other spheres, such as education and parenting, are far more easily and effectively accomplished. However, as she also points out, the ADHD teen may have numerous complications that require intensive psychological assistance. She rightly emphasizes that this assistance is far more effective with a foundation of appropriate medical therapy from the beginning. If appropriate medical therapy is not first instituted, the consequence is poor results, with a great deal of time, money, and anguish unnecessarily spent.

For the first time since ADHD has reached the bookshelves of the lay reader, specific techniques of rearing teens has been comprehensively provided and illustrated with real-life examples. It is beneficial for parents, grandparents, aunts, uncles, and other family members, as well as teachers, and other professionals to employ not only as an interesting work but also as a tool for daily use. It should be read thoroughly and employed by all who have any interest in ADHD.

This, the second of Ms. Alexander-Roberts excellent guide books on ADHD parenting, is a logical and valuable addition to her first. We can only hope that she will continue the process of adding other works to this list. Merely reading the book is a great comfort and value to anyone dealing with ADHD teens, but it also serves the teen and adult as a reference work for continued use as the teen matures.

I heartily and enthusiastically recommend it to everyone's reading list.

Paul T. Elliott, MD

ACKNOWLEDGMENTS

It is with much gratitude that I express my appreciation to Paul T. Elliott, MD, for his belief in this project from day one and for the many contributions he made to the book. Thank you, Paul, for brainstorming with me long before my proposal was even written and following along with me as I wrote the manuscript. To Louis Cady, MD, and Mark Snyder, MD, I am extremely grateful for the time you spent reading and editing the manuscript, offering suggestions, and for the contributions you made, despite your own work schedules. The three of you are very special doctors, a credit to the medical profession, and I'm thankful to have had the opportunity to work with you on this book.

My gratitude is also extended to George Lynn, MA, CMHC, for generously sharing his brilliant insights on ADHD and his willingness to share his own writings with my readers. Thanks, George, for everything.

I gratefully acknowledge the assistance of Tony Hallett, a freelance writer and close friend, who helped me write the proposal for this book and provided the resource materials I needed for several chapters. Tony, you were a great inspiration and I thank you for everything you did for me. Howard Morris, and his mother, Sandra Morris, were both immensely helpful in providing insight into areas I was unfamiliar with. Howard, I thank you for all your words of encouragement and support over many months. It meant a great deal more than you realize!

I would also like to express my gratitude to the many members of CompuServe's ADD Forum who offered tips, suggestions, and ideas. In particular, Mark A. Stein, PhD, Dale Hammerschmidt, MD, Rob Gray, MD, Brenda Wilder, PhD, Stephen Katz, MD, Pamela Darr Wright, MSW, Thom Hartmann, Carla Nelson, Janie Bowman, Pam Jacobs, Bill Crews, John Schumate, Andrew Gil, PhD, Susan Jaffers, and, of course, Drs. Elliott, Cady, and Snyder.

Special thanks to Charles Davenport, MD, child psychiatrist at the Medical College of Ohio in Toledo, for loaning me his many reference books; Stella Francis, PhD, director of the Psychoeducational Development Center in Toledo, Ohio; Joan Kemper, information specialist for the National Information Center for Children and Youth with Disabilities; and Daphne Kent of CompuServ, Inc. Daphne, I cannot adequately express my gratitude for all the help you provided while I researched this topic.

Many thanks to my former editor, Lorena Jones, for the tremendous amount of help she gave me while writing my first three books, and to Macy Jaggers, my current editor at Taylor Publishing, who took over this book near its completion.

To my wonderful, bright, creative sons, Christopher and Blake, I want to say that I'm proud of you both and thankful to be your mom! Special thanks to Heidi Wymer, who provided pages of information on what it feels like to be a teenager with ADHD. Lastly, a special thanks to my mother and father for the help they provided and their love and support through the years.

Colleen Alexander-Roberts
May 1995

INTRODUCTION

Imagine you and your teenager standing on top of two leaking gasoline drums, fumes rising and each of you holding a cigarette lighter in your hands. Who is going to "flick their Bic" first?

This gigantic game of "chicken"—played out on emotional, physical, and sometimes legal grounds—is the natural consequence of untreated or poorly treated attention deficit hyperactivity disorder (ADHD) extending into adolescence. This incendiary situation does not have to exist.

ADHD is the best understood psychiatric diagnosis of childhood, having been studied for the better part of this century. It has had many names: "minimal brain damage," "minimal brain dysfunction," and "hyperkinetic syndrome of childhood" are a few. Unwary parents and teachers tend to label this condition more colloquially. They call children suffering from ADHD lazy, unmotivated, stupid, uncontrollable, wild, mean, and vicious—and that's just on a good day! A bestselling book on the subject of ADHD going undiagnosed until adulthood reveals the terrific emotional pain and acceptance of labels from which ADHD children suffer. The book's title, appropriately and tragically, is *You Mean I'm Not Lazy, Crazy or Stupid?*

However, there are two sides to this issue. This duality of reality reminds me of the story of the incompetent pilot who had gotten hopelessly lost in the air. He got on the intercom to tell his hapless passengers, "Ladies and gentlemen, I've got some good news and some bad news. The bad news is that we're hopelessly lost, I don't know where I'm going to land, and we'll all probably die in the plane crash. The good news is we're making darn good time!"

In ADHD, like life, we can sometimes get distracted by all the bad news. In 1995, however, there is abundant cause for celebration if you, your child, or a loved one has ADHD. Here are some of the reasons:

- At no time before in history have we known or understood so much about this condition; we didn't have PET scanners up until the last few years to understand the biological basis of this condition.
- At no time in history have we had such a wealth of scientific studies that show clearly, indisputably, and undeniably the beneficial effects of medication for this condition. We have also never before had the studies to clearly and consistently show what happens to ADHD children who are not treated with medications—and most of it is not good.
- At no time before in history have we had the success with psychotherapy, talk therapy, or counseling for children, teens, and their parents as we do now (given that a child is well controlled on medications). Studies have shown beyond a shadow of a doubt that counseling and talk therapy work far better when children can think and reason.
- At no time before in history have we been able to really understand why a child may appear "lazy, crazy, or stupid." We now know that ADHD is not a "moral defect" and is not caused because the child is trying to misbehave or deliberately enrage us.

- Finally, at no time previously have we had an explanation or theory about the adaptive quality of ADHD and how children with ADHD can think exceptionally creatively and come up with novel solutions to problems that will make them superstars in business and entrepreneurial pursuits. We have Thom Hartman and his hunter theory of ADHD to thank for that new insight. And that theory has just been published in the last few years.

This leads the well-informed and logical among us to the conclusion that ADHD is a biological problem. Biological problems (diabetes, hypertension, gall-stones, heart disease, and so forth) have biological solutions. Therefore, ADHD has a biological solution. In other words, it's a medical condition, just like diabetes. You treat medical conditions with a medicine. You wouldn't deny a child with juvenile onset diabetes his dose of insulin because "you ought to be able to get control of yourself, kid," would you? Therefore, the mistaken notion that the child's misbehavior is the result of his not trying hard enough—which, in turn, leads to blaming the child for a problem not of his own making—must be cast aside. That augurs well for the child because children will get enraged if they are blamed unjustifiably for things that they did not do or are beyond their control. No matter whose fault it is, if children are not controlled and cannot learn productively they will have disastrous lives—especially considering the increasing technological demands of today's society.

The book that you are holding is not a book about "medicating children"; rather, it is a book that takes you, step by step, through virtually every conceivable twist and turn of the roller-coaster ride of parenting a teenager with ADHD. It is assumed, and from my reading of her work Ms. Alexander-Roberts assumes, that as a given the child is on medication and well controlled on medication if he or she has a moderate to severe case of ADHD. Certainly not all children need to be on medication! For those children who have a mild case of ADHD, cognitive restructuring and other techniques can be quite helpful, and often medications do not need to be used. In fact, they should not be used. For those children who have moderate to severe ADHD, however, virtually every technique you will read about in this book (or any other book) will most likely fail if the child is not on an appropriate course of medication because the child will not be able to internalize and grasp the concepts.

Russell Barkley, PhD, one of the most published psychologists on ADHD, has ruefully commented on these medication issues. In a lecture at the Mayo Clinic that I attended during my residency there, he noted that "we as psychologists, trained to do all different types of therapy, have always been hoping that some form of therapy would work better than medication for ADHD. The plain truth is that nothing works better than medication. Nothing." It should also be noted just as plainly that medication is frequently not the whole answer.

This book is the rest of the answer. Ms. Alexander-Roberts has already struck pay dirt once before with her excellent book, *The ADHD Parenting Handbook*. But parenting teenagers is a whole new ball game. To the baseline wigglesomeness and lack of attention, you now add a case of raging hormones. Boys discover girls, girls discover boys, and the ever-present, loud, and frequently anarchistic music suggests that they have sex with everybody, overthrow the government, and disobey their parents on top of it. They "wanna be me, wanna be free." They have hit the phase of personality development called "separation-individuation," or, more colloquially, they are finding their own identity. They are going to test limits. Sometimes, they will break limits. That's a normal part of adolescence. Stir in some untreated ADHD, however, and you have a recipe for disaster.

Ms. Alexander-Roberts has reviewed a number of vexing issues confronting parents of ADHD teens that simply must be taken into account. Because of the significant hereditary transmission of ADHD, she rightly calls into question whether or not the parents may have undiagnosed ADHD, which sets them up for more hostile, impulsive, and emotional acting out with their children. Inattentiveness certainly does not bode well for point systems or contracts. In my experience working with teenagers, they are all budding little F. Lee Baileys who will argue their way out of any tiny logical inconsistency with you. You must, above all, be attentive. And you must be consistent. Ms. Alexander-Roberts also discusses the emotional consequences of dealing with an ADHD child day in and day out.

Ultimately, this book is appropriate for many different people:

- for bamboozled and exhausted parents—it'll let you know what your teen has been doing to you for so long and how to cope with it.
- for physicians and psychiatrists who may be expert at prescribing medication but either aren't up on or don't have time to review the latest limit-setting techniques with parents and their hyperactive charges—this book is a gold-mine resource that should be "prescribed" right along with any medication.
- for astute, competent therapists, there is something in here that you haven't thought of—I guarantee it! Ms. Alexander-Roberts has craftily collected a wealth of parenting strategies from examining what has worked not only in her life but also in all the lives of the parents and experts she reviewed for this book.
- and, in the final analysis, this book is really for the teenager with ADD or ADHD. It is about helping them, guiding them, and channeling their hyperactive or inattentive minds into a lifetime of achievement and success. Despite all of the medication talk and therapy talk, that is what all of us who work in the ADHD field want to see happen. We want to see the need for pills and counseling fade away as these children mature, and we want to see our hyperactive charges graduate into a lifetime of accomplishment and happiness.

Read this book attentively, study it, and apply it. A superb level of accomplishment and happiness is possible in your child's life . . . and that truly is the good news about ADHD. Good luck and good parenting!

Louis B. Cady, MD

PAY ATTENTION: HYPERACTIVITY IS NOT JUST FOR YOUNGSTERS

Over a decade ago few people had heard of attention deficit hyperactivity disorder (ADHD). Today it is the single largest reason that children and adolescents are referred to mental health clinics, making ADHD the most frequently diagnosed behavioral disorder identified in the United States. ADHD is not, however, limited to children. For years it was assumed to be a disorder of childhood that faded with the onset of adolescence. It is now known that most children with ADHD become adults with ADHD.

Although the current media blitz on ADHD is finally catching the attention of many parents, teachers, and other professionals, ADHD has been referred to as the "yuppie" disease of the 1990s much like chronic fatigue syndrome was in the 1980s. This is unfortunate for all individuals who face the daily challenges of living with ADHD. A "yuppie" disease it is not, as any parent raising a child or adolescent with ADHD can attest. Adults can testify as well to the many challenges they face every day as a result of having ADHD. Although there are many positive aspects to having ADHD—as you will discover in chapter 3—it is considered a disability and, as such, falls under several federal laws regarding the schooling of children with ADHD (Individuals with Disabilities Education Act [IDEA] and Section 504 of the Rehabilitation Act of 1973). Adults and children with ADHD are also covered under the Americans with Disabilities Act (ADA). Under ADA, discrimination against those with disabilities is prohibited in the workplace.

Attention deficit hyperactivity disorder is a complex, bewildering neurological syndrome characterized by severe and pertinacious difficulties that result in symptoms of inattention, impulsivity, distractibility, hyperactivity, or any combination of these, which are excessive or inappropriate for the age level of the child. It is a broad sequence of challenges in tempering motion, mood swings, and paying attention. ADHD often surfaces at an early age (usually around three) and lasts through adulthood, although it may not be diagnosed until the child enters elementary school. Sometimes it is not diagnosed until the preteen, teen, or even adult years. This is especially true for those individuals with attention deficit disorder who do not exhibit overactivity or behavior problems. Such individuals are typically referred to as having attention deficit disorder (ADD), a term used by many professionals that means without hyperactivity. Throughout this book, however, the term ADHD will be used for consistency for all individuals whether they display hyperactivity or not. Additionally, terms such as "ADHD teenager" or "ADHD child" will be replaced with "the child or adolescent with ADHD." Although more cumbersome to use, the latter emphasizes that these individuals are people first, and their ADHD is secondary.

Children or teenagers who have serious debilitating distractibility or attention inconsistencies but exhibit no behavior problems are often not identified. They suffer in silence. They are the daydreamers who may appear lethargic, unable to activate themselves, and are often labeled "stupid" or "lazy." As a result of their challenges, they are unable to complete school work, tasks, or follow directions; they pay attention to everything except what they should (the teacher, for instance). Children and teens who have high IQs and do not demonstrate hyperactivity are at an even greater risk of not being identified simply because their brightness permits them to perform adequately. However, it should be noted that bright children are the ones that most often hear, "I know you could do better than this if you would just apply yourself," which makes the child more vulnerable to failure. When ADHD is coupled with a high IQ and creativity, individuals develop methods of compensating for its disruptive effects, finding mental and physical strategies to attain the state of high stimulation they require.

The primary symptoms of ADHD (inattention, impulsivity, distractibility, and hyperactivity) do not always appear together. Some preteens and teenagers may only experience attention inconsistencies, while others may exhibit difficulties in all areas. For most children and teens with ADHD, symptoms will persist into adulthood at varying degrees of severity. In other words, ADHD is now known to be a lifelong condition, and some clinicians and psychotherapists are now concentrating their efforts on identifying ADHD in adults who have struggled through years without understanding why they have failed in many areas of their lives. As one forty-year-old patient who had just started on medication said to his doctor, "Why in the world didn't I know that something was wrong?" His doctor replied, "Because you grew up inside your own head and didn't have any other frame of reference."

"ADD was previously believed to be a condition rarely persisting into adulthood, but it is now recognized that it very frequently persists throughout life, though in a modified form with perhaps changing symptoms," says Paul Elliott, MD, a Dallas physician who has been treating patients with ADHD for over twenty years. "Persons with ADD should in no respect be thought of as diseased, mentally defective, brain damaged, or psychologically unbalanced."

HOW NEW IS ADHD?

ADHD was first described in medical literature in 1905. However, over 150 years ago a German physician, Heinrich Hoffman, wrote a tale ("Struwel Peter") that described a child with ADHD. And back in 1762 John Locke wrote the following: "A proper and effectual remedy for this wandering of thought, I would be glad to find."

ADHD is not a new syndrome. It has been affecting generations of families for hundreds of years. If your teenager has ADHD, there is a good chance that either you or your spouse, or possibly both of you, have it also. After reading this book you may find yourself saying, "That's me" or "That's my spouse." Many parents of children with ADHD are now being diagnosed because the genetic basis for ADHD is becoming more widely recognized and received in the mental health field.

DIAGNOSING ADHD

An accurate diagnosis of ADHD is obtained through evaluations, parent-child interviews (including the child's history), classroom observations, and a thorough medical examination to rule out vision and hearing problems and neurological disorders. There are no laboratory measures such as blood or urine screens that will diagnose ADHD. It is essential to accurately diagnose ADHD because other medical conditions, such as bipolar disorder, anxiety, or depression, can mimic some of the symptoms of ADHD. In fact, gifted children display many of the same symptoms or characteristics. Many individuals with ADHD display one or more comorbidities, furthering the need for a thorough, accurate diagnosis and treatment approach by specialized professionals that often cannot be provided by pediatricians or internists. "It is estimated that less than fifteen percent of children and adolescents with ADHD experience just ADHD," says Sam Goldstein, PhD, a clinical instructor in the Department of Psychiatry at the University of Utah School of Medicine. "The majority experience at least one comorbid problem . . . a significant minority [experience] two to three additional problems."

It is important to realize that not all attention deficit disorders are the same. "There are many types," according to Thomas E. Brown, PhD, clinical supervisor in the psychology department at Yale University, "depending upon which of the many cognitive functions are impaired and what additional disorders are comorbid."

Ideally, there are several professionals involved in the management of a teen's ADHD. Successful treatment depends on continuous feedback from parents, teachers, physicians, and other professionals who work together to provide comprehensive services for the teenager. Treatment often includes an individual educational plan (IEP), behavioral management techniques, pharmacological therapies, skills training, parent training classes specifically for raising children with attention deficit hyperactivity disorder, counseling and support for the parents and adolescent, and parent-adolescent problem-solving and communication training

Medications (such as the stimulant Ritalin) improve alertness, attention span, and concentration, reduce impulsive and disruptive behavior, and decrease non-compliant behavior, so medications should almost always be used as a treatment method. However, the medications used for the treatment of ADHD do not offer a cure; they simply improve some symptoms and reduce or decrease other symptoms. Although medication helps seventy to seventy-five percent of those diagnosed with ADHD, most studies show that few benefits are long term especially in the areas of social adjustments, academics, and thinking skills. "However, it should be noted that these studies were based on how children did later—once off medications," says Dr. Louis B. Cady. "Had these children stayed on medications, there would certainly have been notable benefits."

Dr. Steven R. Plizka said in an article in *American Family Physician,* "Generally, a primary care physician should refer a child who does not respond to a stimulant agent for psychiatric evaluation because nonresponders . . . often need further psychological assessment or psychotherapeutic intervention." The use of medications in individuals with ADHD is still the most effective and widely used treatment currently available for those with moderate to severe symptoms. Also significant is the fact that not all individuals with ADHD need medication. Individuals with ADHD whose symptoms are in the mild range can often function without medication, especially when the environment is responsive to their needs. Children and teenagers with mild symptoms in structured environments often do well with just behavior modification and some classroom accommodations. In other words, a diagnosis of ADHD does not automatically indicate a need for medication.

WHAT CAUSES ADHD

A single cause of ADHD has not yet been identified. But, in a landmark study directed by Dr. Alan Zametkin at the National Institutes of Mental Health and published in 1990 in the respected *New England Journal of Medicine,* a biological basis for ADHD was traced to a specific metabolic abnormality in and around the frontal lobes of the brain (reduced metabolic activity in those parts of the brain that control movement, emotion, and attention). Bruce A. Pasch, MD, FAAP, Director of the Children's Center for Learning and Development in Toledo, Ohio, says, "Dr. Zametkin and colleagues documented in the adults they studied with hyperactivity that (1) there seems to be a significant inheritance basis, and (2) relevant biological variances in brain metabolism can persist even into adulthood."

Despite much controversy, there is no scientific proof that ADHD is caused by gies, food-related problems, sugar, or additives. ADHD is a chronic developmental disorder that, in almost all cases, is a matter of genetics—a biological predisposition that often has hereditary origins.

recent study conducted at the University of Chicago, researchers believe have isolated the gene responsible for ADHD. The significant results need ted with an independent sample, according to Mark A. Stein, PhD, and associates. This study used a novel statistical approach to test for an association between the dopamine transporter locus and ADHD. In general, genetic studies of complex psychiatric disorders are limited by the imprecision of psychiatric disorders (relative to diagnoses based upon laboratory tests such as those used in previous research on diabetes or cancer). A second pitfall of previous research has been the various comorbid conditions that are often identified with ADHD, making a hereditary comparison more difficult.

WHAT ADHD IS AND IS NOT

ADHD is *not* a learning disability, despite what some people believe, but learning disabilities often coexist in at least one-fourth to one-third of the children diagnosed with ADHD. Educational assessments indicate that children with ADHD, who do not exhibit hyperactivity, may have comorbid learning disabilities more often than children who are hyperactive. ADHD is *not* an emotional disorder, although it can cause emotional problems in both children and adults. Psychiatrists Edward Hallowell and John Ratey, authors of *Driven to Distraction* and *Answers to Distraction*, explain that it exists in the brain and central nervous system and its characteristic problems stem from neurobiological malfunctioning. They also stress that ADD is not willful misbehavior, moral failing, or lack of trying.

The inability to regulate behavior coupled with poor self-monitoring skills places teens at a high risk for academic failure and poor peer relationships, and, to a lower but relevant degree, antisocial behavior. Some young people with ADHD are more likely than non-ADHD children to demonstrate social conduct problems, such as oppositional behavior. Children and teens with ADHD who are significantly hostile, aggressive, or defiant at an early age are at the greatest risk for developing oppositional defiant disorder (ODD), conduct disorder (CD, a more serious degree of ODD), or both. ODD and CD are often associated with poor parent-child interactions such as ineffective parenting methods, parental problems (psychiatric disorders or psychiatric distress are found more often in the immediate and the extended families of children with ADHD), and marital disharmony. These parental issues—situations that present difficulty, uncertainty, or perplexity for the adolescent—can prognosticate the outcome in adolescents, especially for juvenile delinquency. However, according to some research, the tendencies of the child such as a difficult temperament and defiant, aggressive behavior are more powerful contributors to CD than are parental influences. In contemplating marital conflict, you must consider whether the marital distress is a result of the effects of the child on the parents or a separate issue unrelated to the behavior problems of the child.

Research has shown that girls with ADHD are more inclined to have poor peer relationships, low self-esteem, high rates of cognitive (memory and learning impairment, depression, emotional problems particularly as they approach adolescence, and a lesser degree of oppositional behaviors than boys with ADHD. Mothers suffer less often from depression in families of girls with ADHD than mothers boys with ADHD, and marital discord is seen less frequently in families with girls with ADHD than in families with boys with the same disorder. Therefore, it is reasonable to expect that girls with ADHD are less apt to be diagnosed with it because there is often little, if any, family disruption or behavioral disturbances. Genetic studies have shown that boys with ADHD have relatives that are at greater risk for ADHD. Relatives of girls with ADHD, research shows, are at higher risk for anxiety disorders, antisocial disorders, and major depression.

Although the primary symptoms of ADHD are not caused by poor parenting skills, parenting skills have a direct impact on a child or teenager. In other words, the type of parental strategies and techniques used influence the child's behavior. Poor parenting skills, such as trying to control the teenager, inflicting harsh punishments, or taking a negligent approach, can make a situation much worse than it has to be. On the other hand, parents who establish clear rules and boundaries with their teenagers and consistently follow through with appropriate consequences and rewards for behavior will set the stage for positive development. Although most scientists presume that the cause of ADHD is genetic or biological, they also recognize that the environment a child grows up in can determine (or predict) particular behaviors in individual children.

ADHD is considered a serious and persistent developmental disability. It affects all aspects of the life of an individual with ADHD, especially in today's society that is uncompromising and rigidly delineated. "American society continues to value and enforce conformity . . . punish[ing] its children for being unusual," says Carol Landau, PhD, a clinical professor of psychiatry at Brown University. "The ADD child often experiences rejection and confusion in a traditional school setting."

A LOOK INSIDE

Living with ADHD is a daily challenge for all individuals who are affected. Newly diagnosed adults with ADHD relay stories of lifelong frustrations of not knowing why they couldn't pay attention, why they failed academically despite a high IQ, and why they had difficulty making friends, sticking to projects, and completing tasks. Many have changed jobs frequently and have moved from one relationship to another. They talk of the inner pain and turmoil they have experienced, the humiliation they suffered as a result of constant failures, and the misunderstandings of parents and teachers. They talk about the low self-esteem they carried for twenty, thirty, or forty years before being diagnosed with ADHD. For most individuals the realization that they have ADHD comes as a relief. The diagnosis puts a label on their lifetime struggles and gives them answers to questions they have searched for for years. Adults who choose to take medications for ADHD marvel at the clearness of thought they now experience. They become more organized at work and in the home, complete tasks, and find they can successfully manage their daily life. Relationships with spouses or significant others improve. Bills get paid on time, the checkbook gets balanced, and the grass gets cut.

For people who do not have ADHD, it's hard to describe what it is like for those that do. George T. Lynn, MA, a certified mental health worker in Bellevue, Washington, offers readers a remarkable look inside the child with ADHD (Lynn describes these children as attention "different" children): "Raising an Attention Different child is a crucible experience for parents. These children can be extremely oppositional, hot tempered, impulsive, totally disorganized, and hard to manage. Like chemicals in the alchemist's crucible [which is heated by fire], parents will be pushed to their limits and will be changed by the ordeal. To master this challenge, we must first understand the radically different way our kids see the world and how their unique perceptual style limits and empowers them.

"When people pay attention to something, they select it out of the thousands of bits of competing stimuli around them and mute all other stimuli. Perceptual psychologists say that this object becomes our 'figure' while, at the moment of perception, all else is 'ground.' Children with attention differences have an abnormality in the way they perceive stimuli. They tend to selectively focus on discrete things (figure without ground) or are flooded by all stimuli in their environment (ground without figure). Children with ADHD often have an unguarded openness to all external stimuli (ground). These kids may also show a capability for white hot focus on figural things that capture their interest and they do this better than normal. It's as if they are simply more comfortable on the 'extreme' ends of the bell curve.

"I call the children who possess these figure/ground characteristics 'attention different' to denote that their way of perceiving things and learning is different from the norm. These persons are not 'deficit' but simply show a variance of perceptual style that make their lives difficult in our highly routinized culture. I do not suggest a change in terms to minimize the suffering we and they experience as a result of their differences, but a change in how we see these kids is needed if we are to create a positive vision for healing. That being said, it's clear that attention differences are a powerful challenge to personal well being that must be dealt with medically and with psychotherapy if an individual is to have a happy life.

"To succeed in their day-to-day management of their attention different children, parents must also understand their kids' internal emotional experience of the world and how this experience is a 'double-edged sword,' that carries the challenges and gifts that are these kids' genetic legacy. Living perceptionally open to internal and/or external stimuli, attention different kids face several challenges. First, they may feel 'stimulus starved.' They have so much stimulation that life becomes excruciating monotonous. Numbed to the pleasures of ordinary stimulation, they may seek extremes and are susceptible to addictions and will take unsafe risks.

"Living this open, they may also experience a chaotic inner environment. It's as if the limbic or animal brain has greater say in their lives than the cortical or civilized brain. Their cortical brain functions are inhibited in certain areas essential to living in crowded modern society: short memory, personal organization, and impulse control. Like tigers in the zoo, attention different children may feel a enormous amount of pent-up energy but may be distressingly unable to focus it control it. To reduce the pressure of this energy and focus themselves they r aggressively provoke people around them. This provocation does not come from malice but from the need to bring attention to a point and relieve a sense of internal chaos.

"These children also possess gifts that are mirror qualities of their neurological challenges. Because they have so much information to work with, they have the ability to solve problems very creatively. Because they live open to experience, they may feel a deep ecological and spiritual connectedness with nature and a sense of awe around natural phenomena. They are also able to experience and express a variety of emotional states and contain a joie de vivre that makes them remarkable and interesting people to be around. Their great energy, enthusiasm, and creativity can also fire a strong sense of purpose. Most successful entrepreneurs show some qualities of attention difference. To survive until adulthood, all attention different people must develop a strong will, strong enough to rein in their innate wildness and impulsivity.

"Thom Hartmann, in his book *Attention Deficit Disorder: A Different Perception,* says that ADD is a throwback in human history to the age of hunters. He argues that the ADD constellation of traits is that of the hunter; alert, intuitive, resourceful, living in the moment. Hunters played a vital role in the survival of ancient human civilization. Attention different children bring similar powerful gifts to the task of our cultural survival today. These children are very strong and challenge all conventions and rules. This is their nature. Being this strong and lacking skill in self-control, they must get equal quantities of love and structure if they are to grow up to realize their considerable potential. Parents who can give them these things will they themselves be changed, for they will have met and transcended the challenge of their lives."

PREVALENCE OF ADHD

Due to the difficulties in diagnosing ADHD, the exact prevalence is uncertain. Nevertheless, it appears that there are approximately twenty-five million children and adults in the United States with ADHD although some experts sense that estimate is low believing that as many as thirty-three percent of the general population in the United States may be affected. Even though boys are more likely to be diagnosed with ADHD at an earlier age because of hyperactivity and other more visible symptoms, it appears to affect males and females equally. For years, it has been thought that more males than females have ADHD—studies often cited a 6:1 ratio—and that may well be the case. However, at least one nationally recognized expert, Thomas Phelan, PhD, believes otherwise. In his book *All About Attention Deficit Disorders,* Dr. Phelan places the ratio at 1:1, based on his belief that as many females as males have ADHD. Females are more apt to be diagnosed at a later age because their symptoms may be more subtle, or they may never be diagnosed. However, when comparing the ratio in diagnosed adults, there appears to be little difference in the number of males and females affected with ADHD.

PREPARATION FOR ADULTHOOD

While there is no cure for ADHD, it can be effectively managed with medication and other interventions. Educational strengths and weaknesses and the particular learning style of the individual must be identified. Behavioral effects of ADHD must be pinpointed and understood. Early recognition and appropriate supervision of ADHD are more likely to prognosticate a better adolescent outcome.

Children with ADHD will face many challenges as they move from childhood to adolescence to adulthood. The first step parents must take to help their child make a successful transition from one stage of development to another is to accept and understand that ADHD is a part of the child's internal make-up and it will affect the developmental stages of adolescence.

Education is the key. Children and teenagers with ADHD do not choose to act inappropriately. They are not "lazy" or "bad" or "stupid." They, like most other kids, want to please and obey their parents and teachers and they want to control their behavior.

Once parents can accept the realities of ADHD, they can stop blaming themselves or their children and begin an effective treatment plan. Children and teenagers with ADHD may require many interventions before reaching independent adulthood. But they can develop their abilities, learn to control facets of their behavior, discover ways to structure their time and prioritize what needs to be done, and meet success in school and in the home. Low self-esteem, which can lead to a path of failure, can be prevented with appropriate interventions, such as medication, counseling, interventions in the classroom, behavior management, and, most importantly, the assistance of supportive loving parents. Identifying teens' strengths and helping them to magnify and expand on those strengths builds self-esteem and provides the confidence needed to face present and future challenges. With a team approach and parental support, teenagers can develop strategies and techniques that permit them to function effectively despite the challenges of ADHD.

HOW THIS BOOK WILL HELP YOU

Facing the daily challenges of living with a teenager with ADHD can, at times, ᵇ overwhelming. When the teen's ADHD is pure ADHD (without coexisting me⸀ problems), parents may have little difficulty raising their adolescent and fir⸀ the challenges are manageable. Still, even the best of parents can become b⸀ ents with a sound knowledge base of this syndrome and an understand⸀ it affects adolescents. Parents can begin by increasing their commu⸀ problem-solving skills, as well as improving their parenting abilitie⸀ more fully adjusted family organization.

However, if the teen is failing in school, rebellious and runs with a wrong crowd, we are discussing an entirely diff⸀

problems. Families with teens with comorbid (coexisting) conduct disorder (CD), oppositional defiant disorder (ODD), or other psychiatric disorders can cause the family organization to break down. Aggressive teens with ADHD/CD or ADHD/ODD are at a significantly higher risk than their non-ADHD peers (or peers with milder symptoms of ADHD) for behavior and conduct problems (suspension from school, truancy, antisocial activities, substance abuse, etc.). The final chapters of this book will address how these types of problems develop and what can be done to manage them.

It is important that parents realize that most teenagers with ADHD do not develop serious conduct problems, especially those that may lead to juvenile delinquency or criminal behavior in adulthood. The opposite is actually true. Many individuals with ADHD are creative, energetic, and natural-born leaders and entrepreneurs. If you or someone you love has ADHD, you are in good company. Thom Hartmann, in his book *Attention Deficit Disorder: A Different Perception,* speculates that such individuals as Thomas Alva Edison, Benjamin Franklin, and Ernest Hemingway, all who accomplished great things in their lifetimes, had attention deficit hyperactivity disorder.

This book will offer you valuable insight into your teenager, help you to identify ADHD problem areas that need to be addressed immediately, provide warning signs for such things as depression, offer suggestions for coping, and teach you to become a better parent to your teenager with ADHD.

My hope is that you will gain considerable insight into the life and mind of a child or teenager with ADHD and learn ways to improve your parenting skills, placing you in a position to assist your teenager in reaching her highest potential in life. Parenting a child or teenager with ADHD is not always easy, but parents must remember that they are their child's best, and often only, advocate. The parental role is far more important than most parents realize.

This book is for parents who have a preteen or teenager who has been diagnosed with ADHD. However, some of you may be reading this book because you suspect that your child or teen may have ADHD. Or you might suspect that you, or maybe your spouse, also have ADHD. With that in mind, the following is a list of criteria defined in the *American Psychiatric Association's Diagnostic and Statistical Manual of Mental Disorder,* Fourth Edition, 1994 (DSM-IV).

Diagnostic Criteria for Attention Deficit Hyperactivity Disorder

ither (1) or (2):

/or more) of the following symptoms of inattention have persisted for at
~6 months to a degree that is maladaptive and inconsistent with devel-
al level:

's to give close attention to details or makes careless mistakes in
'. work, or other activities
iculty sustaining attention in tasks or play activities

(c) often does not seem to listen when spoken to directly

(d) often does not follow through on instructions and fails to finish school-work, chores, or duties in the workplace (not due to oppositional behavior or failure to understand instructions)

(e) often has difficulty organizing tasks and activities

(f) often avoids, dislikes, or is reluctant to engage in tasks that require sustained mental effort (such as schoolwork or homework)

(g) often loses things necessary for tasks or activities (e.g., toys, school assignments, pencils, books, or tools)

(h) is often easily distracted by extraneous stimuli

(i) is often forgetful in daily activities

(2) six (or more) of the following symptoms of hyperactivity-impulsivity have persisted for at least 6 months to a degree that is maladaptive and inconsistent with developmental level:

Hyperactivity

(a) often fidgets with hands or feet or squirms in seat

(b) often leaves seat in classroom or in other situations in which remaining seated is expected

(c) often runs about or climbs excessively in situations in which it is inappropriate (in adolescents or adults, may be limited to subjective feelings of restlessness)

(d) often has difficulty playing or engaging in leisure activities quietly

(e) is often "on the go" or often acts as if "driven by a motor"

(f) often talks excessively

Impulsivity

(g) often blurts out answers before questions have been completed

(h) often has difficulty awaiting turn

(i) often interrupts or intrudes on others (e.g., butts into conversations or games)

B. Some hyperactive-impulsive or inattentive symptoms that cause impairment were present before age seven years.

C. Some impairment from the symptoms is present in two or more settings (e.g., at school [or work] and at home).

D. There must be clear evidence of clinically significant impairment in social, academic, or occupational functioning.

E. The symptoms do not occur exclusively during the course of a pervasive developmental disorder, schizophrenia, or other psychotic disorder and are not better accounted for by another mental disorder (e.g., mood disorder, anxiety disorder, dissociative disorder, or a personality disorder).

If these symptoms sound familiar, it behooves you to seek an evaluation from qualified professional who works with individuals with ADHD. A local CHAI chapter (Children and Adults with Attention Deficit Disorders) can refer you to specialists in your area. (See the appendix for the address and phone numb CHADD, a national organization.)

MEDICAL MANAGEMENT OF ADHD IN ADOLESCENTS

by Paul T. Elliott, MD

In adolescence, the symptoms of ADHD are impossibly entangled with the changes of puberty. However, in the patient with ADHD, much of the oppositional behavior, impulsivity, difficulty with interpersonal relationships, addictive, thrill-seeking behaviors, and plummeting self-image and grades are often reduced by the effective and complete treatment of ADHD.

The goal of any treatment program should be directed toward achieving full access to and control over the patient's full inborn intellectual ability. Too often, we satisfy ourselves with only partial achievement of this goal. The results of the most effective treatment of ADHD in this age group are often the most dramatic of any age group. Since this is an important foundational period of life, optimal treatment of the ADHD symptoms can produce profounds benefits for the remainder of the patient's life. Benefits are considerable not only in view of the doors this treatment opens for the patient, but also in terms of the severe consequences for the person left untreated.

The teen with ADHD, as at earlier stages of life, may seek high-intensity, externally stimulating environments, such as athletics, loud music, or role-playing games. On the other hand, they may never seem to be performing up to their potential, appearing inactive and passive with "lazy" or "daydreamer" labels applied to them. Particularly if they have the nonhyperactive type of ADHD, they may be diagnosed with a learning disability or learning difference, and it may never be suspected that the real problem is ADHD.

The person with ADHD usually has a poor sense of the passage of time. This ca create tremendous test anxiety because the person worries over how much time passed, and whether he will have time to finish. Anxiety may produce substant lower test scores than the person's knowledge level of the subject would reflect same poor sense of the passage of time may result in being late for appointm missing curfews. Thrill-seeking behavior, acting out, or similar behaviors are also characteristic of this stage of life.

Once the diagnosis is made, methods of treatment must be carefully considered. As the use of medication is discussed, it is essential to keep in mind the goal of treatment: To grant the patient full access to and control over his inborn intellectual ability. For the first time, full access and control may be experienced by the teens and people around him as an exciting and reassuring event.

TEENS' ATTITUDES TOWARD TREATMENT

Teens frequently do not want to take medication in the first place. They want to feel normal and avoid anything that might set them apart from their peers. As a result, they will often resist the diagnosis of ADHD and the use of medication. They often feel that taking medication is admitting that they are "diseased." This is understandable in the overall context of adolescence but can remain an obstacle to the effective control of ADHD. Parents, teachers, and physicians must be sensitive to this reaction and try to work within this framework. This may not be easy, and it may take some time before the teen is willing to take appropriate medications.

More can be gained if the teen recognizes the self-serving benefit of taking medication. Try to see the teens' issues from their perspective. Learn of the teens' fears, concerns, likes, dislikes, etc. When we understand these issues better, the need for medications can be couched in familiar terms the teen finds more acceptable. Eventually, the teen may be amenable to the use of medication with the understanding that her grades may improve, even though the parent may secretly wish that the oppositional behavior will be better controlled as well. Better grades may, in turn, allow the teen to participate in sports or other extracurricular activities. Many scenarios are possible depending on the circumstances of the individual teen.

Sometimes an adolescent insists there is no need for medication. In such cases a contract may be helpful, such as, "We'll try medication for this semester to see what the effects are. If you wish, you don't have to take the medication after that." Most often the teen will appreciate the benefit of better grades and choose to take the medication beyond the contract period.

Teens will often report that they don't like the way the medication makes them feel. This must be explored carefully to determine exactly what sort of feeling the teen is experiencing. Perhaps the medication is causing a feeling of depression or nausea. However, it may be that the teen doesn't seem as spontaneous or funny to himself or his peers. Often, the teen has developed a reputation as the class clown, a comic, or an airhead. With the use of medication, the teen is able to think more deeply about subjects, no longer requiring humor to cover up for a poor understanding of the subject matter. When this is the case, the teen must be handled with and concern, so he does not develop the idea that to take medication is to be a permanent nerd.

A therapist with whom the teen communicates comfortably can be invaluable in such situations. Therapy can also help with the myriad of other issues the teen struggles with during this phase. These issues can almost always be appropriately managed with careful, concerned communication and medication changes.

TREATMENT OVERVIEW

While medications are an important cornerstone in any treatment of ADHD, they must neither be considered the only treatment nor be thought of as a permanent solution. Effective parenting techniques are essential and cannot be replaced by medication. Nor can poor parenting be overcome by medication. Furthermore, medication can deliver ability or capacity but cannot deliver a skill. I'll use a bicycle as an analogy. I can give a bicycle to a person who has never seen one and say, "You sit here, make it go with the pedals, and steer with the handlebars. Now ride away!" and give the person a shove. Of course, the person will probably wind up in the ditch on the first try because he lacks the skill, though he has the ability to learn it.

This also applies to anyone with ADHD with good medical control. The ability may be there to do a particular task, but the person may never have been trained in the skill. This often applies to teens' study habits. A parent may feel that, because the teen has had special courses in study habits or organizational skills, he should deploy those skills once medicated. However, if the training was given before the medical control was achieved, the teen may not have learned the skills effectively because of the ADHD. Once medical control is present, the teen will need retraining. With medical control, the teen will now be able not only to learn the skill but will also be able to put it into practice with consistency until it becomes a habit.

While on medication, acquiring skills and developing habits is wise. These basic skills will remain with the teen and benefit him for a lifetime, though medication may be stopped in the future. Medication will not make the teen something he is not. It will not make him more intelligent or a better athlete, though his performance may be dramatically improved in those areas once on medication. That improvement, however, is merely the acquisition of full access and control delivered by the medication.

I am frequently asked how long the patient must continue medication. The medication is needed only as long as the benefits are needed. I do feel that the teen should take medication throughout the scholastic process of formal education, since most schools from the preschool through the PhD levels are designed to teach and test the average brain rather than the ADHD brain. The ADHD brain does have the wiring to do things the way the average brain does, it simply lacks complete access to and control over that function. This is what the medication can deliver.

Patients and parents are understandably concerned about the risks of medication, from the standpoints both of physical side effects and the possibility of addiction. Medical complications are few when the medications are carefully prescribed and appropriately followed. Concerns about long-term complications of hypertension, coronary artery disease, and growth retardation have been laid to rest. While Ritalin may cause a temporary slowing of growth, the teen's growth rate will eventually speed up even while the Ritalin is continued. Though there are a few reports of permanent growth retardation, it is unclear whether the medication was the cause.

It is still widely believed that the stimulant medications are addictive, that is, habituating like alcohol, tobacco, narcotics, cocaine, crack, etc. They are not. There is no evidence of, nor have I encountered in over twenty years of practice, any cases of true physiological dependency. Amphetamines do have such a reputation, but it is unfounded. One of the reasons the amphetamines have the reputation for addiction is that they can be so dramatically effective. As you might imagine, if the medication had allowed you to make dramatic changes in your life previously marked by struggles and failures, you would be strongly motivated to continue taking it. Of course, this is not addiction, but it can appear so to the uninformed.

Like any prescription medication, however, stimulants can be abused. However, the properly medicated teen with ADHD has far greater benefits when Ritalin is used correctly than she would get by abusing it. Therefore, there is no incentive for misuse. A patient may take these medications in high doses, nonstop for years and cease them abruptly without harm. There would probably be a five- to ten-day period of noticeable fatigue and perhaps some transient depression. However, this is a down modulation pattern unassociated with a drug craving. Certainly, someone whose life has improved after years of struggle will want the medication to avoid returning to the previous life, but this is not a drug craving as seen in patients addicted to truly habituating drugs. Nevertheless, since about one-third of all teens with ADHD will abuse habituating drugs (including alcohol), I feel it is essential to properly medicate them in hopes of relieving the need they feel to misuse other substances.

Probably the most bothersome issue of medical complication is the development of tics or movement disorders similar to Tourette's syndrome. This disorder occurs in about one out of seventy-five to one hundred patients when medication is started. Tourette's syndrome is found more often in patients with ADHD, and its symptoms often begin in the teen years. When the symptoms begin with the initiation of medical treatment, there is dispute whether this merely represents the unmasking of an underlying tendency or a symptom caused by the medication. Rare cases do not go away after the medication is stopped. It is unclear whether these cases were going to develop and remain permanent regardless of the medication.

More and more physicians are feeling comfortable with the continued use of medication for control of the ADHD symptoms while reducing the dose or adding some other medication to control the tics.

ASSESSMENT

Physicians must carefully assess the presence of ADHD and related disorders prior to initiation of any sort of medication. Impulsive or disobedient school behavior alone is not sufficient reason to use medication. Information must be obtained from as many sources as possible, including parents, teachers, and the patient.

A physical examination and laboratory studies may reveal other general medical conditions, such as diabetes or thyroid imbalance. Vision and hearing tests may be necessary to exclude poor vision or hearing as contributors to the problem. While the diagnosis of ADHD is basically made from the history obtained from the patient, family, and teachers, other testing may be necessary to identify the degree of difficulties experienced by the patient. Diagnostic educational testing may also be necessary to assess the presence of associated learning disabilities.

Psychological testing helps to clearly identify the teen's areas of struggle. Such testing may help identify other psychological or psychiatric conditions coexisting with ADHD. Tests may include but are not limited to the WISC-R or WAIS, Bender-Gestalt, and possibly the MMPI psychological tests.

INDICATIONS FOR MEDICATION

A diagnosis of ADHD is not an automatic indication for medication. In mild cases, modifications in family and classroom structure may be sufficient. Medication should be considered in all severe cases, particularly if a child is causing significant family disruption or is at risk for expulsion from school. Medications for ADHD are expensive, but they are much less expensive than psychosocial interventions or the failure to treat.

When families or teens are hesitant to try medication, they should not be coerced into using it. Similarly, medication should not be given if the family is unable to comply with a plan for monitoring its effects. The potential for benefit from medication should be considered in any patient with ADHD. It is a mistake to attribute a teen's behavioral difficulties to emotional problems or conflicts in the teen's environment. Family conflicts, school disruptions, and peer rejections often improve dramatically once a teen is properly medicated.

MEDICATION

Medication is the most frequently used and successful treatment of ADHD. The medications found to be useful fall into several categories. These include psychostimulants (often referred to only as stimulants), some antidepressants, other psychotropics, and other medications such as lithium, Klonopin, clonidine, and guanfacine.

Stimulants

Stimulant medications have been known to improve attention span and decrease disruptive behaviors in children with ADHD since the late 1930s. In the ensuing years, stimulants have been given to hundreds of thousands of children with no evidence of significant harm or long-term risk.

Stimulant medications currently on the market include methylphenidate (Ritalin), dextro-amphetamine sulfate (Dexedrine), a mixture of d-amphetamine and amphetamine salts (Adderall, previously known as Obetrol), methamphetamine sulfate (Desoxyn), and pemoline (Cylert). A person who fails to respond or has a bothersome side effect to one stimulant frequently will do well with another.

The Drug Enforcement Agency controls the manufacturing and supplies of these medications in an effort to reduce the diversion of legitimately manufactured medication into the streets. These efforts cause shortages of these medications from time to time for those patients who truly need them. This is most noticeable at the end of the calendar year and the first part of the next year—approximately December through February.

Side Effects

Any medication can cause side effects. Physicians, parents, and patients with ADHD must do an assessment of risks versus benefits to determine if the risks of taking a medication outweigh the potential benefits. When considering these issues, however, it is also important to remember that failure to treat ADHD also carries significant risks whose lifelong consequences are well known: failure to get an education, poor self-esteem, substance abuse, and antisocial behaviors that become habitual and can contribute to "failure at life."

The most common side effects of stimulants are appetite loss, restlessness, headaches, stomach aches, weight loss, and sleep problems. These side effects usually go away after several weeks or with dose adjustment. The usual process is to start with a low dose, allowing the patient's body to adapt to the side effects, and gradually increasing the dosage to a level that allows the brain to function at its best.

ADHD Rebound

ADHD has been jokingly described by some researchers as a sleep disorder. The reason is that most patients with ADHD have an abnormal sleep pattern with a lot of thrashing, position changes, throwing off the bed covers, sleep talking, and snoring. In childhood they often experience sleepwalking and bedwetting as well. Both children and adults with ADHD may awaken during the night to play, work, or merely surf the channels, before going back to sleep for the remainder of the night.

After beginning medication, with proper pacing of the brain chemistry during the day, the pattern of sleep takes on a more normal form. However, early in the treatment people with ADHD seem to have more difficulty getting to sleep or become more restless during the night. This increase in sleep disturbance is frequently incorrectly attributed to too much medication. In fact, most often it is due a rebound of ADHD symptoms after the medication wears off. During this period of rebound, which usually lasts from two to eight hours after the dose of medication wears off, the symptoms of ADHD may actually be worse than they were before treatment began. Unfortunately, the rebound usually comes at about the time a person wishes to go to sleep.

There is a time window I refer to as the "sleep window" beginning about thirty minutes prior to the end of the medication dose and extending thirty, but no more than sixty minutes beyond the end of the dose. This gives a sixty- to ninety-minute period of time when the patient can lie down and drift into restful sleep. If the delay is longer the rebound symptoms may be fully present, which then prevents a person from going sleep. The result is an apparent overstimulation insomnia that is not related to too much medication, but to a drop in blood level of the medication.

The solution to this is to time dosages so that the drop in blood level of the last dose corresponds more closely to the time the patient would like to go to sleep. If this is not possible or does not work, a small dose of the primary medication, such as Dexedrine, Adderall, or Ritalin, can be used at bedtime to reduce the rebound symptoms, but it should be small enough to avoid causing insomnia due to the stimulatory effect of the medication. This can also be used if the patient has persistent restless sleep throughout the night, as is occasionally the case. Ordinarily, the patient's brain chemistry will settle down when the dosage is appropriately balanced and no sleep disturbance will exist.

Another method of tailoring the day's response pattern is often needed in children and teens with ADHD. Frequently, the dose of medication must be given just before leaving home to maximize its benefit at school. This may mean that the teen is up for forty-five to ninety minutes before the medication is given. During this period of time, teens can be sluggish, disorganized, argumentative, or even combative.

A common solution is to wake the teen approximately one hour before he needs to get up and give him a small dose of the medication. Then when he does get up, the medication has already begun to take effect, relieving many of these ADHD symptoms. Since this is a smaller dose given at an earlier time, it usually does not require alteration of the initial dose of the day, which should remain the same.

Antidepressants
About three-fourths of patients with ADHD will respond to certain antidepressant medications. They may be used when a teen has significant depression or anxiety in addition to ADHD. They may also be used to broaden the effects of the stimulants or relieve some of their side effects. Antidepressants are also used when a patient cannot take a stimulant.

The most commonly used antidepressants for ADHD are the tricyclics: imipramine (Tofranil), nortriptyline (Pamelor), and desipramine (Norpramin). The group of antidepressants known as the SSRIs (Selective Serotonin Re-uptake Inhibitors) is being found to be helpful as well. These include Prozac, Zoloft, Paxil, and Luvox. Others in different groups that may be helpful are Wellbutrin and Buspar. ADHD symptoms sometimes improve with antidepressant doses lower than required to treat depression.

Typical side effects of the antidepressants include dry mouth, constipation, nervousness, and drowsiness. The tricyclic antidepressants have caused irregular heart beats in some rare cases. Safety can be improved by monitoring EKGs and blood levels of the medication.

Clonidine and Guanfacine

Catapres (clonidine) and Tenex (guanfacine) are medications used in the treatment of high blood pressure, but they are also particularly useful in ADHD.

They are effective in decreasing hyperactivity and impulsivity but are less effective than stimulants in improving attention span. The combination of one of these and a stimulant can be useful, particularly if a patient suffers from sleep problems. They are an effective treatment for tics and can be used alone or in combination with stimulants or antidepressants if teens develop motor tics or Tourette's syndrome. Clonidine is less expensive than guanfacine, but guanfacine is less likely to cause drowsiness throughout the day.

The principle side effects are decreased blood pressure and sedation. These frequently subside after some period of use. When a patient does not have hypertension before treatment of ADHD, the drop in blood pressure is rarely sufficient to require discontinuing the medication. Night terrors may occur after several days or weeks on either medication, particularly in younger patients, and usually will not subside with continuation of the medication. While they are not of medical significance, they can be very disturbing to the family.

Other Medications

Other psychotropic medications have use in certain cases for the management of ADHD. Monoamine oxidase inhibitors (MAOIs) are a class of antidepressant that has been useful in children and adults with ADHD. Use of MAOIs require dietary restrictions that are often not practical with younger patients.

Several antipsychotic medications, notably thioridazine (Mellaril), chlorpromazine (Thorazine), and haloperidol (Haldol), are useful when patients show severe, unmanageable aggression or impulsivity. Antipsychotic medications have been demonstrated to be superior to stimulants in ADHD patients who also have a low IQ.

Those who use lithium carbonate or citrate for control of their bipolar disorder, or some of the more aggressive, abusive tendencies that can accompany ADHD, will often report a jittery or internally shaky sensation associated with the medication, even though the blood levels of lithium may be completely within the normal range. Since lithium is handled in the body as is potassium, a potassium supplement will often alleviate the side effect without causing any others. This relief can be obtained even though the blood level of potassium is in the normal range. This requires prescription medication, since most over-the-counter potassium preparations are too weak.

Stopping Medication

While there is no medical necessity for stopping treatment at any time, many parents and patients prefer to stop for a period when the benefits of the medication are not necessary. The most logical time to do this is in the summer. However, it should be emphasized that it may be unwise to stop if the teen is going to camp, taking some additional educational programs, or in summer school.

The practice of stopping on the weekends is generally counterproductive. One of the reasons for starting at low doses and gradually moving up as therapy is initiated is to allow the body to adapt to the side effects of medication, permitting the dose to be raised to the point where the brain is functioning at its best. This process of adaptation takes several days at a minimum. If medication is stopped, the readaptation process begins as soon as it is resumed. Unfortunately, this often produces an unpredictable and unreliable result. The readaptation process can also be accompanied by bothersome side effects, which interfere with daily activities and performance.

It seems unwise to stop the medication during scholastic breaks, such as spring break or during the holidays. These times usually bring more family contact in a more stimulating environment. The accompanying stress will certainly aggravate the usual ADHD person's symptoms at a time when they need to be under better control. Therefore, I recommend that the medication be continued during these times.

Medication Choices

My first-choice drug is Dexedrine. This is manufactured in capsule form in five-, ten-, and fifteen- milligram strengths. The manufacturer, Smith Kline Beecham, has trademarked the name Dexedrine Spansule for its twelve-hour timed-release capsule. It is also manufactured as Dexedrine Tablets, a 5 mg tablet that lasts four hours. The generic name of the drug is dextro-amphetamine sulfate; and other manufacturers, such as Richwood Pharmaceutical Company, Inc., produce a five-milligram tablet form, but there are no other manufacturers of a sustained-release form.

Dexedrine Spansules are my first medication of choice for most ADHD patients for several reasons:

- It is among the most successful medications in producing global control. By this, I mean it is one of the most effective drugs for relieving all of the bothersome symptoms of ADHD.
- It is the least expensive of the most effective medications on the market. When contemplating taking a medication for many years, a difference of several hundred dollars a year takes on considerable significance.
- It produces a rapid effect, which means its benefits can be quickly assessed. The advantage of the predictable twelve-hour release mechanism is to avoid extra doses throughout the day, either at school or at work. In a busy day it is often difficult to get in additional doses of medications, such as Ritalin, that require dosing every three to four hours for maximum effectiveness.

About 15% to 20% of teens will not need a second dose of Dexedrine at the end of the twelve-hour period. They simply notice that the benefit of the medication fades away, with a gradual return of the ADHD symptoms. The remaining 85%, however, will notice a rather abrupt drop-off in the effect of medication, with a rapid return of the ADHD symptoms. In fact, many often experience a rebound of the ADHD symptoms that is actually amplified above the premedication level. I refer to this as filtered rebound. By this, I mean that even though the medication's effectiveness has subsided, a small amount of the medication remains in the blood stream and can modify the symptoms as they return. This filtered rebound lasts anywhere from two to eight hours but is more likely to occur toward the eight-hour end of this range.

Ritalin
Traditionally, Ritalin has been used as the main drug of choice for the treatment of ADHD in both children and adults. There are several reasons for this. Ritalin is not technically an amphetamine, though it functions in a similar way in the brain. Traditionally, it has been felt that Ritalin had less value on the street and, therefore, had less abuse potential. The only evidence for this is indirect, in that Ritalin does not have as high a value on the street. However, this is disputed among college students who frequently purchase Ritalin from classmates in order to get their ADHD brains to work well for exams or writing papers.

The disadvantages of Ritalin include its short duration of action, which is never more than four hours and frequently not more than two. As a rule, if it lasts only two hours it is usually due to too low a dose to begin with. Increasing the dose will often give a benefit more closely approaching four hours. However, each teen varies greatly in his response to the medication. Although this is the case with many medications, it is particularly true of the psychostimulants.

Other drawbacks include the need for a noon dose in school children. The need to go to the principal's office or the nurse's office for medication during school can become stigmatizing at about age eleven or twelve. At this point, adolescents with ADHD who used to go together arm in arm to the office in earlier years now sneak furtively in hopes that nobody notices. The strong impulse to be completely average is universal among teenagers. A definite need exists for preparations that do not require in-school dosing.

Ritalin has a sustained-release form called Ritalin SR, which is available only in the 20 mg preparation. Although it is supposed to last for eight hours, it frequently lasts no more than six. Furthermore, its blood level during the release period can vary considerably, producing fluctuating effects. Another unpleasant phenomenon noticed by a small percentage of patients is a spiking of the dose when it is taken initially.

This initial increase in blood level can produce symptoms of too much medication, followed by symptoms of an inadequate level of medication. The blood level after this initial higher spike drops below the therapeutic threshold and remains there for the rest of the day. This often necessitates another dose in one-and-a-half to two hours and possibly a third dose to get the residual blood level to stay above the therapeutic threshold for the entire day. Therefore, even the sustained-release form of Ritalin is only effective for about two hours for some patients.

Another disadvantage of Ritalin is that it has a tendency to produce more bothersome side effects. While this will vary from person to person, it is simply an average finding. These side effects are the same as with other medications, including agitation, nervousness, jitteriness, a sense of pressured performance, intolerance of other people's slowness, a hyperfocused or glazed appearance of the eyes, nausea, and a general dysphoria. It does not have a tendency to produce tachycardia or blood pressure elevation in teens although these effects may be found in adults. Various cardiac arrhythmias, which may be nothing more than aggravation of previously existing tendency, due to MVP (mitral valve prolapse) for example, may also be found in adults.

The dosage of Ritalin varies up to 1 mg per kilogram of body weight in three to four divided doses per day at four-hour intervals. I have experienced good results and no adverse effects in adults with as much as twice that amount. As with any of the psychostimulants, the medication must be increased gradually and with caution, monitoring blood pressure, pulse, and overall physical condition.

COUNSELING

Behavioral therapy has its merits. However, it works far better if a person is under control first with prescription medications. Behavioral management is a method of structuring the teen's life and offering training skills that allow him to avoid problems. These techniques maintain a narrow and short-termed focus, allowing the person to work around some of the difficulties of ADHD. Unfortunately, these skills are more difficult for the person with ADHD to learn and implement consistently unless adequate medication control is achieved first. The differences in behavioral therapy between medicated and unmedicated patients can be dramatic.

Psychotherapy alone has little merit in the management of ADHD patients. Active medication management obviates the necessity of much psychotherapy, particularly in childhood. Psychotherapy is no more effective in assisting the control of ADHD symptoms in adults than in children. However, teens, like adults, may have made a number of poor life choices because of their ADHD. After the best medication control, psychotherapy may be required to assist the person in unraveling and managing the problems caused by these poor choices. At that point the results of psychotherapy can be dramatic since the person with ADHD can now not only understand the recommendations and their logic intellectually but also implement them in his life consistently until they become ingrained as habits.

The real goal of counseling or therapy for teeens with ADHD is to train them in behavioral skills that they may have missed out on at earlier, more appropriate stages of life. The counselor should help the teen establish appropriate patterns of behavior and develop them into habits of living.

Since the ADHD thought process is not time based, one of the first skills to acquire is time management. Some of the other skills include organization, listening, goal development, and self-discipline. These can be obtained from a variety of sources: books, tapes, conferences, and personal coaches or trainers, an industry that has risen rather rapidly as the compelling need for it has become obvious.

VITAMIN AND MINERAL SUPPLEMENTS

Many treatment approaches employing vitamin and mineral supplements have been tried through the years. Again, the occasional person will achieve substantial benefits, but most people will notice little or no detectable difference. Another difficulty with nutritional supplements is that they often do not offer good global control. By global control I mean controlling all of the symptoms of ADHD rather than a few.

Oil of evening primrose contains essential fatty acids, which have been demonstrated to improve cell wall function of the brain cells in laboratory animals. The British have done several studies that illustrated improvement in hyperactivity among teens with ADHD, but they did not demonstrate improvement in grades. Their studies did not examine the effects of this treatment on other ADHD symptoms.

Herbal preparations may contain Ma-Huang (known by its English name Ephedra), which contains ephedrine. Ephedrine is a stimulant/decongestant that was widely used prior to the development of pseudoephedrine (brand Sudafed). While some will tout it as a "natural substance," it is simply another source of the drug. The contention or implication is that natural substances are better. Tobacco and alcohol are both natural substances, but they can have adverse medicinal effects.

Vitamins such as niacin (sometimes in the form nicotinic acid) and B_6 can cause a stimulant, or a stimulant-like effect, that can be enhanced by stimulant medications to the point of increasing the unpleasant side effects of nervousness or jitteriness and can be avoided or taken at night if discomfort occurs.

Vitamin B_5 and choline have been reported to help some children with ADHD symptoms. These are patient reports, sometimes referred to as anecdotal evidence. No scientific studies have been reported on these.

FOOD ADDITIVES

The category of food additives involves a wide range of different substances, including preservatives, artificial and natural flavorings, and coloring agents. Some people will have certain adverse reactions to one or more of these or even true allergies to them. Of course, these people will need to avoid the offending substances, but this is a rather small fraction of those with ADHD.

Studies have been done with the Feingold Diet, which was popular a number of years ago. Scientifically speaking there was no detectable difference between those on or off the additives when neither the teen nor the parents knew which diet the patient was on. However, an occasional parent reported that the teen did markedly better when such a diet was followed. In such cases, I encourage the parent to continue the dietary measures. I believe it is important to use whatever seems to work best for each patient.

There are a number of foods that affect ADHD treatment, some of which can reduce the effectiveness of medication. The citrus and cranberry fruits and juices and vitamin C can cause the stimulant medications to be removed from the system more rapidly and reduce the blood levels, producing a less beneficial result.

Citric acid is added to many foods as a flavoring agent. It will reduce the level of the stimulant medications only if it is used in amounts to make the drink or food taste like citrus. It may be used in foods in smaller amounts to slightly alter or enhance the flavor and will not lower the benefit of the stimulants in these cases.

If people wish to eat these foods they should do so in the late evening when the full effectiveness of the medication is not necessary. They should take any vitamins containing vitamin C in the evening or at bedtime as well. This way the vitamins are in the system, do their job, and are out of the system by the next morning when the stimulant medication is taken. Long-acting forms of vitamin C should be avoided since they would not be out of the teen's system by the next morning.

Occasionally, a patient will take an overdose of a particular medication inadvertently, having forgotten that the first dose was taken. When this occurs an uncomfortable degree of stimulation may occur. This is rarely dangerous but can be frightening. A rapid reduction of the effect can be achieved in patients of adult size by giving them 1,000 mg of vitamin C every hour until they are once again comfortable. The amount used for smaller teens is 500 mg hourly until comfortable.

NONPRESCRIPTION DRUGS

Stimulant medications can amplify the unpleasant side effects of other stimulants. Some unlikely products fall in the stimulant category. The most obvious is caffeine, found in coffee, tea, some soft drinks, and chocolate. Less obvious is nicotine. Occasionally, smokers (and those taking prescription nicotine patches or gum) find that after they begin stimulant medications, they get unpleasantly nervous or jittery when they smoke. Happily, this encourages smokers to kick the tobacco habit.

The side effects of over-the-counter decongestants, decongestant nasal sprays, caffeine-containing medications that help people maintain alertness or overcome drowsiness (such as NoDoz and Vivarin), and the brands of ephedrine commonly sold at truck stops and convenience stores may be amplified by the stimulant medications to a level of uncomfortable nervousness or agitation.

It should be reiterated that herbal remedies, especially those containing Ma Huang, actually contain stimulants that may be amplified by the stimulant prescription medications.

EXERCISE

Exercise is helpful in alleviating the symptoms of many teens who have ADHD. Exercise produces an increase of adrenaline, which stimulates other systems in the body. One of the important results of increased adrenaline is an increase in endorphins in the brain. Endorphins seem to play a vital role in the way that the ADHD brain functions versus the average brain. As the endorphins flow, the ADHDer's brain is more able to function in the A mode. This is the logical, sequential, time priority in completion-based method of thought processing. It is the average form of activity that produces better access and control over the teen's inborn intellectual abilities.

The metaphor I have suggested employs the concept of different channels or modes for processing thoughts. In the A-B metaphor, the A channel is the sequential, orderly, linear, and monodimensional thought process that exhibits a good recollection of previous experiences, as well as a far ranging view of future consequences. The person functioning in this mode is able to keep up with the passage of time, continue a logical sequence of thinking, including a deeper attention to and understanding of the issue, and is driven by a sense of priority and a need for completion. These individuals do not have ADHD and appear to have more mature judgment. They act less impulsively and more logically. They have a tendency not to start as many activities, but the ones they do start are more likely to be finished.

The ADHD person has the "wiring" for A-mode operations but does not have good access to or control over these activities. The ADHD person functions in the B mode, which is characterized by a task-based function. In this respect, the person is task oriented with the ability to hyperfocus, even for extended periods of time, on a given task until she has figured out the problem, seen a glimpse of the end result, or satisfied her general curiosity about the task. Since she is not driven by a need for completion, she often will lose interest in the task as soon as she sees the logical conclusion or end result, dropping it when it is little more than half finished. Her life is often characterized by many things started, few completed.

I hasten to point out that this is apparently not the way the brain actually works. However, it does describe many of the observations we make about the behaviorial differences of teens with ADHD. Exercise opens the A channel, giving the ADHDer more complete control over that part of her brain function, since it produces the endorphins that seem essential for this process.

It is interesting to note that the circulating endorphin levels in the brains of people with ADHD are lower than in other people. We do know that one of the actions of the psychostimulants is to elevate the endorphin levels. This appears to be one of the attributes endorphin levels have in common with exercise.

Often parents will notice that a teen has a great deal of agitation, impulsiveness, quick anger, and objectionable behavior until exercising strenuously. The teen is much more calm, logical, communicative, and reasonable after exercising. The only drawback to using exercise as a treatment is that this effect lasts only sixty to ninety minutes. After that, the B mode of processing in behavior returns as before. The sixty- to ninety-minute period of benefit corresponds with the average lifespan of the endorphin molecules in the brain. They undergo a natural process of degradation after this time and are no longer active. This is one possible explanation of the benefits many parents have noticed with strenuous exercise for their teens and the improvement of their dispositions.

I want to emphasize that these comments are purely from my observations and have not yet been explored sufficiently to determine whether there is any true scientific validity for such a metaphorical scenario.

As teens begin their medication and gradually increase it, they sometimes have a diminished tolerance to exercise. This may be even more pronounced if the exercise is done in excessive heat or humidity. Since the stimulant medications can also stimulate the cardiovascular system, producing increased pulse rates and perhaps a mild increase of the blood pressure, I suggest the exercise program be more relaxed during the process of building the medication to its appropriate level.

Unless the teen has other underlying cardiac problems, such as mitral valve prolapse, there should be little if any uncomfortable side effects with the medication and exercise. However, it is wise to increase exercise more slowly while the proper dose is being determined. After a teen has been on a stable dose of medication for a period of six to eight weeks, there should be little effect on the cardiovascular status and maximum exercise can usually be tolerated without difficulty.

If the exercise period is during the summer, it is wise to initiate the medication early in the summer rather than late. If the teen has been on the medication the previous season, simply continue this through the first part of the summer in anticipation of the strenuous exercise in hot conditions that the teen is about to be subjected to.

If the teen comfortably tolerates the exercise, no additional consideration needs to be entertained. However, if some cardiac irregularity persists, a resting pulse rate above ninety beats per minute continues, or a blood pressure elevation greater than twenty points either on the systolic (high number) or the diastolic (low number) occurs, the medication should be altered.

BIOFEEDBACK

Biofeedback is a treatment based on the teen's ability to change his own brainwave pattern. In this case, the brain waves are measured through electrodes placed on the head or scalp and fed into an instrument designed to monitor and distinguish between them. These brain waves can be displayed either as the specific wave form or along with other graphic methods. Teens are encouraged to understand that they can change the pattern and are given an example of what change is desired. By learning that there is a relationship and learning how to concentrate on producing that result, the patient can become quite proficient at these changes.

Biofeedback has been suggested and frequently espoused as a treatment for ADHD. Although it seems apparent that the behavior can be changed in certain areas over a period of time and that this period of time can be extended, it does not appear to provide good global control. By global control, I mean that there is a pronounced improvement in the majority of the symptoms the ADHDer experiences.

Biofeedback has been reported to improve attention span and hyperactivity. However, this appears to require frequent retraining. The research previously reported has not been up to customary scientific standards so any conclusions are tenuous at best. It seems that biofeedback is less effective at producing a good sense of priority, lack of impulsive actions, and an ability for task completion.

Much research is presently going on, and it needs to be continued. However, the expense of biofeedback (in some cases more than $6,000 for six months of treatment) suggests that medications should be used prior to engaging in it. The medications produce better global control, are usually well tolerated if employed cautiously with adequate monitoring, and are often more effective. If medications produce some type of unpleasant reaction or fail to work completely, then biofeedback is an option. The ongoing research will give us more information about this treatment modality, and its appropriate position in the options for treatment of ADHD symptoms.

THREE

ADHD IN THE TEEN YEARS

A ttention deficit hyperactivity disorder is a complex syndrome involving a variety of symptoms as defined by the DSM-IV (*Diagnostic and Statistical Manual of Mental Disorders*). All individuals with ADHD will display a different combination of symptoms, manifestations that will range from mild to severe even in the same individual. For instance, a teenager may have mild attention inconsistencies but be severely disabled with persistent motor activity (inability to sit more than a few minutes, always on the go, nonstop talker, cannot sit and relax). Another teenager may be extremely distractible and insatiable but experience only mild restlessness. Still another may have severe difficulties with inattention but only minor problems with impulsivity. However, it should be noted that some teens will demonstrate an excessive amount of difficulty in all areas, including severe inattention, impulsivity, distractibility, hyperactivity, or a combination of these.

According to Russell A. Barkley, PhD, an internationally recognized expert on ADHD from the University of Massachusetts Medical Center, 70% to 80% of all children with ADHD will continue to display completely their ADHD symptoms into adolescence at a level that is not age appropriate. About 50% to 60% will fully exhibit ADHD symptoms into adulthood. Because adolescence usually brings with it a host of unique issues, considerations, and uncertainties, the preteen and teenager with ADHD will face additional challenges and pressures.

ADHD is known to induce a multitude of challenges, such as academic problems, negative self-image, social difficulties with peers, and a lack of success at extracurricular activities. The teen years of the individual with ADHD may be the most difficult since he seeks more freedom but must display greater responsible conduct. He must deal with identity issues, dating, physical development, and sexuality—additional sources of stress for the teen who is already dealing with the symptoms of ADHD.

"As the [growing] child becomes aware of his differences from others, is shunned or teased by peers, or is criticized by teachers for being unable to remain in control, the child begins to develop a negative self-image, low self-esteem, depression, and anger," says Pamela Darr Wright, LCSW, of Richmond, Virginia. "What significant others (parents, teachers) tell the child about himself has a powerful impact on his developing self-concept. The child begins to view himself as he is viewed by others. Told repeatedly that he 'could do better if he would only try,' he begins to believe that 'I am worthless because I cannot always control my behavior.' Sadly, these negative feelings about the self often persist through life."

The enormity of the problems faced by teens with ADHD cannot be dismissed. About 33% to 50% of teens requiring psychiatric outpatient services are identified as having ADHD, according to an article in the February 1991 issue of *Pediatrics for Parents*. In one study of 244 children diagnosed with ADHD, less than one quarter had unmitigated ADHD uncomplicated by another diagnosis. Other studies have shown that upwards of 85% of children with ADHD will have at least one comorbid condition that complicates the initial diagnosis of ADHD.

ADHD, with or without comorbidities, greatly affects the teen's performance in all areas of his or her life and creates varying degrees of challenges and difficulties. "Most of the problems arise from the fact that they process emotional and intellectual information somewhat differently from non-ADHD children and youth," says Wright. "Our culture places great value on conformity, especially in the training and education of children. If the child with ADHD is raised and educated with an appreciation of his or her uniqueness and strengths, then that child can grow up into a healthy, productive adult."

SYMPTOMS OF ADHD IN TEENS

Teens who achieve success in academics and social relationships in their childhood years are able to develop positive self-esteem, confidence, and a sense of identity. It appears, however, that teenagers with ADHD have limited success as a result of scholastic underachievements, poor or limited peer relationships, poor self-monitoring skills, and unsuccessful extracurricular activities during their childhood. This may carry over into their teen years.

You must remember that ADHD affects all aspects of the teen's life. Although not related to IQ, ADHD impairs the ability to learn, socialize, and behave, to some extent—no matter how bright the teen is. It affects relationships with parents, teachers, relatives, siblings, and friends.

The primary symptoms of ADHD—inattention, impulsivity, distractibility, and/or hyperactivity—are each multidimensional.

Impulsivity
Teens may have little self-control, often acting without thinking first. Poor impulse control can make it extremely difficult to say no to peers who encourage

them to try drugs, have a beer or two before driving to a party, or numerous other problems:

- spontaneous decisions regarding the use of drugs or alcohol
- casual sex resulting in pregnancy (inability to delay gratification)
- reckless driving (due to attention inconsistencies or distractibility)
- failure to recognize the propensity for dangerous, risk-taking, thrill-seeking behavior and the negative consequences of this behavior (the need for highly stimulating activities to reduce boredom is not unusual in those with ADHD)

Equally important, however, is that teenagers with ADHD may also lack the self-esteem and the self-control needed to say no to high-risk behaviors and situations.

Attention Inconsistencies

Children and teens with ADHD also display attention inconsistencies. When engaged in activities they enjoy (movies, sports, a conversation they find extremely interesting), they can easily tune in. This is called selective attention. At other times when faced with a boring, mundane task, an uninteresting class lecture, or a parent making a request, they tune out—their ability to sustain attention is greatly reduced. This inability to selectively attend to a task, such as homework or listening to a class lecture, often leads to underachievement and even failure in school. Constant failures lead to low self-esteem, and many teens with ADHD view themselves as failures, lazy, stupid, or worthless.

A teenager with severe attention deficits may not be able to focus on a discussion. During a conversation, for instance, you may suddenly notice a blank look on her face, because her free association of thoughts and ideas has lead to daydreaming. Other times, something else has caught her attention (a song on the radio, a program on television, a sibling entering the room), and she has literally disconnected from you through no fault of her own. Because many stimuli compete for her attention at the same time, she is unable to focus on the subject at hand. Biological changes during adolescence may also make her more hyperresponsive to stimuli.

Whether in school, at home, or with peers, her ability to pay attention is limited. In school she may literally sit through an entire class and never hear one word the teacher says. She may have to read a paragraph over and over before comprehending it. Books are especially difficult because they appear to be an endless task. Some teens with ADHD complain of constant noise in their head, like a radio playing in their brain that interferes with their ability to pay attention. Fortunately proper medications can relieve these symptoms.

They easily lose school books, glasses, house keys, etc. Homework assignments often do not get turned in either because they forget to hand the paper in or they can't find it. The challenge for parents is to assist the teenager in managing his environment. House keys, school books, etc., should always be placed in the same location upon entering the house. Routines must be set up and followed consistently. Research shows that children and teenagers with ADHD are not able to repeat activity patterns long enough to create routines on their own.

Conscientious parents who are quick to rescue their teenager by doing such things as driving forgotten homework to school or doing things for him that he could easily do for himself, prevent the teen from having to accept that he can and must find ways to become more responsible for himself.

"Many people in the child's future will accept the fact of the ADD; but few will accommodate irresponsibility that negatively impacts them," says Mark Snyder, MD, a psychiatrist in Phoenix. "As the young person matures, he will be taking on adult responsibilities. To be successful as an adult, he'll need to find strategies, aids, devices, tricks, whatever it takes, to keep himself on time, on target, and on schedule. A good time for the young person to practice accepting that responsibility is now. Obviously, the parent cannot or would not just abandon the young person, but slowly shifting the responsibility for his life to him, with help as appropriate, is the best gift parents can offer."

Parental requests or demands may have to be repeated many times before the teen actually hears and realizes that the parent is speaking to him. Before making any requests, you should first get the teenager's attention by establishing eye contact. Then, make your request brief and to the point (for example, "Please wash the window in the kitchen"). If instructions are complex (such as "Wash the kitchen window, vacuum the living room, then run to the store and buy milk, bread, one green pepper, and some laundry detergent"), written instructions are needed. Otherwise, you are setting him up for failure.

Chronic Procrastination

Individuals with ADHD are great procrastinators. They often have difficulty starting a project or task and may put it off until the last minute. A student may have six weeks to work on a science project but not start it until the night before it's due because of the inability to plan ahead. Parents who monitor school work can help their teenager by showing him ways to break a project down into smaller tasks that can be done weekly.

Procrastination can be brought about by the fear of failure or a resistance to do something that he truly doesn't want to. A low frustration level is often seen when the teen attempts to complete a particularly difficult assignment. Tempers may flare as he becomes more and more frustrated. In the same vein, he may disregard stop signs because he doesn't have the patience to stop and wait. Waiting in lines or in traffic becomes almost unbearable.

Instant Gratification

The need for instant gratification is seen in many young people with ADHD. When they want something, they want it now. However, the item they wanted so badly is often discarded a short time later for something else. Because of the difficulty in delaying gratification, rewards for appropriate behavior must be given immediately.

Teens with ADHD cannot wait until the weekend for their allowance like most teenagers because they focus on immediate gains and satisfactions.

Peer Relationships
Those with poor social skills have difficulty making and keeping friends. They are often better talkers than listeners, may frequently interrupt others (for fear of forgetting what they want to say), and may have difficulty reading the reactions of others. Some may be nonstop talkers, irritating those around them. Others may be exceptionally quiet unless they have center stage. Teens with hyperactivity appear more often to be rejected by peers. Those without hyperactivity tend to be ignored or neglected by their peers.

Hyperactivity and Hypoactivity
Restlessness (leg swinging, finger tapping, yawning) replaces the hypermotor activity you may have witnessed in childhood. Restlessness is the least diagnosed form of hyperactivity. It is important to note that many experts believe that all individuals with ADHD show signs of restlessness throughout the life span. Some individuals may actually fluctuate between hyperactivity and hypoactivity throughout the day. A teenager may be hypoactive and appear lethargic, yet still experience bouts of energy in the late afternoon and evening hours. Mental fatigue is also common, but falling asleep at night may be difficult due to a bombardment of thoughts.

Poor Organizational Skills
Most have poor organizational skills, which means their environments are cluttered. Bedrooms are messy with stacks of papers, magazines, clothes, and other items piled on their desks and floors. Their cars may look like they live in them. In school, they often cannot locate a pencil, a book, or a homework assignment, and their lockers are usually messy. They are often unable to plan ahead by determining and setting priorities. Planning homework assignments that are due in one month or longer without having a written schedule to follow is nearly impossible for many teenagers with ADHD. Untidy surroundings, careless reading and writing habits, and incomplete homework assignments are evident. Organizational skills do not come naturally to individuals with ADHD—this usually requires the help of a parent, teacher, or a "coach" (someone outside of the family who checks in with the teenager regularly and helps with organizational management). Structure is difficult for the ADHDer because his brain lacks internal organization. Unlike most people, the person with ADHD must learn to build structure. Therefore it is imperative that parents teach their teen how to manage and organize his environment.

"Give him structure in all aspects of his life," says George Lynn, MA, a certified mental health counselor in Bellevue, Washington. "Use lots of reminder notes, incentives, and posted schedules [calendars, appointment books, use of a computer] to compensate for short-term memory and personal organization problems. Help him organize his space. Use 'reminder language' to give him specific behavioral feedback on what he is doing. He may not remember from the last time."

Poor Concept of Time

Those with a poor concept of time are unable to predict how long a task will take. They might think a book report will take only an hour to write, but in reality it will take them two hours. Predicting how long it will take to drive somewhere is easy, but only as long as it is the same route that they have been driving back and forth for months or years. Ask them how long it takes to drive to the post office (a mile away) and they may not be able to give you an accurate time. This poor concept of time interferes greatly in their lives, from writing a book report to missing social appointments.

The Need for Stimulation

Individuals with ADHD like and seek out highly stimulating activities, yet they often fail to recognize the dangers involved. When bored they often create their own excitement or stimulation. Have you ever wondered why, when everyone in the family is sitting around peacefully, suddenly out of nowhere your teenager directs a ridiculous statement at you or a sibling and an argument erupts? It's actually quite simple. As he sits there he becomes increasingly restless and bored. It's like an itch that needs to be scratched. The pressure builds up and needs to be released. So he starts a fight, and the excitement begins!

Teens with ADHD are starving for stimulation. Although they experience more stimulation than is normal, they are actually anesthetized to the usual stimulation that others experience. Because of this, they often create their own stimulation or seek highly stimulating activities to fill this void.

Poor Internal Self-Monitoring

Poor internal self-monitoring makes it difficult for young people to see the cause and effect of their actions, so others get blamed for their failures or inappropriate behaviors. Some have hot tempers that can be set off by even the slightest irritation. Moods may shift from normal to depression to excitement within a short time and without apparent cause.

Other symptoms you might observe in your teenager are a testing of the boundaries and limits and a fluctuation in performance (maybe he passes a math test on Monday but fails a similar test two days later, frustrating both the student and the teacher). However, despite the difficulties faced by many individuals with ADHD, parents must remember that the use of medications will greatly reduce many of its most difficult symptoms. The teenager whose ADHD is being closely monitored by a physician should take medications as prescribed, decreasing many of the daily challenges she faces.

Teens with ADHD will experience many of the symptoms outlined, but those without hyperactivity tend to be more spacey, lost in their own thoughts, and seemingly unaware of external events. Their awareness is focused inward. They tend to be less disruptive and are seldom oppositional, aggressive, or noncompliant. Memory recall appears to be inconsistent. All people, at one time or another, may display many of these symptoms, especially at particularly stressful times in their lives, but individuals with ADHD experience them daily.

IS THERE ANYTHING POSITIVE ABOUT HAVING ADHD?

By now you are probably wondering if your son or daughter is doomed to fail. The answer is no. With assistance and support from parents and teachers, and medication and therapy if indicated, young people find ways to cope with difficulties in tempering movement, moods, and attention inconsistencies. Through the years, they can learn to compensate for their differences. As an adult, with a job or career ideally suited to their strengths, they often conquer many hurdles and are successful in life.

Too often as parents, we tend to dwell on the negative characteristics of ADHD in our teenagers because we find many of the symptoms overwhelming. However, if we can look beyond the negatives we can identify many positives; albeit, many of the positives may not be seen as strengths by parents and teachers in the teen years but will be more clearly defined as such in adulthood. While not all people with ADHD have the following strengths, these have been recognized in many individuals with ADHD:

- the ability to see the whole picture as if through a wide-angle lens
- exceptional memory for remote incidents
- the ability to think creatively
- affirmative risk taking
- sharp observation skills
- the ability to react swiftly to any change or threat in the environment and to rapidly change course if the situation warrants it
- ability to hyperfocus on a project that is stimulating and interesting
- insightful, discriminating, and perceptive about other people and situations
- often has a high energy level
- often are great negotiators
- extremely persistent
- often intuitive and highly intelligent

Look for and appreciate the positive qualities you observe in your son or daughter. "These qualities can be hailed as strengths in adulthood," says Bruce A. Pasch, MD, director, Children's Center for Learning and Development in Toledo. "For instance, impulsiveness may be seen later as decisiveness, insatiability as ambition, distractibility as creativity or open-mindedness." How we label these symptoms (using positive, rather than negative, terms) can help improve the outlook of parents, teachers, and others working with our teens.

DEVELOPMENTAL PERIOD

Adolescence is a time of rapid and dramatic development involving physical changes, intellectual growth, emotional ability, and behavioral changes, with a variation of what is considered normal. This time of transition from the preteen years to adolescence to adulthood places many demands on the teen and his parents. Transitions are generally difficult for teens with ADHD.

The usual problems of adolescence are compounded in the teen with ADHD and his family in a manner that is out of proportion with the typical course of development. This imbalance is a direct result of the primary symptoms of ADHD and the associated characteristics (social, emotional, physical, and academic) that place a burden on the normal developmental tasks of adolescence.

During adolescence, the teen faces new challenges and demands that he must cope with, all of which will pose specific difficulties for the teenager with ADHD. Some of these include the following:

- the need to establish an identity separate from his parents (early adolescence) and the need to distinguish himself from his peers (middle adolescence)*
- gain independence*
- develop interpersonal skills*
- dating
- dealing with peer pressure
- physical changes in appearance
- new feelings and emotions
- sexual awakening
- exposure to drugs and alcohol
- parental guidance and authority
- more advanced courses in school
- setting life goals (planning for college, vocational school, or a job after graduating from high school)*

  *the primary tasks of adolescence

Obviously all teens must deal with these issues and demands, but teens with ADHD often experience failure in school, social segregation, conflict with parents, low self-esteem, and depression as well. Impulsivity, the need for instant gratification, and the desire for highly stimulating activities often lead to additional problems and high-risk behaviors. Noncompliance, the inability and sometimes unwillingness to tackle daily homework assignments and chores, deficits in communication and listening skills, and greater mood swings than non-ADHD teens add extra challenges to the family unit.

The Parental Role

Because of the many challenges facing the teen and the immediate family, parents must do many of the following:

- re-examine their parenting style
- restructure the home environment
- maintain a parental coalition (or develop a parental coalition if the teen has too much control in the family)
- develop a cooperative relationship with the teen
- learn new methods of handling conflicts within the home
- manage stress and marital discord
- find supportive adults and friends that can provide positive role models for their teen outside of the family
- maintain or open the lines of communication with their teen
- teach their teen as much as they can about the positive and negative aspects of ADHD and help steer them in the right direction
- assist the teen in developing the skills needed to become his own advocate
- set realistic expectations
- observe the teen because medication or treatment strategies may need to be changed or started
- watch for problem or high-risk behaviors
- watch for signs of depression, anxiety, and other psychological problems that may develop

During the time when parents are re-evaluating their parenting skills and making other adjustments in the home, their teen is reaching for independence (or more independence). And rightfully so! The time between childhood and adulthood is the time for parents to begin letting go and yielding to their teen's need for independence. However, this concept is somewhat frightening for parents of teens with ADHD, especially those parents who have been overly protective and overly concerned through the years.

Parents as well as teachers must educate themselves about ADHD, recognize the symptoms, and assist the teen in learning to successfully cope with her symptoms. Involved parents and teachers can help to minimize the increased perils and potential for failure that exist by understanding the specific challenges the teen faces academically, socially, physically, and emotionally. An empowered parent can help the teen recognize and utilize her strengths, assist in identifying problem areas, provide information to the teen so she is better able to understand her challenges, and encourage her to become actively involved in her own treatment plan. Identifying, understanding, and accepting the individual needs of the affected teenager will also provide a parent with realistic expectations of their teen—an important step toward helping the teen experience a rewarding home life surrounded by caring, supportive parents.

Parents who expect perfection will be sorely disappointed. Focus on your teenager's skills, talents, and abilities, rather than dwelling on his shortcomings. Encourage the development of special talents and gifts. Provide opportunities for your teenager to experience success by using his talents creatively. Remember that many of those shortcomings you are witnessing now will become assets for opportunities in adulthood, but for now those challenges are real for your teenager and he still needs your support.

Throughout the ups and downs of adolescence, parents must accept their teenager by showing unconditional love and support. Develop a close, positive relationship with your teen. Many teens with ADHD see themselves as worthless, unappreciated, and unloved. They must know they are loved unconditionally no matter what their strengths and weaknesses, how they act, or how they look. Teenagers are children in transition who need to feel loved and accepted by their parents.

Successful ADHDers often comment that one particular person was responsible for making them feel special and important during their childhood or teen years. Sometimes that person was a teacher, coach, relative, or a parent who showed the child that he was worthwhile and significant. Your child's future depends on your commitment. The power of unconditional love and support is amazing. A close, positive relationship with your teenager can pave the way to future successes in all areas of his life. Don't let the opportunity slip through your fingers. Become the key player is your teenager's life.

FOUR

YOUR TEEN'S EVOLVING IDENTITY

Preteens and teenagers will experience many new feelings and emotions as they move from dependence to independence, establish an identity, and learn intimacy. For many years, families operate on parental rules. Limits and boundaries are set, and parents do their best to make sure their youngsters comply. As adolescence approaches, the family undergoes many changes. The teenager wants and needs more autonomy. Because autonomy goes hand in hand with responsibilities, parents must now begin to let go and trust that their teenagers will make positive decisions for themselves. As expected, parents of teenagers with ADHD will have mixed emotions as they watch their teen test the waters of life.

Although most parents understand this testing is a natural course of development, the symptoms of ADHD can easily obstruct their view, making them reluctant to step back and permit the teen to try on different identities. This may be especially true of parents who have been overly protective, have preconceived ideas of what they expect their teenager to do, or who attempt to control their teenager.

Insightful parents who have watched their child struggle through school, struggle with friendships, and tackle the daily challenges of ADHD, know that their teenager is lacking in certain skills. As a result, parents who have been advocating for their child for years often are overly protective. They strive to spare their child from anything unpleasant, including the pain of failure. As the child reaches adolescence, parents feel a heightened need to protect him from outside influences.

Protecting teenagers from their actions deprives them from learning about the natural and logical consequences of their behavior and how it affects others; therefore, the teenager is not able to discover his own limits or those imposed by others. This protection factor fails to let the teen grow and experience failure. Failing and learning from mistakes is vital as teenagers search and experiment in an attempt to define their own identity.

Overly controlling parents, as well as parents who overidentify with their teenager, restrict their teen by leaving him only two choices. One, the teenager either opposes his parents and acts out, or two, he gives in to his parents' wishes and demands and fails to adopt his own identity. Neither is healthy.

Teenagers must have the opportunity to experiment and explore to form their identity if they are to become healthy adults. Naturally, they will experience both successes and failures. Successes, no matter how small, must be acknowledged and encouraged. When the teenager with ADHD fails, parents can help by brainstorming with their teen to find different ways they might have handled the situation better. As parents, we need to take a step back, give advice only with permission, and always give compliments and recognition when it is earned.

THE SEARCH FOR IDENTITY

The search for identity means that teenagers will try on many hats to see which one fits the best. They begin to look at things differently and question such things as religious beliefs, friendships, and commitments. Their interests change (for instance, art classes or piano lessons of several years may be abandoned). Friendships change, and new ones are formed.

Privacy becomes an issue. During this time, teens become private about their personal lives. They often hang out in their room for hours at a time doing nothing, or so it appears to parents. But this time of reflection and aloneness is much needed for the teen's adjustment.

New feelings often produce complicated emotions that teenagers may have difficulty expressing. Their appearance may become an obsession. They may spend hours looking at themselves in the mirror, styling their hair, trying different clothes on—all in an endeavor to determine who they are and where they fit in. Thinking, questioning, and changing is necessary for the developmental process of adolescence. When the teenager is stifled he is unable to investigate and test, which results in an inability to learn who he really is.

With the exploring and experimenting comes minor rebellion—primarily directed at the parents' values. Families who have always attended religious services together may find that their teen suddenly refuses to go. They frequently do exactly the opposite of what you want. This perfectly normal form of rebellion is part of the their search for an identity.

Minor rebellion usually begins in the home in the form of parent-teenager confrontations. Teens begin finding fault with their parents, disputing the rules, and challenging opinions and values. Challenging rules in the search for identity is normal. However, acting-out behaviors such as stealing, running away from home, or using drugs are not normal rebellious behaviors and require professional intervention. (See chapter 13 for more information.)

THE SEARCH FOR INDEPENDENCE

Moving toward independence includes such things as the teen wanting to take charge of her own life, choosing her own friends, and making her own plans and decisions. Success comes with the recognition of the ability to take charge of her own life and handle responsibility.

Although most normal teenagers manage to make the transition from childhood through adolescence with relative ease, some do not. In a study of twenty thousand nonpatient teens, 80% of the teenagers interacted well with their parents and friends, did not experience unusual stress, and felt comfortable with their values. The other 20% did, however, experience difficulties such as depression, suicidal thoughts, and risk-taking behaviors.

The problem that teens with ADHD encounter are that, while they are expected to take responsibility for their actions and decisions, they face delays in general development such as inadequate self-perception, inattention to details, poor social skills, poor concept of time, immaturity, and impulsive decision making. Their ability to handle responsibility is in essence delayed—they lag behind non-ADHD teenagers in many areas.

LEARNING INTIMACY

As teenagers begin separating from their parents, their friends become their emotional base of support and understanding. Through these friendships teens form their identity, develop social skills, develop trust, learn to rely on others outside the family, and form close relationships with their peers.

Bernice R. Berk, PhD, school psychologist at Bank Street School for Children, says "[I]t's important for kids to learn how to talk to and be comfortable with members of the opposite sex. Failure to learn these skills can interfere with the strength of later male-female relationships." Many teens with ADHD, however, often lack a sense of self-esteem and have poor social skills, making it difficult to establish close personal relationships with peers.

How can parents help? They can begin by opening up their home to their teen's friends and making everyone feel comfortable. Teens who know they can bring friends home and entertain with your permission and cooperation will fare better than those who are not permitted to have friends visit in their homes. Encourage your teenager's involvement in outside activities such as those held at your place of worship, after school projects, volunteer work in your community, a part-time job, joining a health club—places and activities where she can connect with others and develop friendships with peers and adults who have similar interests. Group activities are important for all teens, especially in early adolescence, and encourage the development of social skills.

Avoid comparing your teenager to others her age because many teens with ADHD lag behind their peers. Constant comparison will only depreciate the already lowered self-esteem. Instead, recognize the accomplishments and the improvements you witness. Focus on strengths rather than on weaknesses because this will encourage your teenager to face her daily challenges knowing she has your full support and confidence. In other words, believe in your teen so she can believe in herself!

STAGES OF TEEN DEVELOPMENT

Early Adolescence
In the early stages of adolescence (ages twelve to fourteen), there is a rapid physical change in body development. This age group is particularly concerned about their personal appearance and the physical changes taking place. The need to know that they are "normal" and not different from their peers is particularly important at this age.

Many teenagers with ADHD already feel different and have for years—this awareness alone is stressful enough. Studies have shown that children with invisible disabilities (ADHD, learning disabilities, diabetes, etc.) actually have a lower self-image than children with more apparent disabilities. The reason is that peers and others make allowances for disabilities they can see, but not for those disabilities they cannot see. Teenagers with invisible disabilities look normal and are expected to perform as well as their peers, but they are often perceived by others as different.

While some teens with ADHD are gregarious and popular, others may have insipid personalities that make it difficult to talk to others, listen appropriately, make eye contact, etc.—all skills needed to fit into a peer group. So while one teen is popular, another may be bossy and argumentative, and still another so passive that no one even notices her.

Peer groups are important to teens because they are able to look at others their age and see how they compare. Unfortunately, the teen with ADHD may be looking at the peer group from the outside due to immaturity, the inability to relate because of poor social skills, and low self-esteem. On the other hand, she may be identifying with an inappropriate crowd, but it may be the only crowd that is willing to accept her. Although she may know that these friends are not the type of friends she really wants, her desperation to fit in makes her susceptible to peer pressure. The wrong peer group can lead to inappropriate behaviors particularly with drugs and alcohol and can even lead to juvenile delinquency, especially if the teen has oppositional defiant disorder or conduct disorder.

So what should parents do if their teenager is involved with a wrong crowd? One young woman with ADHD, Heidi Wymer, offered some insightful thoughts:

"Most kids with ADHD do not end up running with the wrong crowd, but some do and parents often try anything to prevent their teen from running with friends who they think are a bad influence. Putting their peers down does not help. It will only cause the teen to turn against the parent and defend their friends, even if the teen has an idea that the friends are not a good influence. Rather than having your teen sneak around, allow him to

*associate with these friends but only in nonthreatening environments, such as school sport-
ing events, supervised parties at homes of friends where parents are home, or invite the
friends into your home. You cannot protect them from peer pressures, but you can provide
them with a home they can always feel safe and loved in—a place to go home to. Teenagers
need to feel that they can call on you if they find themselves in a dangerous situation or
when facing a crisis. They need to feel that they have somewhere to go or someone to talk
with other than their peers. Eventually they will find that these are not the friends they
want to be around."*

Other teens may just withdraw, spending all of their time in their bedroom,
watching television or listening to music. If the withdrawal is persistent, depression
may be the underlying cause and must be addressed. Depression and ADHD often
go hand-in-hand. Seek professional help if depression is a concern because counseling, medication, or both may be indicated.

Since this age group is just beginning the developmental tasks of adolescence,
their identity is far from being formed. However, they are aware of their increasing
sexuality and find adult behaviors appealing. The teen with ADHD may be
extremely impressed by things that are not age appropriate such as smoking, drinking, or sexual activity, especially if she thinks such things will make her appear more
mature. The need to fit in is strong in teens with ADHD. Girls, who feel unloved,
may become sexually involved in an attempt to gain love. Their impulsivity and
insatiability may lead to pregnancy. Boys may become involved with a gang or
engage in destructive acts. Delinquency and promiscuity are common, particularly
if the teen has a history of hostile, aggressive, and defiant behavior. Hyperactive
teenagers usually look down on rules and do not tolerate limits placed on their
behavior.

Middle Adolescence

In middle adolescence (ages fifteen to seventeen) teens remove themselves even further from their parents. They begin to feel better about their body image, and their
appearance usually becomes even more important, although teens with ADHD may
not become interested in these issues until later. Cognitive and conceptual skills in
normal teens forge ahead during this stage along with a growing ability to express
their thoughts and feelings and understand those of others. Cognitive and conceptual skills in the teen with ADHD, however, may be delayed.

According to an article in the *Journal of the American Academy of Child and Teen,*
25 (1986), 50% or more of all clinic-referred children with ADHD have speech and
language disorders that will directly affect their ability to express themselves adequately. While more severe forms of language disorders are usually detected before
the child enters school, less severe forms may not be detected for years.

It is during this time that your teen will often say, "You don't understand."
Many of us do remember and understand, but from your teen's viewpoint, his peers
are the only ones who truly understand. The attachment to peers is particularly
strong; they want to do what their friends are doing and go where their friends are
going, which may not be exactly what you had in mind.

Teenagers are under a great deal of stress in middle adolescence with the demands of school, home, relationships, and their extracurricular activities. The stress alone can lead to risky behavior, but the risks and temptations become even greater for some teens with ADHD.

Late Adolescence

By late adolescence (ages eighteen to twenty-one), the search for an identity is nearly completed. The teen should be successfully handling many responsibilities of adulthood and have an idea of where he is headed in the future. Although he has separated successfully from his parents, acceptance by peers is not as important as it was a few years earlier. By now, he has identified his sexual orientation and is gaining an understanding of sexual desires. The teen is usually more confident of his self-image and his values. His major concern, nevertheless, is skepticism about his future and what path to follow.

Older teens with ADHD on the other hand, may still be struggling with identity issues, striving to manage their environments, and trying to assume more responsibility for their actions. They may not have given any thought to their future, unless you or another role model has been addressing this with them.

Parents play a major role in assisting the teenager in successfully completing the developmental tasks of adolescence and the move into adulthood. Here are some of the parents' tasks:

- learning about, supporting, respecting, and encouraging the identity process and realizing that this is a transitory stage of development
- adapting to the changing needs of the teen
- realizing that hormonal changes can affect behavior and mood changes
- understanding and accepting that the teen is preparing to enter adulthood and is no longer a child
- helping the teen by enhancing his self-esteem or by providing ways he can enhance his self-worth
- respecting the teen's need for privacy but maintaining contact by showing love and support
- negotiating clear, concise rules and limits and consequences and rewards for behavior
- choosing battles carefully
- learning and understanding how ADHD affects the teen's development
- letting the teen know that mistakes happen to everyone and you are willing to give them another try

MAKING THE TRANSITION

How successfully the teen with ADHD makes the transition from adolescence to adulthood depends on many factors including the severity of the symptoms the teenager has, school successes or failures, peer acceptance or rejection, coexisting medical problems, treatment strategies (medication, therapy, etc.), and the parental relationship with the teenager.

Teenagers whose symptoms are in the mild range usually have the best chance of successfully navigating adolescence and moving into adulthood, particularly if they have higher IQs, close friends, come from a higher socioeconomic class, excel in a sport or another interest, feel good about themselves overall, have stable family lives, and have learned ways to compensate for their difficulties. This is not meant to imply that these teens are not at risk for some negative behavior but that the risk is greatly reduced for this group of teens with ADHD.

Teenagers with severe ADHD symptoms, a history of aggressive behavior, and conduct problems will face more challenges. But even with these factors involved, the outcome is still unknown because other variables such as the emotional, social, intellectual, and psychological aspects of the teenager's life—not to mention his relationship with his parents, the home environment, and his peers—all combine to make a tremendous impact on his life. Teenagers with severe symptoms of ADHD, aggressiveness, and conduct problems are at greater risk for such things as truancy, substance abuse, sexual experimentation, running away, violent behavior, delinquency, and defiance, particularly if the family environment is dysfunctional. It is important to note that such behaviors, while deplored by concerned parents and society, may be seen as solutions to some teens, especially those who are suffering from a sense of failure or hopelessness.

Parents of teens with special challenges must provide acceptance and support just like any other parent. They must encourage the teen to explore and experiment and provide the space needed to accomplish these tasks. Yet, at the same time, parents must also take into consideration that their teenager with ADHD will need more time than other teenagers to begin and accomplish these developmental tasks.

Parents can support their teen with ADHD by watching for opportunities to praise the many strengths they observe. ("I couldn't help but notice that you did not give up on that project even though you found it difficult. Your persistence and determination really impresses me.") Focus on the strengths, not the weaknesses. ("Why is it you can sit still and concentrate on that project but not on your homework?")

Parents should also look for and encourage talents, hobbies, and special interests. Many individuals with ADHD are extremely creative and excel in many areas. Help your teen find an area that he can excel in, assist him in fostering the talent, and lend assistance through supportive approval and encouragement. That one talent or special gift can make a tremendous difference in the life of a teen with ADHD—it will not only strengthen self-esteem but will also offer the opportunity to make friends with others who share the same interest. Many teens with ADHD have high energy levels, are inventive, express enthusiasm for new activities and interests, and find novel approaches to tackling tasks—all wonderful traits if the teen is pointed in the right direction.

As stated earlier, many teens with ADHD struggle with poor self-esteem due to the failures they have experienced so, when observing others their age, they often feel that they do not measure up. They often fail to see their strengths, believing they have none or fail to recognize those they have and their shortcomings are magnified. In an attempt to hide their feelings, they may present themselves in such a way as to appear arrogant—often at the expense of making another look inferior—the use of sarcasm and displays of attention-seeking behaviors are common. Parents often describe their child as having a chip on his shoulder; he appears to be always looking for an argument.

Many teens with ADHD are overly sensitive to mild criticism. Sensitive teens with ADHD often hear more than the mild criticism, taking it one step further and blowing it out of proportion. "Dad criticized me, so he doesn't love me." It helps if parents can identify with their teen. "When I was your age, the same thing happened to me . . . " Even with an equal balance of attention to all siblings, parents often complain that their teen with ADHD feels he is never treated fairly.

For example, your son with ADHD is planning to use the car on Saturday night. On Thursday he learns that his sister has asked to borrow the car on Saturday and has been told she can use it. Although you explain to him that he has used the car the last six Saturdays and his sister needs to use it this week, he explodes and complains of being treated unfairly because he truly feels his sister receives more privileges than he. To understand his feelings, you must understand him. Because of the failures he has experienced in the past and the criticisms he has received over the years, he feels like he is always being treated unfairly. To him, handing over the car keys to his sister is just one more example of his unfair treatment.

Parents can encourage their teens to improve their self-esteem by having them make lists of their strengths. "I have two best friends," or "I am proficient on the computer," or "Today I got to school on time." Have your teen add to the list daily. Parents can also encourage positive eating habits and exercise (exercising reduces stress, promotes relaxation, appears to increase the ability to pay attention and focus, and builds stamina and confidence).

No one succeeds until he faces failure. Remind your teen that everyone makes mistakes, even adults, but that ultimately he must forgive himself, but he must still hold himself accountable for the consequences. Having ADHD should *never* be an excuse.

You can teach your teen to feel better about himself. Have him practice deleting negative talk within himself. In other words, teach him to tune into his inner self-talk and recognize the negative thoughts. Teach him how to work to change those thoughts by first making a list of them (this increases awareness), and then teach him how to change negative thoughts to positive ones. "It is my behavior, not me, that is being criticized"; "I'm not stupid because I failed the history test"; or "I don't excel in music, but I'm good at sports." For reccurring thoughts, teach him to say, "Stop! Thinking like this will get me nowhere. I need to dwell on something positive." Remember we all have the ability to control our inner thoughts, some of us just need more help learning how to do this than others. We can choose to think only specific thoughts,thoughts that make us feel good about ourselves.

The combination of ADHD and the developmental tasks of adolescence interact with the relationships within the family and the overall management of the home. Remember, many teens with ADHD have difficulties completing chores and doing school work. They may also have problems getting along with others, including parents. They often lack age-appropriate communication skills, have problems interacting with family members, and have perception difficulties that interfere with the parent-teenager relationship. Hot tempers, impulsivity, and mood swings can hinder effective communications between parents and teens. Distinguishing between defiant behavior and behavior caused by inattention is a difficult task for parents. Understanding parental limits is difficult for the teen at best, and conflicts often erupt. These conflicts can escalate into significant disputes (power struggles) if the teen is not included in the decision-making process of rules and consequences. One of the most difficult tasks for parents of teens is establishing limits and following through with logical consequences and rewards.

Teens whose parents abuse drugs, have antisocial personality disorder, or suffer from depression or anxiety will experience more problems within the home than teens who enjoy a stable home environment, unconditional love, acceptance, and understanding during the teen years.

FIVE

GUIDING TEENS' BEHAVIOR

"What do you mean I can't go out with Kelly tonight?" Amanda screamed to her mother. "You can't tell me what to do."

"Now listen here, young lady. As long as you live in this house you will do as you are told," replied her mother in a stern voice. "I don't care if the president will be there. You are not going out, and that is that!"

As Ann turned to leave, Amanda yelled, "I hate you!" and threw a dish across the kitchen. "I wish Kelly's mom was my mother. You are so stupid. Besides, you never give me money when I want it, and you only let me use the car once in awhile. You are always interfering in my life. Why can't you just leave me alone? I hate you, do you hear me?"

Ann shouted back in retaliation, "If you think Kelly's mom would be a better mother, then go live there. I'll even get your suitcase for you. I've had enough of you to last me a lifetime."

Amanda is the perfect example of a teenager who is testing the limits. She is arguing for her rights and privileges. She wants to make her own decisions and be independent. However, Amanda is challenging and confronting her mother for something she perceives to be her right. Amanda also has ADHD and a low frustration tolerance. She frequently displays a hot temper and becomes aggressive when she's told "NO." Because of her impulsiveness, conflicts with her mother have increased considerably as she's gotten older. Ann, on the other hand, is the perfect example of a parent who is caught in a power struggle, which is a no-win situation. She is just as confused and angry as Amanda.

According to David Elkind, PhD, author of *The Hurried Child* and professor of child study at Tufts University, "Teenagers' power plays are not personal attacks on us and our authority." Confronting the rules is natural for teenagers. They need established rules to determine their own rules and appraise their importance as individuals. So how do you establish the limits? What limits are appropriate for teens with ADHD? When do you know when it is time to readjust the rules? How do you establish consequences for breaking the rules? If you are asking yourself these questions, you are not alone.

WHY LIMITS?

Adolescence is the time of separating from parents and making the transition from childhood to adulthood. It is the time when you must begin to accept that your child has a mind of his own and is no longer willing to do what you say just because you say it.

Teens want and need limits, even if they object to them. Boundaries permit them to explore and challenge the rules—a task of normal development—and learn that their parents care about them and their actions. "It is because young people need to confront our rules that it is so important for us to be firm about them," writes David Elkind, PhD. But how do we set the boundaries and remain firm about rules when we are challenged by a persistent, badgering teenager?

We begin with an effective parenting style. In my previous book, *The ADHD Parenting Handbook*, I describe four types of parenting methods and how each affects our children and teenagers:

1. Dominating parents, or overly controlling parents, have high expectations and expect rules to be followed without much explanation. ("I am the boss in this house, and you will do what I say.") The goal of these parents is total obedience—teenagers are to adhere to the rules without exceptions. Teens with dominating parents often become aggressive and angry. The result of dominating parents is often a teenager who is demanding, disrespectful, rebellious, and has little or no regard for authority and rules. Clearly, a dominating parenting style is the least effective and most negative method for any teenager but particularly for a teen with ADHD, who is already at higher risk for problematic behavior. A dominating parenting style actually encourages the types of behavior problems parents are hoping to ward off or eliminate.

2. Neglectful parents are usually not capable of emotionally supporting their children, nor do they possess any kind of control over them. The neglectful parent's life comes first. These parents often resent the time demands the teen makes—it interferes with their lives. Younger children are often left with baby sitters and teens are left to fend for themselves. This isolation from parents can cause insecurity, low self-esteem, rebellious behavior, and hamper emotional growth in teens. Those with ADHD need guidance, structure, clear-cut rules, and involved parental support to succeed.

3. Lenient parents fail to establish rules and consequences, believing that teens will learn to live in society through choice and experience. They rarely discipline because they usually have a disdain for authority figures.

Because of this, they do not want to be seen as inflexible or unyielding. Children of such parents are often manipulative, insecure, have low self-esteem, and believe that they are in control. They have trouble abiding by society's rules since they usually have no rules to follow at home. Teens with ADHD desperately need rules and structure, something these parents do not believe in establishing.

4. Firm and loving parents establish rules and consequences by involving their teenagers in the actual decision process by permitting them to make choices that encourage independence and promote self-esteem. Teens are more apt to abide by the rules if they have been given the opportunity to help establish the rules. Firm and loving parents also provide unconditional love, support, and spend focused time with their teenagers. They recognize that their teens are emerging adults with developmental tasks that need to be experienced and explored, and they actively encourage them to seek independence, make choices and decisions, and accept responsibility. Teenagers of firm and loving parents naturally feel more secure, loved, and have higher self-esteem. It is easy to see that teens with ADHD will experience more successes in the home and fewer confrontations with parents who are firm and loving.

EXAMINING YOUR PARENTING STYLE

It's worth repeating here that parents do not cause the primary symptoms of ADHD. However, the way parents handle misbehavior, disrespectful behavior, rebellious acts, confrontations, deviance, and even ordinary day-to-day mistakes can make their life with a teen with ADHD either one of harmony or discord. Parents who seem to be always clashing with their teenagers need to stop and evaluate their parenting skills. They must also be willing to make a strong commitment to change. The way a parent responds to problematic behavior, their expectations and whether the teen can meet those expectations, the teen's temperament, and how she reacts to your parenting methods are all factors that need to be examined. Obviously, if parents want to see changes made in the home and with their teens, they must be willing to make changes within themselves.

Authors Jane Nelsen and Lynn Lott, in their book *Positive Discipline for Teenagers,* suggest that parents admit that they might be partly responsible for problems, search for ways that they are part of the problems, try and look at it from the teen's perspective, and then validate the teenager's feelings.

An effective parenting style can have a beneficial impact on behavior as well as encouraging independence for teens. So what steps can parents take to change their parenting method to an effective, loving style? Consider the following suggestions.

Use negotiation. Do not dictate the rules. Instead, mutually establish rules and limits, consequences for inappropriate behaviors, and rewards for compliance. Be sure your teenager knows ahead of time which issues are negotiable and which are not.

Teenagers who are involved in the decision-making process regarding the use of the car, going out on school nights, and doing chores, for instance, are more apt to cooperate and follow the rules simply because they helped establish them. (See chapter 6 for detailed information on using negotiation strategies.)

Ask for his input on other decision-making issues that involve the whole family, such as taking a part-time job, purchasing another television, or arranging for after-school supervision. This permits the teen to feel like a valuable member of the household. It is not necessary for you to disclose your income to your teenager, but certainly let him begin to learn how much it costs to live. Most teenagers have no idea what household expenses involve.

Rather than tightening the reins, begin to relax them. The more control you exert, the more resistance you can expect to receive. The teenager with ADHD can be persistent and demanding and usually won't give up until he gets what he wants. If a rule has not been established, nagging and whining will continue. Or, worse yet, he will do what he wants to do behind his parents' backs if no one takes the time to sit down and discuss the request with him. Again, be willing to listen to what he has to say and seriously consider the request unless it involves an issue of safety or it is totally outrageous.

Change your response. If your normal reaction is to yell or nag when faced with uncompleted tasks, misbehavior, or noncompliance, try speaking softly and slowly. If a confrontation begins, and you usually stand nose-to-nose with your teen, next time tell her you will speak with her in one hour after everyone has the chance to calm down. Then excuse yourself from the room. This allows you the opportunity to think of a better way to handle the situation so there is a positive rather than negative discussion and outcome. The more you walk away from a confrontation or a teen's nagging, whining behavior, the sooner she will get the message that you are not willing to discuss anything with her until she can control herself and speak without demanding, arguing, or whining.

Think before you speak. If the first words out of your mouth when your teenager makes a request are usually negative, you can expect a negative response. Next time, instead of responding immediately, stop and think. Take a deep breath and count to ten, then reply. Without a doubt this takes a lot of practice and patience, especially if you and your teenager are both difficult, demanding, and quick to anger. If you work at it, you can change that initial response to a positive one. Awareness is the first step. Ask yourself, "How do I usually ask a question or respond to that request?" Then change your usual response. If your teenager is seeking attention through anger or demands, don't fall for it. Instead, give him attention when he least expects it. Catch him being good.

Anticipate upcoming problems or difficulties and decide how you will react to a situation so you can prevent it from escalating into a major confrontation. For instance, the summer family vacation, once perceived as fun, may not appeal to your sixteen-year-old teenager this year because she suddenly does not want to be seen in public with you. Prepare yourself ahead of time by brainstorming for possible solutions, such as offering choices if possible (she can stay with her grandparents or a friend's family) or negotiating with her (maybe she'll go if she can take a friend). It is better to think about potential problems ahead of time rather than waiting for them to develop. However, if a situation arises that you have not yet discussed, do not give an automatic no. Give her a time and date when you will respond.

Set reasonable expectations. Think ADHD and you will be less apt to expect perfection. You cannot expect impeccable grades, chores done to perfection, obedience with a happy face, or many other things that non-ADHD teens seem to be able to accomplish easily. Remember, your teenager is a special and unique individual with loads of potential if steered in the right direction. Unrealistic expectations focus on your needs instead of your teenager's inabilities.

Plan scheduled time with him. Like younger children, teenagers like to spend time with their parents. Exercise together, take a walk, watch a baseball game, hit a few golf balls in the backyard, or just sit and talk. The length of time you spend together is not as important as how you spend it. The greatest need a teenager has is to have your focused attention. Unfortunately, in today's hyperactive society, which manages to keep us all busy, parents do not give their teenagers the focused time they need. Often parents give gifts, grant privileges, and do favors under the guise of attention. Although these things are nice, there is no substitute for genuine focused attention from parents. Teenagers who do not receive focused attention from their parents feel like everything else in their parents' lives is more important than they are. Insecurity, anxiety, inability to cope, and impaired psychological and emotional growth are often the results. He may become dependent on peers, for example, and more susceptible to peer pressure.

Be patient. This is perhaps one of the greatest gifts we can give our teens with ADHD. Whether doing chores around the house or working on homework, it is important to remember that the symptoms of ADHD, especially distractibility and inattention, will get in her way. It may take longer to start and complete a task than it would a non-ADHD individual.

Concentrate on her strengths and abilities. Look for and encourage skills and talents that are naturals for your teenager. Most teens with ADHD excel or are creative in at least one area. If she expresses an interest or has a special talent in a particular area, especially one that could lead to a career, do everything you can to further that talent. Suggest ways that she might use those abilities to help others in school or at home. Remember to focus on strengths rather than weaknesses.

Believe in him so he can believe in himself. Acknowledge all efforts and improvements, even minor ones. Encourage and express confidence in his abilities by concentrating on his strengths. If you overly protect your teenager or express pity that he has to contend with ADHD, you will discourage him and inadvertently augment feelings of hopelessness.

Identify with her feelings. If your teenagers is depressed because she wasn't invited to a party, listen to what she has to say and acknowledge those feelings. Tell her how it felt when you were growing up and you weren't invited to a school dance or flunked a test that you should have passed with ease.

Choose your battles carefully. If you insist on getting your own way all the time, you will constantly be in a power struggle with your teenager. Decide what issues are the most important ones to address and leave the others behind (hair styles, clothing, music, etc.). Don't turn your home into a war zone by reacting to normal mishaps or mistakes as if they were major catastrophes. Bill Crews, the father of a teenage girl, says he and his wife choose their battles carefully. "We ask ourselves 1) Is this hurting us in any way, and 2) is the house on fire? If we answer no to both of these, it is not a catastrophe."

Talk to him about difficulties he may encounter. Let him know about the problems and temptations he may encounter concerning peer pressure, the use of drugs or alcohol, sexual activity, etc. Discuss with him how his impulsiveness may come into play and the choices he will have to make. Teens are more apt to listen to your advice before a problem develops than after.

Don't be afraid to let her fail, but resist the temptation to say, "I told you so." Instead, let your teenager know that everyone makes mistakes, even adults. If you suspect she is going to make a poor decision, it's okay to ask, "Have you thought about this from every angle? Can you think of how you might be able to handle it differently?" If she does not want to discuss it, drop the subject unless her decision endangers her safety, the safety of others, or is totally against your values or beliefs. Let her take responsibility for her actions and make her accountable when she fails.

Be sure she understands that your love is unconditional. If she makes an impulsive decision to go shopping when she was supposed to be running errands for you, be sure she understands that her behavior was irresponsible and inappropriate but that you still love her. Unconditional love means that despite a mistake, an impulsive decision, poor judgment, choice of clothes, or poor grades, she is still very much loved and cherished by you.

Avoid criticism, nagging, ridiculing, and yelling. Your teenager deserves respect. The teen with ADHD has a fragile ego and will react strongly and negatively to parents who use this approach. Fragile egos are difficult to repair. A damaged ego can have lifetime effects on your teen. If he insists on arguing, walk away from him. To avoid having him think you are walking away because you have given up, tell him you will talk to him later. James Windell, author of *8 Weeks to a Well-Behaved Child,* writes, "While [parents] do not cause a behavior problem, the . . . response . . . considerably affects whether that misbehavior continues . . . whether it gets better or worse." When teens "start to get scoldings, criticism, and . . . parents' devoted attention to the undesirable behavior . . . the behavior continues and sometimes gets worse." Teenagers with ADHD see any attention as positive, even if it results in objectionable consequences. Pay attention to how many times you say something similar to the examples below:

"You're sixteen years old, I shouldn't have to remind you of this everyday."
"When I was your age I was baby sitting. I have to remind you to take a bath."
"If you had only listened to your father. He was right, you know."

"You just have to try harder. Math was easy for me."
"Sometimes you seem so stupid. Use your brain once in awhile."

Each of these statements will affect the teen's self-confidence and self-esteem and may further energize the behavior you are trying hard to eliminate. Instead of commenting on undesirable behaviors, comment on and praise the desirable behaviors you witness. Encouragement and praise are positive reinforcers. Criticism, nagging, and yelling are negative reinforcers, but reinforcers just the same. The teen with ADHD sees all attention as positive simply because you or someone else has reacted to the behavior.

Avoid using labels. Do not call your teenager things such as lazy, stupid, bad, or dumb. Do not constantly remind him of things he cannot do. Teenagers who hear such remarks eventually begin to believe they are stupid, bad, and incapable of learning.

Always present a united front. It is imperative that parents present a united front. To do so, you must discuss the rules and boundaries, the consequences and rewards, then decide how you will react to certain misbehaviors. When a teenager sees that her parents disagree on the rules, when one parent is more apt to walk away and leave the other parent to handle the situation, or when one parent names a consequence and the other reduces it later, she is encouraged to play one parent against the other. Or she may assume that the rules are really not that important because even Mom and Dad can't agree on them.

Be a good role model for him. Teenagers learn from their parents so practice positive role modeling. Parents who lose control, for example, when angry and become aggressive towards other family members are not exhibiting positive role modeling. Parents who get angry and throw things teach their children that it is okay to express anger in a physical manner. Parents who listen attentively and show respect for their teenagers are positive role models. Similarly, if parents handle anger appropriately, their teens will learn how to express anger in an acceptable manner. Teens learn by observing your actions and those of others.

Try to distinguish the difference between noncompliance and incompetence. This is not an easy task and in some situations you may not be able to tell the difference. Noncompliance is deliberate defiance, whereas incompetence is the inability to do a task, follow directions, etc. If, for instance, you have asked your teenager to stop an annoying behavior and he complies but then several minutes later you notice he's doing it again, you are witnessing incompetence. If the same request is given and he continues after several seconds, you are usually witnessing noncompliance, unless you did not get the teenager's full attention before making the request. When in doubt, incompetence is usually the culprit.

Work on developing effective problem-solving and communication skills. Again, not an easy task if parents are caught up in a vicious circle. Therapy may be needed to break cycles and teach problem-solving and communication skills.

Let her know how her behavior affects you and other family members. Most teens with ADHD do not realize the impact their behavior has on others. Calmly and gently explain using "I" statements rather than "you" statements.

Don't embarrass or criticize him in front of others. If he has done something that you find unacceptable, take him off to the side and explain how you feel. Never address unacceptable behaviors in front of his friends or others.

Practice forgiveness. All parents make mistakes and some of those mistakes can damage a teens' self-esteem. We cannot undo these mistakes, but we can learn from them. Forgive yourself for your mistakes, and forgive your teenager for his. Don't dig up the past.

ESTABLISHING GUIDELINES AND LIMITS

It can be difficult to establish rules and follow through with consequences. By the time children with ADHD reach adolescence, parents are often burned-out from the challenges faced through the early years. So burned out, in fact, that some parents may have already given up. They have thrown their arms up in the air, frustrated and feeling inadequate about behavior problems, and proclaimed that they can no longer handle their teens. Have these parents really given up? No, most of them have not. Instead, they are hoping and praying that their teen's behaviors will change. It rarely does without intervention.

Instead of looking at the teen and wondering how to change him, parents should look at ways they can formulate changes in their relationships with their teens. If what you are doing is not working (trying to control him, overly protecting him, nagging, preaching, etc.), then you must change these actions or responses and replace them with more appropriate ones. Try different approaches (establishing more democratic rules, resolving conflict with negotiation, or responding differently to misbehavior) and don't be afraid to seek professional help.

Fortunately, it is never too late to set limits and guidelines, although it certainly is much easier if you have established rules and consequences and have worked with your child consistently on these issues before he reaches adolescence. Whether you have been setting limits and enforcing consequences for several years or you are just beginning the task, the fact that your teenager is no longer a child must be kept in mind. Demanding compliance just does not work with teenagers, particularly those with ADHD. They want to know the reasons they cannot do something and often will continue to argue and badger until they receive a satisfactory reply. In fact, teens who adhere to all the rules without questioning them often experience many difficulties in adulthood, because the developmental tasks of adolescence were not completed. They may experience low self-esteem, an unhappy marriage, psychological problems, physical ailments, inability to have intimate relationships, difficulty standing up for their wants and needs, and dissatisfaction with their jobs.

Teenagers today are faced with issues that parents did not have to face in their youth, such as drugs, street crime, violence in schools, AIDS, and strong media messages. Parents must be mindful of the changes that have taken place since their teenage years and become proactive, rather than reactive, parents.

BEGIN WITH NEGOTIATION

The first step parents should take is to examine the areas of difficulty they are experiencing now with their teenagers, as well as those issues they may expect to face in the future. Remember, this will include negotiable and nonnegotiable issues. The following are areas of discussion that are negotiable items in most families: use of the car, the telephone, chores, extracurricular activities, allowance, and dating.

Before beginning any negotiations with your teenager, you should examine the issues to be discussed and evaluate them (how they apply to the family situation, how they apply to the teen with ADHD whose mind is usually far behind their physical development, and parental values, beliefs, and expectations). Decisions should be made as to which issues are negotiable and which are not. Then decide what parts of an issue are negotiable and nonnegotiable (your teenager may use the family car but friends are not permitted to drive it). The following are examples of a few areas you may want to explore first with your spouse (single parents may want to seek the assistance of another adult) then with your teenager.

Use of the Car
All teenagers want to drive because it is a sign of maturity. For parents of teens with ADHD, this may be a troublesome decision, depending on the level of maturity displayed by the teen and his ability to take on responsibility and follow through. For teenagers, driving means a great deal of freedom—for parents it means a loss of control, often at a time when they are reluctant to let go. (Since teens are less apt to react negatively to corrections from a stranger, you may want to have a professional teach your teen to drive).

Before he runs out and gets his driver's license, there are issues you should discuss first. Look over the following list of questions in this section. There are no right or wrong answers since each family situation is unique. These questions are meant to be used as guidelines for parents preparing to negotiate with their teenagers.

- Is he mature enough to take on the responsibility of driving? Teens with ADHD are three to four times more likely to have an accident than non-ADHD teens. Research indicates that teenagers with ADHD are more likely to have their licenses suspended, drive without a license, be involved in one or more accidents in which they are at fault, receive more traffic citations especially for speeding, and suffer more bodily injuries from these accidents.
- When should he be permitted to use the car? To drive to school? One night on the weekend? To drive to a part-time job? Unlimited access? No permission at this time because . . . (fill in the blank)?

- Who else in the family needs to use that particular car? What days and times?
- What responsibilities should he have regarding the car? Pay his own insurance? Use his own money for gas? Wash the car once a week?
- Who is allowed to be in the car with him? Only one or two friends? No one in permitted in the car with him because . . . (fill in the blank)?
- Determine the rules he must follow when using the car. (Make a list, such as no driving if you have been drinking, no speeding, how far is he permitted to drive, etc.)
- If he is stopped for a traffic violation, what will the consequences be? (Make a list of the possible consequences to be discussed and negotiated with him.)
- If he is involved in an auto accident in which he is at fault, what are the consequences? (Make a list if you have some ideas but be prepared to discuss and negotiate with your teen.)
- In exchange for using the car, should he be expected to run some family errands or pick up a sibling from school?
- Does he need to ask permission to use the car?
- Must he tell you where he is going and how long he will be gone?
- Is he allowed to let anyone else drive the car?
- Because the cost of automobile insurance is high for a teenager, who will pay for the insurance? Are you willing to pay for it? Or should he pay for part or all of it?
- Should he be restricted to daytime driving?

When established rules are broken regarding the use of the car, a firm but fair punishment should be delivered immediately. A teenager who has the family car and returns home two hours past his curfew should loose the privilege of using the car but not for weeks on end. For instance, a fair punishment would be not permitting him to use the car the following weekend.

For the teenager who is impulsive, distractible, and cannot yet understand the connection between cause and effect, a car may become a source of concern and may even invite trouble. Proceed cautiously. Perhaps waiting another year before permitting him to get his license or before letting him drive alone may be the best and safest course to take. If your teenager has moderate or severe symptoms of ADHD, medication should be taken while driving.

Be sure your teen understands that he is at risk when driving. Most people with ADHD enjoy driving because they are in control of something that stimulates them. Driving fast is risky for anyone but especially ADHDers because it is a highly stimulating thrill.

In today's society, where parents are overtaxed with increasing demands, providing the use of a car to a teenager decreases some time demands placed on parents. Let's face it, it's convenient when we no longer have to play chauffeur. State your expectations clearly and advise him that the consequences for irresponsible behavior is a loss of driving privileges. But realize that if the rules are broken, the privilege must be taken away no matter how inconvenient it may be for you.

Using the Telephone

Using the telephone is a social function in early adolescence. The telephone is a link to friends. The problem usually seen during this stage of development is the amount of time spent on the phone and how it infringes on the rights of other family members who also need to use the phone. Here are some issues to be discussed:

- How much time should she be permitted to use the phone each day?
- Is the use of the phone currently interfering with the completion of homework? If so, what limits should be placed on the phone? No phone calls during homework time? No phone calls except between certain hours (you and your teenager decide the hours together)?
- Should long distance calls be limited? How many calls per week? How long can the teenager stay on the phone when making a long distance call?
- If calls are interfering with parents' telephone calls (whether business or personal), should you add another phone line reserved for teenagers and other children in the house? Who should pay for this extra line?
- What will be the consequences of abusing phone privileges?

Chores around the House

No one likes to do the household chores, but they must be done. Some teens with ADHD are especially resentful of chores and when asked to do them often lose their temper or flatly refuse to comply. Although, to avoid a confrontation, it is certainly easier to just do the tasks yourself or have another sibling perform the chores, teens who do not participate in chores are being deprived of a valuable learning opportunity. They must learn these skills if they are going to live independently one day. Teens who are assigned regular household chores and complete them feel like they are a contributing member of the family. They will also acquire self-esteem for a job well done. Here are some questions to discuss about chores:

- How many chores should be assigned each week based on his schedule?
- What chores can be assigned that he can complete successfully on his own? If you assign chores you know he will have difficulty with, he may once again experience failure. However, he should never be excused from a chore based solely on the fact that he has ADHD. If there are chores you would like him to handle but he lacks the knowledge or ability to, then let him assist with certain tasks until he learns to do them on his own. For teens with sequencing difficulties, provide written instructions or pictures to follow.
- Should you rotate chores weekly among all family members? (Remember, your teenager with ADHD may become extremely bored doing the same chores every week.)
- What are some consequences for failure to do chores as agreed?

Extracurricular Activities

After-school activities (and the friendships that are formed as a result) are extremely important for teens with ADHD, who often have difficulty making and keeping friends. It is important to remember that some teenagers with ADHD are quite popular because of their gregarious personalities while others have difficulty with peer relationships. Popular teens may be involved in several after-school activities. However, the teen who is so involved with extracurricular activities may easily fall behind in school work. After-school activities and the time commitments they entail should be monitored carefully by parents. On the other hand, teenagers who have difficulty with peer interactions will benefit greatly from one or two after-school activities particularly in areas in which they excel.

Teenagers who are involved in too many after-school activities and not keeping up with school work need your support and guidance. Arrange a time when you can all sit down and discuss her schedule. At the designated time, gently explain your concern about her many commitments and how they appear to be affecting her grades. Ask if she has any ideas about how she might keep her grades up, yet still be involved in the extracurricular activities. Have her make a list of her activities in order of priority and see if there are any that might be dropped indefinitely. Can she think of other times she could study (Saturday mornings, for instance). Is she making proper use of study hall time at school?

Many teenagers with ADHD benefit from the assistance of a coach to help them keep priorities straight and help with the organization and management of their time. The best coach is someone outside of the immediate family who is willing to spend a specific amount of time a few times a week with your teen, whether in person or on the phone, helping her organize and manage school work or other activities.

It is essential that parents help their teens in these areas (they cannot do these things on their own) so they will eventually be able to develop their own skills to manage time and schedules. No doubt, most individuals with ADHD will have to make use of planners, bulletin boards, calendars, and personal daily lists for school, work, activities, and tasks for their entire lives. Help your teenager learn these basic strategies by encouraging her to make lists of things she needs to do each day. Show her how to breakdown school projects, such as term papers, over several weeks and listing what needs to be accomplished each week to meet the deadline. Have her list on a kitchen calendar or bulletin board her chores for each day, after-school activities, supplies she needs to take with her to school, etc.

As your teenager matures and proves that she can be responsible, trustworthy, and demonstrates appropriate behaviors, rules can be adjusted and redefined with more privileges granted.

Allowance

Teenagers need to learn the value of money. Whether you choose to just give an allowance or make your teen earn it is your personal decision. For teens with ADHD the approach that appears to work best is to give them an allowance with conditions attached. Although many professionals advise against paying a teen for doing chores around the house, emphasizing the need for him to learn responsibility and contribute to the family in a meaningful way, this is not the case with those with ADHD. Their ability to follow directions and complete tasks is restricted. Paying a teen with ADHD an allowance to take on the obligation of household chores teaches responsibility and follow through. For instance, if he is paid to complete chores, he receives positive reinforcement for accepting the responsibility and following the task through to completion. The difference between non-ADHD teens and those with ADHD is that the one with ADHD must receive positive reinforcements immediately and consistently. Whereas the non-ADHD teen can wait until Saturday to receive his allowance in one lump sum, the teen with ADHD may need to receive the monetary compensation immediately following task completion because of the inability to delay gratification. This usually means paying him for chores completed on a daily basis. How much money you give a teen for an allowance depends on a few factors:

- The family budget and what you can afford to pay. No family should attempt to give what they cannot afford just to satisfy their teenager.
- What the allowance is meant to cover (gas for the car, lunch money, spending money, etc.).
- How much money the teen earns on his own.
- How hard he is willing to work around the house. If it's a constant battle to get chores done, then you must decide what they are worth. If a particular chore cannot be completed in one day, pay him for the work he has done that day. Pay him the difference when the chore is completed, but let him know there is a time limit in getting the work finished. If he cuts half of the grass, for instance, he must complete the rest the next day, not next week.
- As your teenager gets older, allowances may be increased to include clothing expenses, extra spending money, money for dates, etc., again, with stipulations attached.

Remember, the point of an allowance is to help your teenager learn how to manage money effectively and to prepare him for independent living. Many parents monitor the spending of allowance or a teen's salary from a part-time job. Teens do not yet know how to manage their money. Have them set aside a certain amount each week to deposit in a savings account. And, yes, you have the right to veto purchases that you are uncomfortable with. You might also want to tell him that he must first consult with you on purchases over a certain amount.

If your teenager spends all of his money at the beginning of the week, he will be in for a big surprise when he cannot go to the football game on Friday night or take his girlfriend out because he has no money. What should a parent do if their teenager runs out of money by the weekend? Of course, you could give him some extra money, but that will not teach him the lesson he needs to learn. On the other hand, you could advance him the extra money from next week's allowance. If it is not paid back, then no further loans should be made available. If he spends all of his money on CDs and has no money left for lunch, then he'll have to pack his lunch that week or go without. Consequences teach responsibility.

Curfews: Negotiable or Not?
Depending on the teenager and his family, curfews may or may not be negotiable. If a curfew is negotiable in your family, tackle it through negotiation. Discuss curfew times and reach a consensus.

Teens in early adolescence should have a curfew that you are comfortable with. This curfew can and should be negotiated between parent and teen in the same way you negotiate the use of the car, dating, chores, etc. If your teenager requests a later curfew than you are willing to concede to, you have the right to say no. A special occasion should be considered carefully. Depending on the circumstance (prom night, a homecoming dance), parents should talk with other parents whose teenagers will be attending the same event and going out afterwards. Be sure you know who your teenager will be with, where, and what time he will be home.

Encourage your teenager to call home if he expects to be late. This call should not be made minutes before the curfew deadline. Teenagers who break the rule and come home late should be left to face the consequences. ("The rule we agreed to was that you would call us if you were going to be late. You did not. Therefore, next weekend you will be expected to be home thirty minutes earlier than the agreed upon curfew. I hope you make that deadline next Friday night.") Do not raise your voice. Do not argue. If you have negotiated the rules and your teenager has a copy, you need only to point to the clock when delivering the consequence. If your teenager makes the curfew the following weekend, then return to the original curfew.

IN SUMMARY

Negotiating allows teenagers to express their feelings about all of your expectations. This, in return, promotes collaboration and willingness to comply with the guidelines. Sometimes a consensus can be reached, sometimes not. It is important, however, that your teenager knows you are listening to what she has to say and that you are weighing her opinions carefully. This shows her that you have confidence in her, and it helps her make sure she understands what has been agreed upon. Provide written guidelines, if necessary.

It is extremely important that parents be concise and state exactly what they expect. Saying "I want your room cleaned every Saturday" is not specific enough. Provide your teenager with a list of what is expected:

- Room cleaned by noon on Saturday
- Sheets removed from the bed and taken to the laundry room
- Clean sheets put on bed
- Clothes folded, hung up, or taken to the laundry room

- Books, papers, etc., put in the proper places
- Vacuum and dust the room
- Empty the trash can
- Room check will be made at noon

A list will reduce the bargaining or bickering that might otherwise occur. Post guidelines in her room and periodically review them. As the teen with ADHD matures and becomes more responsible for her own actions, guidelines can be reviewed and revised as needed, with the teen actively participating in the discussion. This is best accomplished at weekly family meetings (discussed in the next chapter).

Specific ways of handling your teenager can either reduce conflict within the home or escalate disruptive behaviors. It has been shown that parents who are firm but loving may actually reduce the number of behavior problems or conflicts within the home. "The family's handling of their child or teenager, as well as overall family function, undoubtedly affect the eventual outcome of these children," says Paul Elliott, MD. It is not easy to change our parenting ways, but change we must as our teens mature and move toward adulthood. Letting go is not easy, but your teenager has the best chance at succeeding if she is brought up in a home where she is respected for the individual she is, is granted freedoms when she is prepared to handle responsibilities, and knows she is loved unconditionally. As Dr. Elliott so wisely points out in chapter 2, medication, when indicated, will help your teenager abide by the rules and guidelines established. When routines and structures are set up in the home, along with clearly defined guidelines, confrontations between parents and teenagers will be greatly reduced.

POSITIVE DISCIPLINE

Younger children with ADHD respond well to time-out, token systems, positive reinforcement, reward systems, and stickers and charts. However, as your child matures and moves into adolescence, the effectiveness of most of these strategies lose their strength. Parents can no longer dictate the rules and expect them to be followed on the basis of, "Because I told you so." This approach does not work with teenagers—they want reasons for the rules. This makes it absolutely necessary for parents to find other techniques and strategies that work while maintaining respect for the teenager who is entering adulthood.

Teenagers want and need the freedom to make their own decisions and choices. As much as teens desire freedom, however, they still need their parents to set rules and boundaries that will help guide their behavior to adulthood and prepare them to live in a society that expects rules to be followed. Parents know their teenagers need freedom to grow, but many parents of teens with ADHD fear this stage of development. For them it means letting go—letting go of a child who has required much guidance through the years and still requires assistance and management in several, if not many, areas. How do committed parents let go? They do it by taking one step at a time.

LETTING GO STEP BY STEP

Before granting new freedoms, such as using the car, dating, staying out late, etc., parents must look closely at their teenager and determine how ready they are to accept the responsibilities that go hand-in-hand with new privileges. As was mentioned previously, a teenager may look physically ready for dating or driving but may not have yet developed the necessary skills and abilities to meet the responsibilities of these freedoms.

If your daughter is basically compliant, has followed the rules with little problems through the years preceding adolescence, she is no doubt ready and capable of accepting more latitude. This does not mean rules and limits are not needed—they are.

On the other hand, if you have had ongoing problems with compliance—your teen is often not where she says she'll be or doesn't call when you have asked her to—then she is not ready to be granted more freedom. She must be taught that following the rules will get her the freedom she desires. This does not mean she is to be exempt from all activities by any means, only that she needs more structure (not control) and guidance in learning how to follow the rules so she can eventually be granted the freedom she desires.

Step by step means just that. If your teen wants to use the car and stay out until midnight and you are not comfortable with that, then you might permit her to use the car until 11:00. If she can prove that she is responsible enough to follow the rules for several weeks, then renegotiate the curfew rule (but only if you are comfortable with a later curfew). When a teenager with ADHD follows the rules, she must be commended and praised (positive reinforcement for compliance) when she arrives home. ("I'm very pleased to see you are home on time tonight. It shows me how responsible you are.")

It is important to remember that if you give your daughter every privilege from the start she has nothing to work for—nothing to earn as she proves she can handle greater responsibility. Even worse, you will have few resources available to teach her to be worthy of your trust and learn the merit of taking responsibility for her actions.

Besides giving verbal praise, you can use physical praise such as a smile, a pat on the shoulder, or a wink. Some other positive reinforcements include an extended curfew for one night, a day off from chores, and using the car on a school day. It is important to remember that some positive reinforcements work for a short time only. If you find that your daughter is no longer interested in specific rewards, you must substitute other positive reinforcers for appropriate behavior. Remember that teens with ADHD are bored easily, so changing rewards often is essential.

To further reinforce compliance in an area that is sorely needed, give your teenager one token (or point) for every time he complies with the rules. After accumulating a specific number of tokens, these can be exchanged for additional rewards. Here are some ideas: his own telephone line, a television or VCR for his bedroom, a compact disc player, a computer, etc. Remember to encourage the behavior you want to continue and provide little or no attention to the inappropriate behavior you want to eliminate if the behavior is not dangerous or life threatening. A balance needs to be struck between ignoring behavior and a teen taking this as tacit approval.

Consequences that are established beforehand allow you to address the infringement calmly. For example, he loses his telephone privileges for one night if he abuses them, is assigned an additional chore when his chores are not done as agreed, or his stereo cannot be played for one day if he has played it louder than agreed without considering other family members. When establishing consequences, remember that the penalty must fit the crime. If a teenager comes home fifteen minutes late, he should not be grounded for several weeks. This is an unfair and unjust punishment for being slightly late.

WHAT NOT TO DO

Too often parents react hastily and take away the first thing that comes to their mind—usually, whatever is most important to the teenager. If your teen has a special talent or interest, such as playing football or the piano, do *not* take this away from her. This one precious gift is just too necessary for her self-esteem to be used as a punishment for undesirable behavior. (Often the undesired behavior can be changed with the loss of another privilege.) Restricting her from something so important will only produce negative results. If she has an activity or talent that she feels good about, she is more apt to have positive feelings about herself, her schoolwork, and her family. If you take away that one activity, she may feel like she has nothing worthwhile left.

If your teen has a part-time job that she enjoys, do not force her to quit. If she's falling behind in schoolwork or is working too late, you may ask her to reduce her hours. Parents should consider the job's role in fostering their teen's sense of independence. Not only does a job teach her responsibility, but it also enables her to acquire valuable skills and knowledge and earn and manage money.

OTHER STRATEGIES THAT WORK

There are strategies that work especially well with teenagers who have ADHD, but not all strategies will work with all teenagers. Try one strategy at a time over a period of a few weeks, then evaluate its effectiveness until you find those that work best. If you need to, modify your plan. Remember, it is impossible to change behavior overnight no matter how hard you try.

Negotiation
Plan a meeting with your teenager to negotiate rules and consequences. Provide him with a list of negotiable and nonnegotiable issues so he can study the list before you sit down to discuss it. After he has had a chance to look the list over, set a time for a meeting that is mutually acceptable to you both. As you go down the list, ask for his input. Listen carefully to all suggestions, and do not reject any as silly or ridiculous (even if it is). At this point you are brainstorming for solutions together. Take notes. When a consensus has been reached on an issue, have him repeat back to you the established rule and consequence. Make sure he fully understands what he is consenting to. Once you are sure that you are in agreement on an issue (the curfew on weekends is midnight, for example), put it in writing.

Be ready to compromise on issues that do not endanger his safety, your family, or others. If you agree that it is okay for your sixteen-year-old daughter to go out one school night a week, how important is it for her to be home by 9:30 if she is asking for a 10:30 curfew? In such a situation, you may want to compromise by suggesting that she be home by 10:00 P.M.

Say yes to as many issues as possible but don't be afraid to disagree. If a satisfactory compromise cannot be reached on a specific issue, set it aside for a few days and think about it. Sometimes a solution isn't obvious until a day to two later.

Rules should always be negotiated between the parent and teen. (See chapter 4 for more information on negotiating the rules.) If he wants to attend the football game on Friday night, make sure he understands what time he is to be home. If he fails to make his curfew that night, don't scream, threaten, nag, or criticize. Overreacting will cause more harm than good (you may reinforce the noncompliance simply by giving it your full attention). Calmly tell him that he has abused the privilege so he must now face the consequence that was agreed upon for insubordination. This may mean that he cannot attend next week's game or he can go to the game but must come home immediately afterward. Let him know that the week after, he will once again be given the opportunity to prove that he can follow the rules. It is important that you respond to misbehavior or noncompliance immediately, consistently, and calmly (no matter how upset you are). Teens with ADHD must learn that noncompliance will result in immediate, predictable, but fair consequences. Your job as a parent is to provide the necessary tools to help your teen's development through adolescence. Some of those tools include consequences, positive reinforcements, brainstorming, negotiating, problem-solving, agreements, choices, solutions, and follow-through.

Family Meetings

The family meeting works especially well when several family members have ADHD. The purpose of a weekly family meeting is to discuss anything of relevance that affects family members. Plan a family meeting for the same day and at the same time each week, taking into consideration other family members' schedules and commitments. This meeting is not just for your teen with ADHD but for all members of the family.

Each week a different family member conducts the meeting and a secretary is appointed to take minutes (you may want to tape record the meeting also). Before the first meeting establish the rules:

- only one topic at a time will be discussed
- all family members will have an opportunity to speak so no interrupting is allowed while a family member is speaking during his predetermined allotted time
- no arguing or shouting; angry feelings must be expressed in an appropriate manner; a family member may leave the meeting to get himself under control

- only "I" statements are acceptable ("I feel angry when Michele does . . . ."); "You" messages must be avoided ("You always take my stuff without asking.")
- while brainstorming for solutions, ridiculing or criticizing ideas presented is not allowed
- all possible solutions will be evaluated by the entire family (record everything)
- all family members will work together to find the best solution (look for obstacles that may prevent the plan from working) and together the family will determine how the plan will be implemented
- negotiation and bargaining techniques will be used, but if a solution is needed quickly and the family members cannot reach a decision, a parent will make a decision that will be upheld until the next meeting where it will, once again, be presented as a topic of discussion
- respect is to be shown for all family members including the youngest child who needs to be heard also

Family meetings are the appropriate time for the following:

- focus on issues that were unresolved from the last family meeting
- renegotiate household rules
- negotiate new rules or agreements
- share in each other's feelings, concerns, and interests
- settle disputes between family members that are adding stress to the household
- set up times to complete household chores or establish a new routine
- decide whether to make a major purchase that would make things easier for all, such as a another car for the teenager to use or an additional television
- plan a family vacation or recreational activities
- examine unusual situations that arose during the week that had never been addressed before
- address problem behaviors between siblings that they have not been able to resolve on their own and assist them in reaching a compromise

Family meetings encourage collaborative problem-solving, permitting children to see themselves as part of a solution rather than the cause of the problem. They are also the time to set clear and consistent family rules. Parents must realize that as children grow and mature, routines, schedules, and rules will need to be revised accordingly. In other words, do not expect that rules that were established when your teenager was thirteen will hold up when she is sixteen.

Grounding

Most parents are, no doubt, familiar with being grounded (who wasn't grounded at least once for breaking the rules as a teenager?). If your experience with grounding was extremely negative (you were grounded once for the whole summer), you may not see the benefits of grounding your teen for noncompliance. When grounding is used properly, however, it can be extremely beneficial as a consequence.

The problem is that many parents do not use grounding appropriately because they don't understand how it is meant to be used. Grounding a teenager for a month because he was on the phone during homework time is not using grounding effectively. It is also an unjust consequence for a somewhat minor noncompliance to the rules and totally unrelated to phone use (not permitting the teen to use the phone for a day or two would be appropriate for phone abuse). It will also enrage your teenager, encourage further acting out, and jeopardize the parent-child relationship.

Grounding a teenager with ADHD for long periods is detrimental to his social life. So what, you ask? Children and teenagers with ADHD often have enough problems with peer relationships. If your son has a few friends, he has worked hard to maintain those friendships. Cutting teens with ADHD off from their friends for several weeks may cause their social network to collapse. They may also rebel, become resentful, seek revenge, or become depressed as a result of reduced self-esteem. Besides, grounding your teenager for weeks on end is hard work for parents. Can you really monitor your teenager twenty-four hours a day? Would you actually want to? If you can't manage it perfectly, it only encourages internalization of "the rules don't apply to me."

Grounding works best (and produces better results) when rules have been established first and the teenager has been warned that if he is late arriving home he will be grounded next weekend. Grounding is most effective when used for short periods of time.

Offer a Choice

Offering a choice is especially helpful with teenagers who are oppositional. ("Would you prefer to cut the grass or rake the leaves?") Be sure your teen understands that if she does not choose one or the other, you will make the choice for her. Mini-choices are appropriate for nonnegotiable rules. ("Would you like to do your homework in the kitchen or in your bedroom?") The wonderful thing about offering choices is that they cannot be answered with a "yes" or "no," but don't be too surprised if you hear a "but."

Write a Note

Writing is an effective way of getting a teenager's attention. If you come home only to find a chore not completed and your daughter is nowhere to be found, calm yourself down by grabbing a piece of paper and writing her a note. The first note may have to be disposed of because of your angry feelings, but the second note should do the trick. Post it where she will find it.

Here are two sample notes:

Dear John,

Our agreement was that you would set the table for dinner on Tuesdays. I was very upset to see that the table was not set because I was already running late for my class tonight. I think we better have a short meeting at 7:30 tomorrow evening. Please let me know if that time is all right with you.

Mom

Notes can also be used to reinforce appropriate behavior and build self-esteem.

Dear Sarah,

Imagine my surprise when I came home to find you had folded the last load of laundry. Thank you for being so responsible. I am proud of you.

Dad

Notes are a great way to urge a teen to do something she is supposed to do, because teens are great at tuning out when parents want them tuned in.

Write a Contract

A contract is a negotiated agreement between parents and the teen that can be used to elicit compliance and reinforce positive behavior. A contract can be used for any number of things. The following is an example of a rather detailed contract between a sixteen year old and his parents, but contracts can be any length covering as many issues as need to be addressed. If you should find it necessary to use a contract with your teenager, be sure to write one tailored to the specific behaviors you are dealing with.

I, Matthew, enter this agreement with my parents on September 24, 1995. I promise to fulfill the terms that I have agreed to and, in exchange, will receive an allotted number of points for the privileges below.

2 points every time I meet my curfew

1 point for making my bed everyday before school

1 point for leaving for school on time each morning

4 points for doing my weekly laundry between Thursday evening and Saturday afternoon (This includes washing, folding, putting clean clothes away, ironing when necessary, and washing my sheets once a week)

4 points for doing my homework during the designated time (If there is a conflict with my schedule, I will speak with Mom and Dad about this as soon as possible

before my homework time. If I fail to speak with them ahead of time, I will receive only 2 points for doing my homework.)

2 points for cleaning the bathroom immediately after using it. (This includes rinsing out the bathtub, putting my personal items away, putting dirty towels and wash-clothes in the laundry room, and leaving the bathroom presentable for the next person.)

2 points for completing my daily household chores

3 points for any additional chores I do around the house

3 points for running errands for Mom and Dad

4 points when my room is cleaned on Saturday before noon (1 point if it is not cleaned by noon but later in the day)

I also understand that lying, acting-out behaviors such as profanity, stealing, and aggressive actions toward family members are prohibited. Compliance to these rules will result in a reward of 20 additional points each week. Each offense will result in a fine of 5 points per episode.

Points may be exchanged as follows:

10 points for use of the car

2 points for use of the telephone per call

8 points for an extended curfew of one hour

7 points to attend a party, a sporting event, a movie, etc.

5 points to rent a movie

5 points to have a friend spend the night

5 points to spend the night at a friend's house (if parents approve of friend)

6 points for the use of the computer for something other than homework

5 points for one hour of television or video games

1 point for a junk food snack

4 points to have friends over for an evening

I acknowledge that I have read this contract and understand it. Therefore, I agree to abide by the terms and conditions.

Signed on September 24, 1995:

Teenager's signature_____

Mom's signature _____

Dad's signature _____

If you are working on changing one particular problem, you may be able to use a short contract. Remember the purpose of contracts is to encourage good behavior or eliminate annoying behavior.

I, Julia, agree to help with dinner five nights a week without complaining, whining, or arguing. Every day that I do this, I will receive one point. Once I have earned 5 points, I can go out for pizza with my friends.
Signed,

_____

Use Grandmother's Rule
Grandmother's rule is basically a simple arrangement that says, "When you do what is expected, then you may do what you want to do." For example: "When you wash the car, then you may use it." or "When your homework is finished, then you may call your friend." Grandmother's rule is easy to use and works well for children of all ages. However, never substitute the word "if" for the word "when." Using "if" will only invite your teenager to say, "If I don't do it, what will happen?" The reason Grandmother's Rule works so well is that you are never saying, "No, you cannot." Grandmother's Rule is a positive way to communicate with your teen.

Cost Response
Teenagers with ADHD appear to do well with a cost-response system. Instead of earning privileges and rewards, the reward is given first. For instance, you might tell your teenager that he can use the car for six hours on Saturday and six hours on Sunday. He then works to keep those hours. Inappropriate behaviors then lead to a removal of time from his weekly allotment.

A similar arrangement can be used with an allowance given one week in advance. On Saturday you tell your son that he is now working to keep next week's allowance of ten dollars. If all goes well over the next seven days he will receive the full ten dollars. Be sure you discuss with him how much money he will lose for inappropriate behaviors and define those behaviors (much like you would do when using a contract).

Use Praise with a Hidden Message
You can praise positive behavior while making reference to inappropriate behavior at the same time. "I was so pleased to see that you picked up your bedroom this morning, rather than leaving it a mess" (resist the temptation to say "like you usually do"). Be sure you acknowledge the effort in an encouraging, upbeat tone. Using this technique to praise appropriate behavior should not be sarcastic in any way.

Use "I" Statements
"I" statements can be used whenever a consequence of an unacceptable behavior interferes with your needs. "I" statements have three parts: behavior, feeling, and consequence. "When you do not call me to say you will be late (behavior), I begin

to feel frightened (feeling), because I do not know if you are okay (consequence). Do not use "I" messages all the time. If they are used too often, eventually they will reinforce the inappropriate behavior.

"I" messages can also be used to send positive messages: "When I came home and found the kitchen clean, it made me feel so good to know that you cared enough to help me with something I usually do. Now I will have time to fix an extra special dinner tonight."

Allow for Logical Consequences
Teenagers can learn desired behaviors by allowing natural and logical consequences to occur. For instance, it is her responsibility to get up for school and leave on time. It is not your job to wake her up each morning—that's what alarm clocks are for. If your daughter fails to get up on time and consequently arrives at school late, having to stay after school is a logical consequence of not getting up in time.

If the same teenager jumps out of bed, throws on a T-shirt and a pair of jeans, grabs a lightweight jacket, and leaves the house without checking the temperature and weather forecast, she'll learn through natural consequences that she is not properly dressed for the weather.

Allow for Mistakes
Whether you buy sports equipment, clothes, or a compact disc player for your teen, it's tempting to tell them how to use it (not to loan it out, for instance). It's important to remember that the item belongs to them; therefore, it is their responsibility. If they loan it out and it's never returned, or they lose it, the responsibility is theirs to claim it back or purchase another from their allowance.

Remove Privileges
Removing privileges (use of the car, telephone, video games, computer, etc.) is an effective discipline technique for teens with ADHD. It is important to remember that when you withdraw a privilege, it must be something the teenager values. If you tell her she can't buy a new dress, but she borrows one from a friend and is quite content with doing this, the consequence is of no value. On the other hand, if she misses a party she was looking forward to attending, the consequence is effective. If you tell a younger teen that she cannot use the computer for game playing for one night, but she has access to a Super Nintendo, how effective is the consequence? It's equally important that the withdrawal of the privilege be directly proportional to the unacceptable behavior (don't take away a meaningful privilege for a minor violation) and that the consequence be delivered as soon as possible after the infraction.

WHEN STRATEGIES FAIL

If you find that your technique is not working, ask yourself the following questions that were presented in my first book, *The ADHD Parenting Handbook:*

- Did she clearly understand what behaviors were not acceptable before the management plan was initiated?
- Did she understand the consequences of exhibiting the inappropriate behaviors?
- Were the consequences (both reward and punishment) important enough to her?
- Was I consistent and immediate in delivering rewards and punishments?
- Did my spouse (or other caretaker) fail to follow the management plan or follow it inconsistently?
- Were we trying to modify too many behaviors at the same time?

If necessary, modify your plan and start over again. If repeated attempts at modifying your plan result in failure, you should seek professional help.

PARENTAL TRAPS

Beware of parental traps. These traps exist, and you may be an unknowing victim.

Manipulation Strategies

Children learn at an early age how to manipulate their parents, so it is up to parents to cease manipulation strategies in their home. Probably the most noted manipulation strategies are the ones teenagers use: "Dad said it was all right for me to stay out until midnight tonight, as long as it is okay with you," or "Mom has been really mean to me today, and now she won't let me stay out until midnight." Before you know it your daughter has been told she can stay out until midnight, or your spouse is asking you why you've been so mean to your daughter. Be on guard for manipulation techniques by planning ahead with your spouse. Encourage your spouse to say, "We must include your mother/father in this discussion before we can give you an answer."

Our Way vs. Their Way

Who ever said that adults have all the answers? If you listen to some adults talk to their teenagers, you may be tempted to believe they do! Some parents seem so convinced that their way is the right way— the only way. Certainly as parents we have had many more life experiences than our teenagers, but our way is not the only way nor is it always the best way. It is simply our way of doing things. Even if one or both parents have ADHD, what works for them may not work with their teen. We can offer suggestions, with permission of course, but ultimately our teens with ADHD must find ways that work best for them. Parents become so accustomed to telling their children with ADHD how to do things that as our children mature, we fail to realize that they may have found their own way to handle life's challenges. Remember, we do not always need to be right, nor do we always need to get the last word in. Do not get into a power struggle with your teen over who's right and who's wrong. Accept the fact that we all have our own way of doing things that works best for us.

Fear
If you have struggled with a hyperactive, impulsive, fearless child through the years, your fears usually carry into the teen years. How do we forget the many trips to the emergency room for stitches and broken arms, the holes in the wall when our youngster lost control of himself, or the time he jumped off the high dive when he hadn't learn to swim yet? We don't, but we also do not have to become a victim of our fears. We must remember that adolescence is the time for us to start letting go. That doesn't mean we will worry any less. What it does mean though, is that we now have to look at a situation and ask ourselves, "What is the very worst thing that could happen and how likely is it to happen?" Don't be afraid to talk with other parents of teens with ADHD or express your concerns to a therapist. Talking will help you face your fears so you can begin taking control of your feelings. Loss of control over your feelings can interrupt your teenager's normal developmental tasks.

"Letting go is most difficult for the parent with the greatest imagination," says Mark Snyder, MD. "If you've seen your child do inappropriate and/or dangerous things before, it's very easy to extend that image to even more frightening proportions as he grows older. While you do have an obligation to safeguard your child, it's still far better for him to grow through the challenges of adolescence and the teenage years at those ages. To prevent them from completing these basic and essential tasks of adolescence, only to have to learn them in the adult years, greatly delays their ability to handle adult tasks with maturity and success."

Giving Unwanted or Unsolicited Advice
If you remember your teenage years, you may remember how many times you tuned out when your parents were speaking with you ("Here she goes again. I've heard this before."). Instead, when you have advice to offer, ask for permission to speak with your teen and remember to establish eye contact first. ("Michele, I can share some information about that with you, but only if you are interested. Would you like to hear what I have to say?"). You'll be surprised to learn that most teenagers will answer "yes," simply because you asked for their permission to speak. As to be expected, however, if they disagree, they'll probably tune you out.

Talking too Much
Unfortunately, most parents talk too much. When teenagers misbehave, many parents begin their usual speech or lecture ("How many times I have told you . . . ?" or "When I was your age . . . "). Without thinking, it is easy to fall into this parental trap. As a result of the constant speeches and lectures, our teens eventually expect us to nag and lecture. When we react as they expect, we reinforce their misbehavior. When faced with unacceptable behavior that must be addressed immediately, say what you must in as few words as possible. Otherwise you will be speaking to deaf ears and drawing attention away from the misbehavior. If you tend to talk too much, try to say what you must say in fifteen words or less. Then gradually reduce the number of words each time you must address your teen's behavior.

Dwelling on the Past

No one likes to have past mistakes brought up again and again, including adults. Unfortunately, some parents use every opportunity to bring up issues that point to previous failures instead of adhering to the present and the future. If past mistakes must be raised, they should be discussed only in terms of finding a solution.

Escape Technique to Avoid Requests

It is safe to say that teens learn to use inappropriate behaviors for any number of purposes, one of which is escape. If you ask your teenager to do something and he begins an argument, he is reacting in this manner to escape your demand because he has learned that this strategy works. For instance, you ask your son to cut the grass and a confrontation ensues. You repeat the request several times but eventually walk away saying, "I'll be back when you are in better control of yourself." A few hours later you return to find that the grass has not been cut, and your son is nowhere to be found. So you get out the lawnmower and start cutting the grass. Your son returns later to find the grass is cut. V. Mark Durand, PhD, in his book, *Severe Behavior Problems,* points out that his behavior has once again been reinforced by his parent's withdrawal of the request. You have fallen into another parental trap. The solution is to have him cut the grass by flashlight if necessary!

Social Attention

Social attention to inappropriate behavior also maintains problem behavior. For instance, aggression or temper tantrums in teens may continue simply because they have been positively reinforced by the attention of others. Studies have shown that not responding to these types of behaviors will decrease the number of episodes. "Social attention can have negative effects if it becomes a regular consequence for these [types of] behaviors," says V. Mark Durand, PhD.

The Inner Voice

The next time your teenager does something inappropriate, listen to what you are saying to yourself. ("I can't take this much longer." or "She is rejecting my advice because I am not a good parent.") We all have preconceived ideas of how things should be or could be, so it's easy to fall into the trap of feeling disappointed, discouraged, and sorry for ourselves. When we permit our feelings to overrun us, we cannot effectively relate to our teen. Try to turn those negative thoughts into positive feelings.

Choose Your Words Carefully

Parents often say whatever comes to mind first especially when dealing with teenagers who easily become defensive or hostile. It's important for you to speak calmly and choose your words carefully to avoid a confrontation. Be sure to remember your tone of voice and your body language also indicate how you feel. Avoid the following, which will decrease self-esteem, create anger, and build resentment:

- **Put-downs:** "You act so stupid at times."
- **Commands:** "Because I am the parent and you will do what I say."
- **Criticism:** "Can't you ever fold the clothes the right way?"
- **Sarcasm:** "Well, that was a really smart thing to do. I thought you knew better."
- **Moral Preaching:** "Remember the fourth commandment says to honor thy father and thy mother."
- **Skepticism:** "Now tell me where you really went tonight. Don't lie to me because I know what you did."
- **Unsolicited Advice:** "If I were you, I'd dump the guy. I know more about this stuff than you do."
- **Shaming:** "You know better than that. Imagine what people will think when they hear this."
- **Intimidation:** "You're report is already overdue. You'll be lucky to pass this year."
- **Dictating:** "How many times have I told you that isn't the way it's done . . . "

The Last Word

Some teens with ADHD are arguers. No matter what you say, they will find something to argue about. Unfortunately, it's easy for a parent to be pulled into an argument. If you find that your teen argues with you constantly, she probably enjoys the stimulation. Arguments with teenagers are no-win situations so change your tactic. Instead of always trying to get the last word in, let your teenager have the last say once in a while. Or simply look at your teenager and say, "I refuse to argue with you. When you are ready to discuss this with me without arguing let me know. I'll talk with you later." Then leave the room.

PARENTAL TRAPS THAT CAUSE BREAKDOWNS IN FAMILY STRUCTURE

In their book, *Negotiating Parent Teen Conflict*, authors Arthur L. Robin, PhD, and Sharon L. Foster, PhD, identify five common patterns that may occur in "severely distressed, rigid families." The following events "take place within the context of ongoing sequence of interactions between family members."

Cross-generational coalition refers to a developed pattern where one parent sides with the teen against the other parent. In the case of a single-parent family, a grandparent, for example, may side with the young person against the parent. Cross-generational coalitions often "become problematic when they persist rigidly in the face of developmental changes that require flexibly restructuring relationship patterns to resolve conflicts . . . , " note Drs. Robin and Foster. "The parents' effectiveness as disciplinary agents diminishes because they are divided with the teen's influence thrown in one direction." Such cross-generational coalition may result in one parent receiving more attention from the teenager than the other. This often allows the teenager to escape consequences and gain more privileges or misbehave with one parent but not the other. Again, this illustrates the necessity of parents providing a united front.

"In yet another pattern, two members of the family disagree over an issue . . . and each tries to enlist the support of the third member; the third member vacillates between supporting each of the others, not consistently taking one side (otherwise the pattern would be coalition)," explain Drs. Robin and Foster. "The rigid persistence of triangles promotes conflict and hampers family adjustment." Triangles can place Mom, Dad, or the teen in the middle. Triangulation occurs in all families but is particularly recognized in stepfamilies where the biological parent may be trapped between the stepparent and teen.

Refocusing parents' attention is another effective ploy that can develop due to marital discord in the home. Rebellious behavior on the teenager's part may temporarily suspend marital disagreements as parents focus on the teen's behavior instead of their own problems. However, as marital problems increase so does the rebellious behavior. The continuation of the marital conflicts fuels the misbehavior of the teenager, thus acting as a negative reinforcement. In families in which spouses literally do not speak to each other except when absolutely necessary, the misbehavior of the teenager serves yet another purpose.

When parents are unable to present a united front, another pattern emerges: the teenager dodges punishment and consequences for inappropriate behavior. Drs. Robin and Foster define weak parental coalitions as "the inability of the parents to take effective, joint action against their out-of-control teen." It is relatively easy for teenagers to escape disciplinary measures if one parent imposes a consequence and tries to remain consistent, but the other parent disciplines in a different manner causing a disagreement. The teenager is aware that the parents cannot agree, so he disregards both parents' attempts to modify his behavior and the misbehavior continues while the parents recommence arguing. Many parents just give up at this point to avoid the arguing and frustration. Remember, teenagers with ADHD need parents to present clear rules and consequences that must be delivered consistently for noncompliant behavior.

It is extremely important for parents of teens to begin relaxing the rules. But what happens when parents relax the rules and then find that their teenager has gotten into trouble? They often panic and become overly protective, making even stricter rules. When parents pull in the reins, their teenager often becomes more rebellious. The more the teen rebels, the tighter demands the parents make. The teen responds in any number of ways from increasing his demands for more freedom to ignoring parental boundaries. According to Drs. Robin and Foster, the increased parental demands cycle until the teenager gets into serious trouble and a social service agency (the police, for example) is called in, the parents give up and relax the rules and positively reinforce the teen's misbehavior, or the teen gives in to the parental requests and gives up his autonomy, which, as was pointed out in chapter four, is detrimental to completing teens' developmental tasks.

Overly protective parents believe that if they don't remain strict, the teenager will automatically get into even more trouble. If the cycle is not stopped, it will only continue to increase. Therefore, it becomes necessary for the parents and teenager to reach an agreement. The parents offer some freedom (relaxing the curfew rule, for instance) and the teenager agrees to comply and act responsibly. The conditions are that the parents will continue to give more freedom as the teenager continues to comply with the rules. If you recognize any of these patterns in your family, please seek professional intervention. These are complicated issues for parents to handle on their own and can easily result in displays of more negative behaviors.

Since studies show that hyperactive, defiant, quick to anger, aggressive teens with ADHD are more apt to develop oppositional defiant disorder or conduct disorder if parental management of the teen is aggressive, adverse, or submissive, parents must seek intervention as early as possible.

Following Through
The importance of following through with positive reinforcers or consequences cannot be stressed enough. Parents must follow through in a respectful manner because teens with ADHD need the stability of knowing what to expect. Teens and parents who have worked together through negotiation to reach agreement on rules expect the rules to be followed. As a parent you expect curfews to be met, the car returned with gas in it, and so forth. Your teenager learns to expect that when he does not comply to the rules he will have to face the consequences. When a parent does not follow through and deliver a consequence as agreed, the teen learns that he does not have to keep his end of the agreement because you did not keep your end. In other words, you don't really mean what you say, and they do not have to be accountable for their actions. It also frustrates the teenager, whether or not they are aware of it ("Maybe Mom and Dad don't really care about me—afterall, they didn't even seem to notice").

Gentle Reminders
So what do parents do when their teenager does not keep her end of the bargain on less important issues such as household chores? You gently remind them. You do not lecture, criticize, or nag. Consider the following scenario:

Andrea had agreed to run the vacuum and dust each Saturday morning and have this chore completed by 11:00 A.M. On Saturday morning at 10:30, Andrea's mother realized that she was still in bed. She woke Andrea up and reminded her of the agreement they had made.

"But Mom, I got in late last night," said Andrea. "I need my sleep."
"I expect you to uphold your part of the agreement," replied her mother.
"Just let me sleep another hour and I'll do it then," begged Andrea.
"I expect you to uphold your part of the agreement," her mother repeated.
"Oh, for crying out loud. I can't believe you won't let me sleep another hour," yelled Andrea.
"I expect you to uphold your part of the agreement," Andrea's mother said for the third time.
"Okay, okay," said Andrea getting out of bed. "You made your point."

It's important to note that Mom did not argue, criticize, or make any degrading statements to Andrea. She also ignored Andrea's excuses and comments. Instead, she continued to remind Andrea calmly of the agreement they had made in an appropriate, respectful manner (the broken-record technique). She did not attack Andrea by saying, "You promised to do this and I expect you to do it now." Was Andrea thrilled about having to jump out of bed and start her chores immediately? Absolutely not! But she did, and there are reasons why she did.

At this point many parents may be thinking, "My daughter wouldn't get up that easily. She would still be arguing with me." Remember, your teen cannot argue unless you willingly become a participant in an argument with them.

Let's back up here and look at this situation differently. Andrea and her mother have negotiated rules and made agreements in many areas, not just those areas that concern chores. Together they decided that Andrea would clean the house before 11:00 on Saturday, and Andrea agreed. The rules were written up and Andrea had a copy of the rules. Similarly, her mother has agreed to do such things as letting Andrea use the family car or date on a school night and has never told Andrea she couldn't do something based on a prior agreement. In other words, Mom has always kept her side of all agreements and Andrea knows that her mother always follows through. She knows that if she argues or complains she will get nowhere. Andrea also knows that if she does not comply to the agreement, she will have to face the consequences that she has previously agreed to. If Mom had not followed through, it would have been a great disservice to Andrea.

As parents of teenagers with ADHD, we must explore different discipline strategies with our teenagers until we find those that work. We must remain firm and loving with teens by negotiating rules and consequences and following through consistently and immediately with either rewards or consequences. To not do so places our teens at an even greater risk of defiant or rebellious behavior.

WHOSE RESPONSIBILITY IS IT?

By the preteen and teen years we no longer have absolute control over all aspects of our children's lives. Until we realize and accept this we are often caught up in a cycle that tells us that we must guide and direct him, provide everything for him, keep him safe, protect him from failure, see that he is dressed properly, behaves the way we expect him to, and goes to school.

Granted, our teenagers with ADHD may still need help with structure, routines, problem-solving, organization, and time management and may need interventions in the classroom. But it is imperative to remember that our teens are no longer helpless creatures who must depend on us for everything. We should not be doing things for our teenager's that they can do for themsleves.

Despite what you may feel or think, good moms and dads do not clean their teens' bedrooms, do their laundry, and pick up after them. Knowing that their teens need to be able to take care of themselves adequately and independently someday, good moms and dads turn personal responsibilities over to them so they can develop the skills they need. Good parents let their children fail, so they can learn from their own mistakes.

Getting up in the Morning

Some teenagers with ADHD have absolutely no problem getting up for school in the morning. They may go to bed late and rise early on their own—they tend to need little sleep and are full of energy from morning to nighttime. Others do not fare as well. Their problem is getting up in the morning. No matter what time they go to bed, no matter how many hours they sleep, they just cannot get moving in the morning. If you find yourself running around in the morning popping your head in your teen's bedroom every few minutes pleading with her to get up, you have a problem. Or do you?

By the time your daughter reaches her preteen years, mornings should be her responsibility not yours. After all, that is what alarm clocks are for (you know those things that wake you up each morning). Oh I know some children throw their alarm clocks across the bedroom, or ignore them and fall back asleep, but making sure your teenager gets up and ready for school is not your responsibility. It belongs to her. If your teen is not using an alarm clock or clock radio get her one today.

Won't work you say? Then sit down with her and address the problem. Tell her that it is hard to keep running into her room while you are trying to get dressed for work and get everyone else out of the house on time. Ask for ways that she thinks might help her get up on her own. Brainstorm for solutions. One alarm clock set for one time, followed by the clock radio going off ten minutes later (set at full blast, of course, with her favorite station on). A friend calling her in the morning (her boyfriend, perhaps). A special tape she has made with her own voice telling her to get up. Or have a friend record a "Good Morning" tape. Keep brainstorming until you find a few ideas that might work. Then negotiate. "On mornings that you get up on your own, I'll give you an extra fifteen minutes of phone time that day."

Expect some resistance, expect that some mornings she will miss the bus, and expect some days when she just may not make it to school. But let her know you believe in her. Remind her that she is capable of getting up in the morning on her own. If she misses the school bus, walking or riding a bicycle is an option. If she receives a detention for being tardy, that is her problem, not yours.

Inform the school that from this day forward, your daughter is now responsible for getting up for school. Explain why you are doing this (to teach responsibility) and ask them to handle her tardiness by either a detention or extra homework. Remember her tardiness is not your responsibility.

Close the Door

If you find yourself constantly nagging about the appearance of your teenager's bedroom, close the door and resist the temptation to peek in. At the next family meeting, add this issue to your agenda. Then negotiate and reach a consensus: the bedroom will be cleaned every Saturday by noon, for example. Provide a list of what is expected. If the room is not cleaned, he then faces the consequences that you and he have agreed upon.

As much as you may be tempted, cleaning your teen's bedroom is not your responsibility. Sooner or later, this is a chore he must learn to do. There is also the issue of privacy. Bedrooms are private places that belong to each and everyone of us, including our teens. So unless you hear mice scampering around in there, all of your plates and dishes are missing, or the room literally stinks, stay out! The only exception is if you suspect your son or daughter is using drugs or has been stealing. Then you have every right to enter this private space and are encouraged to do so. However, should you find that you absolutely must clean the bedroom for whatever reason, be sure your teenager understands that you expect to be paid for this job. The fee should be determined ahead of time and agreed upon (for example, one third of his allowance should be enough to motivate him to clean his own room).

Laundry

When children are young we must launder their clothes. As they mature, we need to teach them how to sort clothes, use the washer and dryer, and iron their clothes. By the time your child reaches adolescence, his laundry is his responsibility. Like other chores, negotiate a time and day he is to wash his clothes. Resist the temptation to sneak in his room and gather the laundry. If he runs out of clean clothes, this is his problem. And what a problem it will be the first time he has a special date, and the clothes he planned to wear are found stuffed under the bed or in a heap in the corner of his bedroom!

Borrowing

If you don't mind if your teenager borrows your stuff, skip this section. If you do mind, then read on. First, if you do not want your teenager borrowing any of your personal belongings (clothes, jewerly, make-up, hairdryer, shaver, or whatever), then these are nonnegotiable items that should be added to the list you have made of negotiable and nonnegotiable issues. If there are some things you don't mind sharing, then make a list of things that may be borrowed. Also make a list of items that are not to be borrowed. Items included on the not-to-be-borrowed list are those things of value or items that hold special memories.

Because these are your belongings, it is your responsibility to decide and clarify what may or may not be borrowed. You also have the right to set the terms for the use of these items, such as when they are to be returned, in what condition they are to be returned, if they may be loaned to her friends, and what the consequences are for losing items (such as paying for them).

Long Distance Phone Calls

You open the phone bill and gasp. Your son, who's into computer games, has made numerous phone calls to 900 numbers for game tips without your permission. Those 900 calls total close to $150, and you're steaming. The bottom line is that teens who enjoy playing computer games also enjoy getting these extra tips. Despite warnings that children under eighteen must have their parent's permission before calling a 900 number, some children place the calls anyway. The costs add up quickly. What should you do?

First call the telephone company. Explain to them what has happened, the amount of the bill, that your child did not have your permission to make these calls, then ask the phone company to place a 900 number block on your telephone. Some phone companies will make a one-time consession and remove the amount on your bill but only when you agree to block your line. However, you will be given a code number to use if someone in your family wants to call a 900 number with your permission.

Consequences must be given for telephone abuse. These will vary depending on the age of the teen, but all teens should be expected to pay for the amount of the calls one way or another. They can work the amount off by doing extra chores, giving up part of their allowance, or a certain amount can be deducted from each paycheck if they work (the money can then be used toward other household bills or deposited in a savings account).

The same holds true for teens who call friends long distance and abuse telephone privileges. When privileges are abused, consequences must be given. You can require the young person to pay for the calls or you may wish to take away all phone privileges for a week. This includes outgoing and incoming telephone calls. If you live in an area where almost all calls are long distance, then it is your responsibility to set a limit on the number of calls and the length of calls the teenager may make. If your teenager works, he should be responsible for paying for long distance calls he makes. Remember, you won't always be around to pay his bills.

She Never Picks Up
State what bothers you using "I" statements. "When I find your belongings scattered all over the house, I get very upset." Then make a list of what you expect her to pick up (school books thrown on the floor, dirty dishes and glasses left on the end tables, etc.) and together decide on the consequences for not picking up items and determine rewards for following through. Picking up after your teenager is not your responsibility.

She Never Wants to Do Anything with the Family
Some teenagers are embarrassed to be seen with their families. They may be so embarrassed that they actually slouch down in the backseat of the car. Don't take this personally, because this is their problem. It won't last forever. In the meantime, expect and anticipate! Be prepared to offer solutions (you can bring a friend along, or you may sit with Danielle's family instead of with us). Don't force her to go with you everywhere. Let her off the hook once in a while, especially if it really doesn't matter if she goes or not.

DEVELOPING SOCIAL SKILLS

About 50% to 80% of teenagers with ADHD have significant interpersonal difficulties. Their social interactions are often marked by such things as abruptness, impulsivity, difficulty sustaining interest in conversations, interrupting others, bossiness, insensitivity to feedback, immaturity, little or no eye contact, poor problem-solving skills, and the inability for effortless social interactions. Poor social skills interfere with relationships with parents, teachers, and friends.

However, when teenagers take stimulant medication, studies have shown that both their relationships with peers and social judgement improved. The key word here is "improve." Social skills may still be below those of non-ADHD teenagers. Other interventions are often needed, such as role modeling, anger control, self monitoring training, and instruction in communication skills and problem-solving techniques. Research on social-skills training with teens with ADHD, however, has been disappointing.

Many fail to view the ADHDer's social difficulties as stemming from a skill deficit. In fact, many of these teens are extremely adept at social skills and, as adults, are often quite successful in areas of business such as sales and others that require first-rate communication and social skills.

However, studies have shown that teens with ADHD with aggression exhibit impulsivity and contorted processing of social information. They perceive many situations as antagonistic. In other words, the teenager with ADHD with aggression may become reactive and display hostility or aggressive behavior even if the situation is not adverse. Although stimulant medication such as Ritalin does decrease aggressive behavior, it does not appear to help greatly with social isolation or processing social information.

Parents of teens with ADHD should watch closely for signs of rejection by peers. If your teenager lacks friends and spends a great deal of time alone (private time spent in her room is normal for a teen but only to a point), shows no interest in attending social activities, or complains that she has no friends, try to find out why she is isolated. Talk to people who are around her such as her teachers, neighbors, friends, or relatives. Ask them what they have observed. Is she able to initiate a conversation? Do others say hello to her but she never answers? Does she stay pretty much to herself?

Popularity is important to self-esteem. As was mentioned in an earlier chapter, some teenagers with ADHD are popular and fun to be with, but others lack the necessary skills to make and maintain relevant friendships with others. This often makes them unpopular. Teens who are rejected by peers usually suffer in silence. It behooves parents to pay close attention to what is happening in the life of their teenager. Social problems tend to increase with age and follow the individual into adulthood. Not to be forgotten, however, are the teens who are not hyperactive but are what David Guevremont, PhD, University of Massachusetts Medical Center, refers to as "socially neglected children . . . who tend to be withdrawn and isolated . . . [displaying] anxious or depressive symptoms."

THE IMPORTANCE OF SOCIAL SKILLS

Social skills are not learned overnight. We learn over the years from observation, practice, and feedback from others. Although many teens with ADHD have difficulty taking turns in conversations, maintaining eye contact, paying attention, and developing social skills, they are still capable of learning verbal and nonverbal social cues.

Many teens, unfortunately, become isolated due to a lack of appropriate social skills. Parents should discuss and explore with their teenager how friendships are formed and reasons they sometimes end. If your teenager is willing to role play, practice how to initiate conversations, talk on the telephone, or invite a friend over.

HELPING YOUR TEENAGER MAKE FRIENDS

Some teens with ADHD become so frustrated in their attempts to make and keep friends that they choose to isolate themselves. This section looks at some other ways parents can help.

Be prepared to listen. Socially isolated teenagers with ADHD know they are different than the other teens around them. They hurt inside and want to fit in. They want to be part of a group, to be invited to parties, to have a boyfriend or girlfriend. They are usually aware that they are seen as outcasts but really don't understand why. Their self-esteem is low and they are often frustrated and depressed. Even when they are included in a group, they usually feel like an outsider. Difficulties with following a conversation, making sense of a joke, remembering names, fear of saying the wrong thing, and not knowing how to respond to questions are just a few third-wheel feelings they experience, all of which lower their self-esteem even more.

What they desperately need is someone to talk to who can provide them with helpful feedback. Maybe that someone can be you. If not you, then possibly another adult that they particularly enjoy being around would be willing to be a friend or mentor to your teen. The important thing to remember is that socially isolated teenagers need someone to talk to, someone who will listen, someone who cares and respects them for the special person they are.

Although it is natural for parents to want to protect their teenager from failures, she needs the opportunity to grow socially. Be available to talk to her about difficulties she may be facing socially. When attempts to build a friendship fail, encourage her to try again.

Encourage her to use her talents and strengths as a way to make friends by joining clubs and organizations. Small groups that encourage a noncompetitive activity work best for teens with ADHD, especially if adult supervision is available. Because they will already have much in common with the members of a club or group, it will be easier for them to become an accepted part of it. It's easier to make friends with peers when everyone is working together on something they all enjoy. This will help her build self-esteem and allow her to shine in a particular area. Your daughter may, however, need your help in recognizing the strengths she possesses.

Help your teen find topics he enjoys and show him how he can use them to initiate conversations with peers. Sit with him and make a list of topics he enjoys talking or reading about. These topics can be anything from movies to sports to music to computers. Encourage him to scan newspapers or magazines and listen to the news for current-event topics. If she watches soap operas or shows other teens watch, encourage her to keep up with the programs. Teenagers who know what is going on around them can use these topics to initiate a conversation. They will feel more confident about approaching people if they have topics they can discuss with potential new friends.

Stress the importance of listening. Although it is much easier for many individuals with ADHD to talk than listen, your teenager needs to understand that people who talk about themselves constantly (or don't allow others to participate equally) in a conversation will not be able to maintain friendships. Stress the importance of asking others about themselves, and then listening to what they have to say before jumping in with "me" comments. This is difficult for many individuals with ADHD. Fearing that they might forget what they want to say, they tend to interrupt a lot.

Stress the importance of making and keeping eye contact. It is a fact that many individuals with ADHD have difficulty maintaining eye contact during conversations. Maintaining eye contact may be difficult due to low self-esteem, but they may also be unable to concentrate. If parents and teachers encourage eye contact in the earlier years, many teenagers can learn to do this with ease. Some teenagers with ADHD, however, are still not able to sustain eye contact and may need more help from parents in this area. Be sure your teenager understands that when he talks to others he must maintain eye contact or his friends will think he is not interested in what they are saying.

Work on one problem at a time. Because most teens with ADHD do not usually understand how their impulsivity and lack of attention affect their relationships with others, parents will do best by beginning with a social problem the teenager recognizes within himself (interrupting a conversation, for instance). It is much easier to find a solution when he can define the problem. Once a social problem is identified, help your teen brainstorm for solutions. Choose a solution and practice it with him. Then have him practice it with others and observe him if you can. Decide together if the chosen solution worked or if you need to find another approach. It may be helpful for you and your teenager to make a chart so he can track his progress. Remember, social skills will not develop instantly, but with practice they can become habit.

DAILY SOCIAL SKILLS CHART

Date:

| Social Skills | How Well I Did | | |
	Poorly	Fairly well	Great
	1	2	3
Listened without interrupting	1	2	3
Initiated a conversation	1	2	3
Remembered to say "hi" to those who greeted me	1	2	3
Complimented at least one person	1	2	3
Maintained eye contact during conversations	1	2	3
Remembered to say "thank you"	1	2	3
Ended a conversation successfully	1	2	3
Controlled my angry feelings	1	2	3

Help your teenager make a list of reasons he feels he could be a good friend to someone. Isolated teenagers do not feel good about themselves. Encourage your teenager to take a good look at himself. What qualities does he possess that a potential friend would like? Is he an honest person? Is he loyal? If someone tells him something in confidence, does he respect that confidence? Is he helpful, considerate, kind? Have your teenager write those qualities down and encourage him to reread the list often. The next time he is going to a social event, remind him to look at the list before he leaves the house. To be a friend to someone, you must first like yourself and know that you have something to offer in a friendship. It's a lot easier to make friends if you are not constantly putting yourself down.

Explore with your teenager the type of friends she is seeking. Unfortunately when teens with ADHD feel alienated, their desire to be accepted by anyone is extremely strong. As a result, they may choose the wrong group of friends and end up in serious trouble. They may convince themselves that they are not good enough for the type of friends they truly want. Teenagers with ADHD do not have to settle for friends they would not choose otherwise. Parents should remind their teenagers of their good qualities and urge them to begin making friends one at a time, rather than striving to get into a group. Befriending one person from a group your teenager would like to be accepted in often leads to acceptance by the entire group.

Teach your teenager what it means to be a friend. Once your teen makes a friend, help him maintain the friendship. Remind your teen that friends should always be caring and supportive, loyal and giving. What they give their friend, they will ultimately get back.

Teenagers who have difficulty with social skills will find that when they take medication for their ADHD symptoms it is easier for them to pay attention and participate in conversations, not interrupt others, and control their impulsivity. Using proper medications will make it easier for children and teenagers to make and keep friends.

EIGHT

COMORBIDITY: THE MANY FACES OF ADHD

omorbidity means there is a coexisting medical condition with ADHD. An individual with ADHD might also have a learning disability, conduct disorder, substance abuse, or obsessive-compulsive disorder, to name a few examples. These comorbities make up the many faces, or subgroups, of ADHD.

Medical literature supports substantial comorbidity of ADHD with mood disorders, oppositional defiant disorder, conduct disorder, learning disabilities, anxiety disorders, Tourette's syndrome, and borderline personality disorder, according to a study in the *American Journal of Psychiatry,* May 1991. One reason that individuals with ADHD have a higher rate of comorbities, such as psychiatric disorders, may be genetic. Studies have shown that within the immediate and extended families of teens with ADHD there are more relatives with ADHD and psychiatric disorders than in families without children with ADHD. However, some children with ADHD grow up in less than ideal situations and may be exposed to drugs, alcohol, violence, and gangs. This exposure can increase their chance of developing conduct disorder, for example.

"The advantage of obtaining a clear family history is that it can tell you a lot about 'probabilities', helping to rate differential diagnoses by likelihood of being present," says Mark Snyder, MD, a psychiatrist from Phoenix. "The problem with having a good family history, however, is that it can slant one's interpretation of data to 'fit' higher probabilities pointed out by that history and assume great relevance in the psychiatrist's mind. And perhaps it should! Still, even though having that history is a great help, it mustn't blind you to other possibilities."

Research suggests that teenagers with ADHD with one or more comorbidities may have a different response to pharmacological treatment, clinical treatment, different risk factors, and a different outcome from those with strictly ADHD. For instance, teens with ADHD and conduct disorder are at a substantially higher risk for the development of juvenile delinquency, substance abuse, and antisocial personality disorder in adulthood compared to those who have ADHD but do not have behavior or conduct problems.

It is important that clinicians who are assessing children, teenagers, and adults for ADHD look for comorbid conditions because they are present in 55% to 85% of those with ADHD. Undiagnosed comorbities may seriously compromise the effective treatment of the ADHD. Clinicians should also assess family and psychosocial stressors that can complicate the symptoms of ADHD and other coexisting conditions.

Teenagers who were diagnosed in early childhood or even later with ADHD may not have been evaluated for comorbities. This chapter will provide basic and concise information about some comorbidities that can be seen in teens with ADHD. Because you know your teen better than anyone else, it is imperative that you seek professional advice if you witness troublesome behaviors.

MOOD DISORDERS

Dysthymia (low-grade depression), bipolar disorder (manic-depressive), and major depressive disorder are examples of mood disorders. Anxiety disorders are phobias (fear of school, for instance), panic disorders (terror that lasts for a short period of time), obsessive-compulsive disorder, or generalized anxiety. Both mood and anxiety disorders appear more often in children who are not hyperactive.

Chronic Depression or Dysthymia
The teen who experiences continuous failures in school and within the home, receives criticism from family members and teachers, and suffers from low self-esteem may become depressed. A dysfunctional family atmosphere only makes the child or teen more susceptible to depression, according to several research studies. While most people think of depression as feelings of sadness, loneliness, and lack of interest in things that once were important, teenagers who act out, abuse drugs or alcohol, skip school, and run away from home may also be exhibiting signs of depression. Left untreated, depression may lead to self-destructive behaviors such as substance abuse, delinquency, or suicide. One-quarter to one-third of teens with ADHD will experience one major episode of depression in adolescence.

The common warning signs of depression in teens are listed below. If your teenager displays four or more of the following, call his doctor:

- An I-don't-care attitude
- Acting-out behaviors
- Aggressive or hostile behavior
- Erratic behavior
- Mood swings and sadness
- Expressions of thoughts of death
- A change in eating habits

- Difficulties sleeping (not due to medication)
- Loss of enjoyment in favorite activities
- Irritability and crankiness
- Fatigue
- Physical health complaints (aches and pains)
- A change in academic performance
- Indecisiveness
- Withdrawal and loneliness

Teens with mood disorders often complain of feelings of boredom, hopelessness, or worthlessness. They may have physical complaints, little energy, insomnia, irritability, or loss of interest in favorite activities and hobbies. Since many symptoms of a mood disorder overlap the symptoms of ADHD, it is a real possibility that the mood disorder may go undiagnosed. Individuals with ADHD and other comorbities often have more difficulty in school and forming peer relationships than those with pure ADHD.

Bipolar Disorder (manic-depressive disorder)
The teen with bipolar disorder and ADHD may experience wide mood swings going from the depths of depression to manic elation. Episodes of mania begin suddenly, rapidly worsen, and may last for weeks. The course of bipolar disorder is often erratic; attacks may come one after another or not reappear for several years. Teens with bipolar disorder are likely to be antisocial and aggressive and often show periods of hyperactivity during the manic cycle. Associated problems include truancy, academic decline, and antisocial behavior. Bipolar disorder may be associated with ADHD, panic disorder, phobia, or substance abuse disorders. However, bipolar disorder is diagnosed less frequently in teens with ADHD than is depression.

ANXIETY DISORDERS

Studies have shown that approximately 25% of teens with ADHD will suffer from anxiety disorders (phobias, panic disorders, or obsessive-compulsive disorder). The feelings of anxiety are often exhibited in teens in the form of chronic fears and worries.

Some teens experience school phobia. They may stutter when speaking with others, their hands may shake and feel clammy, or their voice may quiver when giving an oral report in school. Teens with school phobias have a persistent worry about being embarrassed and are afraid that others will view them as stupid or crazy. The anxiety must be chronically excessive and impair the teen's ability to function in school and social situations before it can be diagnosed as an anxiety disorder.

Panic Disorder
Panic disorder is a brief episode of paralyzing terror or a feeling of impending doom. The attack comes on suddenly and usually reaches its peak within ten minutes or

less. The individual may experience sweating, shortness of breath, fear of losing control, trembling, chest pain, nausea, lightheadedness, dizziness, or the fear that he is going to die. (If a teenager is in touch with his feelings, he may feel the attack coming on. One teenager interviewed, who has been diagnosed with panic disorder, said that when he begins to experience that feeling of terror, he runs out of the house and continues to run until he begins to calm down and the attack passes.)

Obsessive-compulsive Disorder
OCD usually begins in adolescence or early adulthood, but it can develop in child-hood. An obsession is marked by a chronic, abnormal focus on a single idea. An obsession is the inability to let go of a disturbing thought that has no usefulness (even though you locked the door you continue to worry whether it is locked or not, or you are so afraid of germs that you won't shake hands with someone).

A compulsion is a persistent, irresistible urge to do something that is usually contrary to your own standards or wishes. Not only do you keep wondering if the door is locked, but you get up out of bed several times to recheck it. This repetitive behavior is a compulsion preceded by an obsessive thought.

Obsessive-compulsive disorder can be crippling in that it may take over a person's life (for example, a person may have to go in and out of the front door, for example, a specific number of times before he can actually get in the car and drive away). OCD is an internal experience of total chaos. It is a challenge because it is grounded in neurology, people are embarrassed to talk about it, and it has a greater impact on life than ADHD. It appears equally in males and females. The good news is that OCD can be treated with medication, behavior therapy, and the help of support groups.

BEHAVIOR DISORDERS

Behavior disorders are often found in hyperactive teenagers. Two behavior disorders that are frequently comorbid with ADHD are oppositional defiant disorder (ODD) and conduct disorder (CD).

Oppositional defiant disorder usually begins before a child reaches elementary school, often before the age of eight, and almost always before adolescence. Children with ODD are noncompliant and oppositional. They argue with adults, annoy others, are often verbally aggressive, challenge rules, and may have hot tempers. Their behavior, although exasperating for parents, usually does not infringe on the rights of others. Conduct disorder is a more severe form of ODD in which the basic rights of others or societal rules are violated—physical aggression toward people or animals, intentional destruction of property, stealing, etc. (See chapter 14 for more extensive information on ODD and CD.)

A common myth is that children who have ADHD will become delinquent in adolescence and criminal in adulthood. Of course, this is not true. Are some children with ADHD at risk? Yes, some are, especially those with CD, but most children are not.

LEARNING DISABILITIES

One-quarter to one-third of teenagers with ADHD also have one or more learning disabilities. The most common learning disabilities are in reading, math, and spelling. These disabilities result in underachievement in school, placing the teen academically behind others his age. There is a significant discrepancy between achievement and IQ. Handwriting difficulties are also common in teens with ADHD.

Communication or language disorders are found in many teens with ADHD. It is extremely difficult for the child to understand or follow a conversation or school lecture or express himself adequately either verbally or in writing. Teens with learning disabilities and ADHD are at higher risk of not getting their ADHD diagnosed. Because the learning disability may be so apparent, the teen may be placed in special educational classes while the ADHD goes unrecognized.

SUBSTANCE ABUSE

Children and teenagers with both ADHD and conduct disorder are at an increased risk for substance abuse. However, the risk for teens with only ADHD is no greater than that of the rest of the population.

TOURETTE'S SYNDROME

Tourette's syndrome (TS) is a physical disorder of the brain. It causes involuntary motor and vocal tics. Both motor and vocal tics must be evident for a diagnosis of TS to be made. About one-half of those with TS also have ADHD and obsessive-compulsive disorder.

IN SUMMARY

If coexisting anxiety disorders are not recognized and treated, a successful outcome is not as likely. A diagnosis of ADHD should always alert parents to the possibility of coexisting conditions. If you are uncomfortable with the problem behavior you are witnessing, follow your instinct and enlist the assistance of a professional. Don't sit back and hope that it will dissipate on its own. Only a professional can determine if a teenager is suffering from depression, anxiety, or any other condition, but only you can act as an early warning system for the health of your teenager.

FAMILY DYNAMICS

There is little doubt that parenting teenagers with ADHD is challenging. It has its rewards, of course, but families with teenagers with ADHD have more conflict, depression among all family members, communication and problem-solving deficits, confusion, and stress than other families. Most families with ADHD require more involvement with their teens in the areas of education, home management, social situations, medical intervention, and day-to-day operation of the family unit.

Parenting is a tough job, a job that is made even tougher when one or more members of the family have ADHD. However, awareness and knowledge of ADHD and how it affects the family can often help alleviate some of the challenges parents encounter with their teens.

The task of raising teens with ADHD, therefore, is often immense as parents try to keep the family balanced as normally as possible with a teen who does not meet the expectations of his parents or society in general. Balance is needed for families to progress, yet the daily challenges of ADHD manage to keep everyone off balance in varying degrees.

The effects of ADHD on family members have been established in numerous research studies. "The family systems theory is based on a general systems theory," says Mary Squire, PhD, "which maintains that a change in one part of the system results in a change in the entire system. Thus, a family can be thought of as similar to a mobile. When one portion of the mobile moves, all other parts move as well. When a family experiences stress in one subsystem, whether it is the marital, sibling, or individual subsystem, the entire family reacts with attempts to adapt or cope with that stress. Some of these adaptations may be functional; others may be dysfunctional. Healthy families are those that are able to make appropriate or functional adaptations in reaction to stress."

In some families, parents virtually give up and decide to get on with their own lives, emotionally detaching themselves from their difficult teenager. In other families, parental authority breaks down completely and the teen ends up controlling the family instead of the parents.

FAMILIES WITH TEENS WITH ADHD VS. OTHER FAMILIES

Research studies have identified many factors that demonstrate that families with one or more teens with ADHD are different in many ways than families without ADHD. Many of those differences are noted here.

Research indicates that interactions between parents and the teen with ADHD tend to be more negative, intense, frequent, and produce more stress than interactions in other families. Tempers flare easily, voices elevate, inappropriate language is heard, and everyone in the household is tense. Parents may feel like they are always walking on eggshells.

Conflicts are more frequent and more intense in families with ADHD. Stress and confusion within the household can develop easily if they are not thwarted by changing parenting styles, professional intervention, or both. The primary symptoms of ADHD—inattention, impulsivity, hyperactivity, and distractibility—are the major source of stress because these symptoms are in direct conflict with parents' expectations. When a parent makes a request and the teenager cannot meet it, conflict often arises. The request may be major or minor, but if the teenager is unable to follow directions or complete a task after much prompting, parental anger is often the result. This anger then elicits more parental directions and demands that the teen is unable to comply with, ultimately having a negative effect on him. In such instances, the more commands he continues to receive, the more likely he is to rebel. The more behavior problems the parents face, the more frustrated they become. In an attempt to achieve compliance, they often begin tightening the rules and boundaries even more, escalating the problem behaviors even more and frustrating parents.

"Parents must take care of their own stress so they do not become candidates for burnout or divorce courts," says George Lynn, certified mental health counselor in Bellevue, Washington. "Parents are vexed by their own stress reaction to behaviors. Thousands of hours of parent education won't make any difference if a parent becomes immobilized or physically abusive in reaction to the child's provocation."

Study after study shows that parents interact verbally with their teens with ADHD more often than families who do not have ADHD. Russell Barkley's research, however, indicates that such interaction is usually in the form of directions, commands, requests, offering suggestions, and expressing approval or disapproval of behaviors. For instance, mothers intervene more often during the time the teen is completing a task because he is more off task than the non-ADHD child, notes Barkley. Parents of teens with comorbid oppositional defiant disorder or conduct disorder are hit doubly hard.

Although noncompliance usually decreases as the teen matures and the ADHD symptoms become significantly improved, the level of noncompliance is still greater than that in families with non-ADHD teenagers.

Most parents of teens with ADHD have been more involved with the school system over the years than other families. Detentions, suspensions, and expulsions lead to additional parental involvement with the school, adding even greater stress to the family. These disciplinary actions are greatest among teens who have both ADHD and conduct disorder.

This is especially evident in families in which the teen is noncompliant, hyperactive, hot tempered, verbally or physically aggressive, or a combination of these. However, teens without hyperactivity who display such symptoms as the inability to pay attention, complete tasks, and follow directions also elicit more unfavorable parental behavior.

Maternal depression is more evident in families with a teen with ADHD, which leads to mothers feeling less positive in their interactions with their child. Their response to the inappropriate behaviors often causes an aggressive reaction toward the mother. Several mothers I interviewed while writing *The ADHD Parenting Handbook* who had clear, unequivocal major depression, found that antidepressants helped immensely. These mothers found that taking an antidepressant not only relieved the depression, but enabled them to interact less negatively with their child, remain more consistent in their management of the child, thus reducing the amount of conflict with the child, and reducing aggression in the child.

Studies have also shown that mothers of teens with ADHD experience more stress, self-blame, marital discord, and feelings of having failed as a parent than other mothers. Russell Barkley's work shows that mothers of teens with ADHD tend to interact far more negatively with them, exhibit more controlling behaviors, and have a significantly higher level of hostility toward their teen.

This is where these mothers frequently get into difficulty, notes psychiatrist Louis B. Cady, who sees children, teens, and adults with ADHD in his practice in Evansville, Indiana. "We know beyond a shadow of a doubt that stress causes depression. Shock a lab rat, drop it into water and make it swim, pinch its tail enough—the rat will get depressed. Stress a human enough, and the human will get depressed. Extend this depression into its common symptoms—including difficulty sleeping, increased irritability, anxiety—and you have a situation ripe for self-medication."

Cady continues: "Many depressed people, including, presumably, numerous mothers of ADHD teens, start self-medicating for their symptoms. A nightcap or two becomes a habit of consuming alcohol before bedtime. Some people get in the habit of using over-the-counter sleep aids. Then, to counteract the fatigue, some folks take 'pep pills' or diet pills, which you can buy all over town. If the parent has ADHD herself or himself, there may be more a tendency to 'fly off the handle' at mild provocations. Hence, in order to 'calm herself down' during the day, a mom of an ADHD child could start low-dose 'medicinal' drinking to steady her nerves. In spite of our 'liberated society' it is still frequently the mother of an ADHD child that will have the most contact with him or her throughout the day."

"The problem with all this," he notes, "is that the self-selected 'treatment' of the symptoms of depression and anxiety which can attend parents of ADHD children becomes, in and of itself, a new and superimposed problem. Now the parent may have depression, possibly ADHD himself or herself as well as chemical dependency. This is a deadly combination, and frequently can't be teased apart without professional assistance."

Dr. Cady concludes: "For the parent of an ADHD child or teenager, the way out of this morass is to seek professional help promptly, right when unacceptable symptoms begin developing, rather than after the 'cure-yourself' program has had devastating side-effects."

On the average, parents of children with ADHD have a history of more substance abuse, learning disabilities, psychological distress, psychiatric disorders, conduct problems, affective disorders, and antisocial behavior than parents of non-ADHD children. Parents are then faced with a further manifestation of vulnerability in their problematic children, because any of these problems interfere with parenting abilities and add stress to the home-based problems of the teen. Studies have shown that parents of teens with ADHD tend to drink more than those in normal families. The use of alcohol and drugs is evident in some parents who may be "self-medicating" their own undiagnosed ADHD or seeking symptomatic relief. When parents have problems with substance abuse, psychological distress, learning disabilities, or psychiatric problems, their parenting style is often inconsistent, affecting the teen with ADHD negatively.

Parents with ADHD themselves can be at even more of a disadvantage when parenting teens with ADHD, notes Dr. Cady. "With relatively uncomplicated 'pure' attention deficit disorder (what is now known as the 'inattentive type'), paying scrupulous attention to any sort of point systems or reward schemes which you and your clever spouse cook up is going to be a problem for you neurobiologically because your brain is just not wired up to 'pay attention' as well as most folks. Give a teenager an inch, and they'll take the proverbial mile. Give an ADHD teenager an inch and they'll take . . . well, you don't want to know what they'll take!"

If you are biologically compromised with the form of ADHD in which you are predisposed to acting out impulsively and rashly, you don't possess what Cady calls the Archie Bunker "stifle yuself" factor—that is, the ability to remain calm, "stifle yuself," and proceed calmly. Cady recommends consulting a psychiatrist who has some experience with ADHD across the age spectrum—frequently, that might be a child psychiatrist because they have completed a residency not only in general adult psychiatry but a fellowship program of study in children and teens. Recognized experts in ADHD in your community, however, are also a good place to start. Check with your local CHADD chapter or call the national hotline for references. Consider going to a major medical center such as Mayo Clinic, Yale, or a similar facility.

"Perhaps more often than not," says Mark Snyder, MD, "adults with ADHD first realize that fact after a child's been diagnosed. Being diagnosed as an adult will frequently have major impact on that parent's life . . . recognizing their own ADHD and seeking and receiving effective care can help that parent improve parenting skills several-fold for all their children, both those with ADHD and those without."

Parents are often blamed for not disciplining and for possessing inadequate parenting skills. Extended family members, friends, and teachers are often quick to blame the parents for the inappropriate behaviors the teen displays. This is usually due to a lack of understanding of ADHD or complete nonacceptance that it exists. Even some mental health professionals search for reasons, other than the ADHD itself, for the teen's behavior. This search is often aimed directly at the parents, creating additional guilt for those who are already exhausted, frustrated, and consumed in guilt.

The contact that does exist between the immediate family and extended family is not always the same quality as in other families. Sometimes extended family members, often grandparents, are in disagreement with the diagnosis of ADHD in their grandchild. Parents may be accused of medicating a teen by others who think it's obvious there is nothing wrong with the teen. (I know of a few grandparents that have actually threatened to call the social service department and report child abuse!) These grandparents may see the attention or behavioral difficulties, but will remind a parent that the teen acts no differently than the parent did at that age. ("You turned out okay without medication. What makes you think he won't?") Although we now understand that, in most cases, ADHD is inherited, grandparents often deny that they had any problems with their son or daughter during childhood, so how could their grandchild possibly have inherited ADHD from their side of the family! The other spouse is then perceived to be the one who can't handle the grandchild or lacks the necessary parenting skills to raise the child, adding even more stress to the family.

Other grandparents may feel guilty that they failed to recognize that their adult child's difficulties in childhood were actually the result of ADHD—an inherited disorder—and now feel even more guilt knowing that their grandchild has been diagnosed with the same.

When the teen with ADHD acts out only at home, parental complaints may be dismissed or rejected by extended family members who see only the other side of the teen. Relatives and friends usually believe what they see, so they may feel compassion for the teenager because they feel his parents do not appreciate him. Younger parents are often cut off from relatives because of strained relationships at a time when they desperately need the emotional (and sometimes physical) assistance of their parents. This deprivation of support is detrimental to the parents' emotional well being.

What about older parents? Are they able to weather the storm between extended families better because of age alone? It certainly is possible. They have been away from the nest longer, feel more confident about their parenting decisions, and may not be as likely to have parents intruding or monitoring their lives as actively as younger parents.

Parents often suffer from isolation. The teen may isolate the parents socially or the parents may isolate themselves from others due to embarrassment or fear of being blamed for the teen's behavior. "Disinhibited behavior is especially problematic in social situations," says George Lynn. "Parents and children become social isolates in an effort to avoid the psychological pain involved in being around other people when the teen begins mouthing obscenities or displaying inappropriate or scatological behavior."

The role of siblings must also be addressed since sibling-child conflicts can also intensify an already stressful situation in the home. Studies have also shown that teens who are close in age are more apt to identify with their siblings than their parents. So a teen with ADHD may greatly influence younger children in the family—the result being that some younger siblings, with or without ADHD, may mimic the older child's behavior in an attempt to receive more attention (whether positive or negative). Or they may see the teen as the primary role model in the family, especially if the parents have lost control of him.

On the other hand, non-ADHD siblings often develop stress-related problems due to the amount of time and attention the teen with ADHD receives. As a result they may feel ignored, unimportant, depressed, jealous, have lowered self-esteem, and may become aggressive and angry also. Factors that will affect the amount of stress a sibling feels, and consequently create more tension in the family, depend on many variables:

- The severity of the ADHD and how it affects the family structure. Does the teenager with ADHD run the house? Has he superseded the parents as the controlling force in the home? Does the family feel isolated from friends and family because of the behavior the teen displays?
- The birth order and age of the teen with ADHD (Is he the oldest or the youngest child for instance?) and the age of the sibling.
- How the parents react to the teen with ADHD. Are parents patient and understanding? Or do they frequently exhibit anger, frustration, impatience, and verbal assaults?
- The temperament and personality of the teen with ADHD. Is he demanding and aggressive toward parents and siblings, sometimes even violent, creating fear and tension in the home?
- Is a younger non-ADHD sibling often a target of abuse by the teen with ADHD (verbally or physically)?

Siblings of all ages living with an acting-out teenager need as much attention and support as the teen receives. Unfortunately younger siblings of aggressive, hyperactive teenagers may also need protection from his wrath.

Parents with a teen with ADHD are three times more likely to become separated or divorced than families parenting non-ADHD children! When parents are stretched to the limits, as is often the case in families in which a teen's behavior interferes with the balance of the family, conflict erupts. Constant conflict, stress, and communication deficits between family members can lead to marital discord or a total breakdown of the family unit. Marriages can be pushed to the limit.

It is not difficult to understand how marital problems can grow in a family system that has not been functioning in a normal manner. (This is not meant to imply that all families with a child with ADHD are dysfunctional, because that is not the case.) When the child with ADHD reaches adolescence many parents are burned out and frustrated as a result of things such as fighting the school system, nightly arguments over homework, handling the daily challenges of ADHD, monitoring medications, etc. Parents who have advocated for years for their child may feel a tremendous sense of failure and loss of control as the teenage years emerge, and they find that things are not better or easier as they thought they would be. If parents do not agree on how to handle the teen, marital discord can result. Social activities may have been limited through the years, so parents may no longer have close friends to lean on for support. In addition, parents may have become so entangled in the difficulties their child has experienced that they have neglected each other's needs and their martial relationship. Marital therapy may be necessary. We cannot underestimate the need for parents to spend quality time together despite the limitations they face.

Adolescence usually arrives when parents are in their midthirties to midforties, which means they may also have their own set of challenges to face. Midlife typically brings some crises as adults look back and wonder if they have achieved all they had hoped to by now. The teenage years can be a difficult time for all families, but they may be especially difficult for families in which parents are experiencing their own personal problems or are overly involved in their careers and less able to monitor their teens closely. Parents with teenagers who also have oppositional behaviors with ADHD may face a number of future concerns since aggressive and disruptive behaviors have been shown to predict criminal and antisocial behaviors. It is relevant to remember that the younger the child is when behavior problems surface, the greater the likelihood the problems will continue. Teens who develop overt (aggressive, confrontational) forms of behavior problems along with covert (stealing, drug use) appear to be at greater risk of one day being arrested for criminal behavior.

Communications and problem-solving deficits are more apparent in families with teens with ADHD, leading to more conflicts between parents and the teen. "Difficulties with effective communication, as well as poor problem-solving skills are found most frequently in families with ADHD children," said Dr. Snyder. "Ironically, the families that depend for survival on these skills the most are families where one or both of the parents suffer from the same problem." Communicating and problem solving are much easier if the members of the family who have ADHD are being treated with medication.

How do teens with ADHD affect their fathers? Research indicates that fathers have less difficulty managing teens with ADHD than mothers. Fathers may experience less difficulty simply because they have less contact with the teen—mothers who are employed full time still spend the most time with their children. Although both mothers and fathers of teens with ADHD tend to give more commands than parents of non-ADHD children—often resulting in increased negative behaviors displayed by the teen—fathers are more apt to deliver a consequence expeditiously, while mothers usually try reasoning or citing the rules first, according to Dr. Barkley.

This natural difference in parenting styles can further jeopardize a marital relationship. Dr. Cady notes, "ADHD children, almost without exception, respond better to limit setting and instructions from their fathers than their mothers. The reason is basically hormonal and evolutionary. Men have more testosterone than women. That means, from a purely biological perspective, they can be more aggressive. ADHD children know, instinctively that 'good ole Dad' can scream louder, hit harder, and is far more likely to do so than Mom. Hence, deep down in their clever brains, they think, 'Hmmm, I'd better do what he says—consequences are far more certain and they're liable to be worse than if I were to disobey Mom.' Mind you, they don't consciously realize that they are thinking along these lines, but they are, just the same."

"This 'differential response' between the male and female parent can ensnare the unwary couple. Dad says to Mom, 'Why can't YOU control him; I don't have any problem with him?'

"Mom, who has had more than her fill during the day screams back, 'Well I'm just at my wits end!! I'm with him (or her) all day. They just don't respect me like they do you because they've gotten used to me!'

"Neither parent is correct," says Dr. Cady. "Both need counseling and education about the different ways ADHD children respond to parents of different sexes. You're getting some of the education right here. Continue your reading, go to CHADD support groups, and talk with other parents of ADHD children to learn more."

Parents who also have ADHD may have difficulties following routines, setting limits, and following through with rewards or consequences—all necessary for the success of the child or teenager. Parents who are unable to organize themselves may not be able to teach their teen organizational skills. Their expectations for their teen may be unrealistic due to cognitive distortions. Promises made to teens may not be kept due to forgetfulness or poor concept of time on the parent's part. Parents may not be able to pay attention to their teen's conversation due to their own ADHD, which may lead the teenager to believe his parent is not interested in him.

Unfortunately, the teen with ADHD and her family are often misunderstood. The teen is often seen as lazy, disorganized, unmotivated, or a problem child. The parents are blamed for not disciplining and controlling their teenager. Parenting, which is difficult under any circumstances, becomes even more challenging because of the symptoms of ADHD and because of the lack of knowledge that surrounds ADHD. Parents must educate family members, relatives, friends, and teachers about ADHD; they must advocate for their teen, cope with the related behavior, and shield their family from the scrutiny of others—all extremely challenging tasks that tax the entire family.

Despite the belief held by some marginally competent therapists that parents are almost always the cause of severe behavior problems, parents of teens with ADHD and professionals involved in their care must realize the profound effect that children with ADHD have on the family, and the impact the family has on the teen as a result of defiant, hostile, and aggressive behavior. Social interactions between the teen with ADHD and other family members vary greatly from the norm in that they are more negative and produce greater stress. The greater the teen's behavior deviates from the norm of socially acceptable behavior, the greater the negative effect on the parents—especially if society sees the behavior as something that could be avoided (such as oppositional behavior or juvenile delinquency).

Society has definite expectations of how children should behave. When a teen deviates from the norm, parents experience frustration and react differently than parents of teens who meet or surpass parental and society's expectations. Parents of teens with special needs, such as ADHD, must readjust their expectations and reeducate themselves as to what is normal for their teen. This disparity between expectations and actuality may induce parental strain, depression, a feeling of reduced control, and less confidence in parenting abilities. However, parents should take advantage of as much assistance as possible from medication therapy. ADHD, at its core, is a neurobiological disorder that can sometimes be so well treated with medication that it becomes almost clinically invisible.

The difficult teenager has a direct effect on the parents, but the effect will vary greatly depending on the individual characteristics of the parents and the teen. Unfortunately, the wealth of literature available on child psychology usually focuses on the effect parents have on their children—seemingly ignoring the significant effect on the parents and the family organization.

COPING WITH THE STRESS

Anyone who is parenting a teenager with ADHD knows that they often carry an enormous amount of stress. A widely acclaimed authority on stress, Dr. Hans Selye, identifies two types: distress and eustress (positive stress). In this section I will offer suggestions for coping with distress because too much of this type of stress can seriously affect your physical and mental health.

Keep the Lines of Communication Open

Although some parents find that they constantly talk about the problems they are experiencing with their children, many parents do not have an open line of communication with their spouse on this issue. One spouse may complain about the behavior problems she is witnessing only to be told that she is to blame for the teen's difficulties. Another spouse may feel that he should be able to handle the behaviors, so, rather than sharing his frustrations with his spouse, he keeps it to himself. The result in all cases is a lack of communication.

Work at keeping those lines of communication open no matter what the circumstances. Parents who work together achieve greater collective strength. It's often easier emotionally to close up, but parents who are facing a great deal of stress should open up and find someone to help carry the emotional burden. If this is not your spouse, then find a reliable friend, relative, or another parent who is going through the same thing you are. There are many ADHD parent support groups in the United States where parents meet regularly. These parents will reach out and help you. If you find that you can't talk it out, write it down. If you find it all too overwhelming, seek help from a mental health professional.

Daily Reminders

Remind yourself every day that no one is to blame for your teen's ADHD. You are not to blame and certainly your teenager is not to blame. Do something nice for yourself each day (a leisurely bath, read, write a letter, spend time on a hobby, call a friend) even if it means getting up earlier in the morning. Take care of yourself. Stay healthy by eating right and be sure to get enough sleep. Look for funny or humorous things each day and enjoy a good laugh. Studies show that when we laugh, our brain releases chemicals that ease stress and promote relaxation. Laughter and a positive approach are vital to your health. Get away whenever you can. You'll come home with renewed strength, a better outlook, and more patience.

"By taking care of yourself, you're better able to meet the needs and demands that all your children place on you," says Dr. Snyder. "Being rested, relaxed, and feeling good also helps your children, too. So if while enjoying yourself you suffer a pang of guilt about your enjoyment, remember: you must do it, for yourself and for your children."

Bad Parent vs. Good Parent

Don't allow yourself to get caught up in the good parent vs. bad parent scenario. If you are making an honest effort to deal with the challenges you are facing, you are a good parent. Considering the challenges you are facing, you are probably doing remarkably well.

One Day at a Time

Do not allow yourself to dwell on the future. It's okay to look ahead for problem areas that could develop (teen pregnancy, substance abuse, etc.) and address those issues now, but to dwell on future "what ifs" can immobilize you. Keep in mind the serenity prayer: God grant me the serenity to accept the things I cannot change, the courage to change the things I can, and the wisdom to know the difference.

Seek Information

Knowledge is power. Learn as much as you can about ADHD and how it affects your teenager and you, and make any necessary changes you need in your parenting style. Join CHADD. If you have a computer, join the ADD Forum on CompuServe (an on-line communication program). Don't be afraid to seek the help of a professional and ask questions. Get the answers you need to build or maintain a healthy family environment. Do whatever you can to balance your family.

Exercise

Individuals with ADHD should exercise daily. It's a great stress reducer and can be a lot of fun—not just for you but for the entire family. Many people who follow a regular exercise program find that mentally they feel more refreshed, their thoughts are clearer, pressure and stress are reduced, depression decreased, and there is an overall improvement in mood swings. For teens with ADHD, exercise is not only a great way to release stress and frustration but anger as well.

Because many parents work and want to be with their teens after work, they often hesitate to leave the house to go to a gym. Yet these parents are the ones who need the exercise the most. (Despite our best efforts to get to the gym a few nights a week, we found our schedules were too hectic. We decided to build a home gym. Every evening my family exercises together—a family activity that we all enjoy.)

Evaluate the Day

When the day is over, evaluate it. Take delight in those things you did right. Compliment yourself out loud in front of your teenager or privately. Don't dwell on mistakes. If you handled a situation poorly, decide how you'll handle it the next time. Remember, mistakes made today and yesterday are just that. Tomorrow is your opportunity to begin anew.

Don't Try to Be a Perfect Parent

Perfect parents do not exist, nor do perfect families. If a family looks perfect, remind yourself that all families have challenges to face. Just because we can't see the problems, doesn't mean they don't exist. If you have a teen who only acts up at home, how many people are aware of the daily problems you face?

Set Realistic Expectations

When expectations are too high they often do not get met, so set realistic expectations for yourself and others in your family. Let go of the dreams you once had. Things will never be perfect, so don't expect perfection from yourself or your teenager. It's okay to have a house that is a little messy, grass that should have been cut yesterday, and laundry piled up.

On days when you feel you just can't handle the stress any longer, George Lynn recommends the following:

- Remember to breathe. A teen's psychological attack may come when a parent is most vulnerable. It is difficult not to react with intense anger. Deep, calm breathing interrupts this stress reaction and gives the person time to think about the best way to deal with the situation.
- Listen to your self-talk. A parent in this situation will often say things to themselves like "That little s.o.b. has gone too far. Now he's going to get it." Sometimes the experience will make the parent feel like she is the teenager, or it might remind her of times in her life when she was bullied or violated. Issues from childhood or a bad day at work may drive the

parent toward action she will regret. She should cultivate awareness of stress-induced mind chatter and deliberately change it by saying something like, "This isn't going to get me down. I'm in charge, he's not. Breathe."

- Remember that he is only partially in control and it is up to you to educate him to control himself by implementing a consequence that he can understand. If you hit him or scream at him, you are teaching him to be violent. The older and bigger he gets, the more this violence will come back to you.
- If you cannot control yourself, call for back-up and give yourself a time out. Separate yourself from him. If possible, call a friend. Involve your spouse. It's okay to sequester yourself and cry. Deal with it later.
- If you do lose your temper, talk with him as soon as you can when things calm down. Apologize if you need to. Don't grovel. Tell him what he did to set you off. Share what it's like living with him. Get over the incident and resolve to do things differently in the future.

Stress research indicates that people who stay healthy and take care of themselves in stressful situations share three characteristics: 1) they have support and love in their lives; 2) they have some kind of work or activity that nurtures them so they hold personally meaningful goals; and 3) they see stress as a challenge, not as a curse or insurmountable obstacle.

If you do not have these three elements in your life, take action as soon as you can. If you are not strong and healthy, you cannot help your teen be strong and healthy. If you are fighting depression, drinking, or using drugs to cope, seek professional help immediately. Don't wait until the situation gets even more out of control.

SCHOOL AND THE STUDENT

Many educators do not appreciate or understand the individual learning styles and the typical needs of teens with ADHD. In truth, the educational needs of youth with ADHD are not "qualitatively different from what other students need—they just need more . . . They may need more monitoring . . . structuring of . . . work and . . . behavior. It is not fair to expect the [youth] to sit still [without being some what restless or fidgety], to ignore visual or auditory distractions, or to [stay] engaged [in mundane] projects for extended classroom sessions." (*The Brown University Child and Teen Behavior Letter*, September 1994). Unfortunately, this is often what is expected of students with ADHD.

Some of the symptoms that educators and parents find annoying now become assets in adulthood. Adults with ADHD are often creative, interesting, high energy people, who are enthusiastic and have tremendous stamina. The difference between ADHD in adolescence and adulthood is that in school teens must sit still, face the boredom of everyday school tasks, and have little freedom to choose what they want to do and not do. In adulthood, expectations change as does social perception. The adult has the opportunity to choose a career that he knows he can excel in, building on his strengths rather than fighting his weaknesses. Unfortunately, before he can shine in adulthood, he has to first get through school—not an easy task for many teenagers with ADHD.

Moving from lower school into junior high and high school is usually difficult for parents and teens alike. Elementary school teachers focus on the child, whereas junior and senior high teachers focus on curriculum. Teens are now expected to be organized, have good study skills, follow directions, complete tasks, and be more independent than before. Upper school teachers expect more from older students, but the student with ADHD has difficulty meeting expectations, thus the gap between teacher's expectations and student performance widens even further.

CHALLENGES FACING THE STUDENT WITH ADHD

Students with ADHD usually have difficulty in the following areas: homework, test taking, sustaining attention, taking notes, long-term projects (term papers), keeping track of assignments, organizing information, remembering to bring books home from school, taking the courses that are required for entering college, vocational school or a career of interest, and defining career goals.

Teens with ADHD are more likely to receive lower grades and scores on standardized tests, especially in math and reading. The risk of school failure for teens with ADHD, who have equivalent IQs to other students, is two or three times greater than the risk for teens without ADHD. By adolescence, over half of all students with ADHD will have failed to pass at least one grade and one-third will eventually drop out of high school. However, as Dr. Elliott emphasized in the foreword (and in chapter 2) and Dr. Cady points out in his introduction stimulant medication, when needed, will greatly improve all areas of the ADHDer's life, including school performance (academically and behaviorally).

WHAT ABOUT RETENTION?

The trend in the United States to retain students is distressing because there is little if any evidence supporting the benefits of retention. "A meta-analysis of research on retention by Holmes and Matthews reported in *Exceptional Children,* May 1992, shows that children who are held back have lower self-concepts, poorer attitudes toward school, and achieve at a lower rate than classmates who were promoted. Retention rates in the United States compare favorably with Haiti and Sierra Leone, while contrasting sharply with most industrialized nations (e.g., Japan and most European nations), where fewer than 1% of the school-aged population is retained each year." Studies show a dramatic increase in the rate of retention in the United States, with some states reporting a 50% retention rate.

More distressing is that one of the leading causes of dropping out of school is being behind in grade level and older than classmates. Children with learning problems are at an extremely high risk. The drop out rate for these teens ranges from 42% to 54%, even if the child was retained as far back as kindergarten for age reasons.

If retention is suggested, remember that a student cannot be held back without the parent's permission. Ask school officials why they are recommending retention and ask them to back up their recommendation with research that will prove to you that holding your child back will benefit her. Look for other options like summer school or tutoring. Finally, make sure your teen is really lagging behind. In upper- and middle-class areas, your daughter may appear behind when she is really working at the national level and the other children are actually working above grade level.

WHAT CAN PARENTS DO?

One of the biggest complaints that middle and high school teachers have is that parents do not seem to take an interest in their teenager's education. Parents of teens with ADHD must maintain contact with the school just as they did when their sons or daughters were younger. Teens will need help in choosing the right courses if they plan to go to college. Left on their own, they will choose classes for the wrong reasons (their friend is taking the course or a certain teacher never gives homework, for instance).

When scheduling time rolls around each semester, call the guidance counselor and set up an appointment. Find out what courses are needed to get into a college or technical school or what courses would best meet your teen's career goal. Stay in touch with teachers and guidance counselors throughout the school year.

ADVOCATING

By the time a student with ADHD enters junior high and high school, he should be encouraged to advocate for himself. He should be able to approach teachers, explain his challenges, and ask for assistance when needed. You may have to role play to teach him how to do this.

The teenager with ADHD who can say to a teacher, "I have ADHD and have difficulty with written expression. It is easier for me to take tests orally. Is this possible in your class?" is one large step ahead of the student who is not able to advocate for himself. Admittedly, it is difficult for many teens (and adults) with ADHD to ask for assistance, so parents should make it clear that all people, not just those with ADHD or learning disabilities, need the assistance of others from time to time.

Teens should be encouraged to ask teachers for suggestions to correct problems. Tutoring may be helpful and advisable, especially for students with ADHD who do not have an Individualized Educational Program (IEP—discussed later in this chapter). If his grades are falling below his actual ability, he should inquire about doing extra credit work. This shows awareness, initiative, and the willingness to work toward improvement. Students should also speak with classmates to determine if others are experiencing difficulties. It's easy to assume that the teenager is having problems because of the ADHD, but sometimes the level of instruction is not what it should be.

Because you are your child's best advocate, monitor school work closely. Be sure your teenager understands what ADHD is and how it affects him in specific areas. Parents should step in if the teen is unable or does not want to approach his teachers.

According to Janet Robinson, RN, PhD, from Sylvania, Ohio, parents can easily step in without embarrassing their teen. "My son has never been able to talk with his teachers, so I draft a letter to each one every year about the third week of school.

In the letter I begin by listing his strengths and abilities, then list the specific problems he has (like disorganization). I make only one request, and that is if he misses more than two assignments that I'm notified. When you are concrete, most teachers are supportive. I've seen them write in their roll book, 'misses two assignments, contact mother.' They don't even have to talk with me personally. They can just leave a message on my voice mail.

"Whenever I see my son going into a self-destructive pattern, I send the teachers a note that says I'm concerned about how he's doing. I put in a self-addressed postcard and all they have to do is make a check mark or fill in a blank." Dr. Robinson's postcard is similar to the one below.

Student's name:_____

____ He's doing fine
____ No changes
____ Not doing so well
____ Missing _____assignment(s)

_____
Teacher's Signature and Class

(from *The ADHD Parenting Handbook: Practical Advice for Parents from Parents*)

Dr. Robinson explains, "Most high school teachers are surprised that parents don't want to be involved in their kid's lives. I think it's essential every parent gets to every parent-teacher conference. It's easy to assume that if kids don't hand in assignments that the parents just don't care. Even when there are problems, stay in touch with the school. I know it's hard to hear the negatives, but parents must be involved in their child's education."

The following is a letter that Mary Squire, PhD sends to her son's teachers.

Dear _____,

_____ has Attention Deficit Hyperactivity Disorder (ADHD). ADHD is a physical/neurological disorder characterized by age-inappropriate levels of attention, hyperactivity, and/or impulsivity. The primary manifestations for _____ are difficulties with attention and concentration, organizational skills, and difficulty staying on task. In a classroom he may disturb other children at times by talking but is not distruptive. His attention difficulties are most evident in math, due to the degree of concentration required for accurate calculation.

His is presently taking medications for this disorder, therefore feedback from teachers is especially important to help us monitor dosage.

Accommodations that improve _____ classroom behavior and academic performance include the following:

_____ should be seated in the front of the classroom surrounded by the attentive students.

_____ will likely require more time on tests and other assignments than the majority of students in the class. He should be encouraged to check his work, especially in math.

If _____ fails to turn in assignments or comes to class without his homework done, it is important to notify me before his grade is adversely affected.

_____ is capable of doing honor-levels work. Superior work should be expected of him, and he should not be placed in lower levels simply because of his attention difficulties. He has high aspirations for himself, and together we can help him achieve them.

If _____ quarter grade average falls below a B (or A in science or English), please call me immediately. I can be reached at home at _____ or work at _____.

Thanks very much for your help.

Mary Squire

(from *The ADHD Parenting Handbook: Practical Advice for Parents from Parents*)

Teenagers who need special educational services should participate in all meetings with school personnel including parent-teacher conferences and those that address Individualized Educational Plans (IEPs) that are addressed later in this chapter. Parental support and persistence in dealing with the school and community resources should be ongoing during adolescence. Involvement in their teen's education may need to be continued through the high school years (sometimes carried out behind the scenes), and many parents may need to assist the young adult with ADHD as they enter vocational school, college, or choose a job.

HOMESCHOOLING

Much of the information in this chapter covers students who are in a public, private, or independent schools. However, there is a growing number of parents who teach their teens at home, including parents of teens with ADHD and other disabilities. There are numerous academic programs available for homeschooling, and each family approaches it in their own way. One thing is certain, families that are homeschooling successfully are enjoying it immensely!

New homeschooling mother Carla Nelson says, "We are homeschooling just in eighth grade English this semester to test drive how it works but will probably do it for all core courses in ninth and tenth grade in a semisupervised independent study monitored by a mentor in the district's alternative high school. My son tests gifted. It's hard for him to read at length from books, and it's torture to do the rote homework the school expects. Even when we get that part sort of handled, too many forgotten papers and missed dates clutter the landscape.

"Instead, I am building his curriculum almost completely on learning software, supplemented by videos like *The Brain* from the Discovery Channel. There is a lot of good information available on CD-ROM and video that makes the classroom experience look so blah. But the key part for kids like ours is self-pacing with built-in validation that learning is taking place. Ironically, the courses we are pursuing are more rigorous than he had in public schools. So we are asking him to do more, not less, but he's more than willing when he can tackle it at his own speed and doesn't have to keep endless reminder lists of things he couldn't care less about. A number of prepackaged curricula exist, but we are doing mix and match for now, working with a teacher's sourcebook of software. In addition to the academics, we are including things like speed reading and eye exercises to address perceptual kinks."

Janie Bowman talks about homeschooling her high school son: "Homeschooling was [mentioned] by a psychologist when our son wasn't adjusting to middle school. I thought he was insane. I felt we couldn't homeschool because, hey, we were worn out from trying to push him in middle school, trying to educate some of the teachers on how to fill out assignment books or even let us know if there was a problem. I didn't think I would survive it. Guess what? I not only survived it, it helped turn my family around, saved my children's self-esteem, and saved lots of time and money in the long run.

"If a homeschooled teenager needs two years to get through algebra, that's not a problem. If he can do it in four months, that's not a problem. Few schools can provide this kind of flexibility. There are some school districts that offer the HALL Program (Homeschool Alternative Learning Lab) where homeschoolers and parents have access to computers, science labs, etc. Additionally, a certified teacher oversees the program. Homeschoolers are typically registered one-half time. There are many places to get curriculum, including the typical educational books that are usually sold only to public schools."

If you are interested in homeschooling, the first step is usually to contact the local school district. Laws vary from state to state. The superintendent is usually in charge of homeschooling. You can usually use the school's curriculum or purchase one from another source.

"The first year is usually a learning experience for parents and student," says Susan Jaffer. "It is wise to be prepared for some stress and possible discouragement. Many families find this experience to be enormously rewarding. I found that I had many more opportunities to share values and information with my teenager. When he was at school, he was hardly ever here and almost never tuned into me. At home, I assign him articles on all sorts of subjects from all sorts of publications from the *Wall Street Journal* to *Yankee Magazine.*"

TESTS, HOMEWORK, AND STUDY TIPS

Most teens hate homework and studying for tests. But the teen with ADHD hates homework and studying even more for several reasons: 1) it is a boring activity that provides no stimulation; 2) there is no immediate gratification for studying; 3) it takes them longer to study than it does the non-ADHD student; 4) it's difficult for them to stay on task because of their internal chaos; and 5) they are easily distracted by visual and auditory stimuli (their attention is easily captured by random, stronger stimuli and they are therefore unable to attend to the task at hand).

Encourage study time every night whether your son or daughter has homework or not. Some parents make a study hour mandatory in the lower grades, and use this time to review the next day's work. Others may devote the time to working with the child in areas where he is having some difficulties. Those parents who have employed this method for several years have found it works during adolescence also.

Set a specific time period and place to study and complete homework. Negotiate a plan and put it in writing. Older students can earn such privileges as use of the car or telephone for staying on task during homework time.

Students with ADHD have difficulty organizing materials, concentrating for extended periods of time, and selecting important information from written and auditory direction. Assignments must be tackled with a game plan.

Notetaking Tips
Encourage your teen to try one or more of the following in class:

1. Use a tape recorder (with permission)
2. Ask another student to share a copy of their notes
3. Take notes even if tape recording the session for double reinforcement
4. Explain to the teacher the difficulty of notetaking and ask if they will share a copy of their notes with them
5. Draw pictures to help make a connection between a fact presented and the picture you have drawn
6. If he says he can't draw, have him visualize a picture of what is being said. When reading, visualize a paragraph's content for easier recall.
7. Write a summary of the lecture from his notes

Sitting Still Long Enough to Read
Without a doubt, those who are taking medication for ADHD will find that they can sit and study for longer periods of time than without medication. Teenagers who have just started taking medications are often stunned to find that, rather than

getting up from their desks every ten minutes or so, they can actually sit for hours and study. Not only can they sit still and concentrate, they also work much faster and get more accomplished during that time.

One teenager has his own approach to studying. He puts music on, unplugs the phone, turns off the television, sits down and begins reading. His goal is to read just one page. If at the end of that page, he feels he can read another, he does. When he realizes that he is no longer concentrating he takes a short break, then returns with the goal of reading just one more page. He does this until he has read the entire chapter. If your teenager wants to try this approach, encourage him to set a timer to signal when short breaks are over. Otherwise, he may get involved in another activity and fail to return to studying.

Reading Chapters in a Text Book
Reading a textbook chapter can appear to be a monumental task to a student with ADHD, but when broken down into sections the assignment becomes less overwhelming and threatening. When studying chapters, students should use the popular SQ3R Method:

S—Scan the chapter
  * Reading the title of the chapter
  * Reading each subtitle
  * Studying any illustrations, graphs, charts, etc.
  * Reading the study guide questions at the end of the chapter
  * Reading the chapter summary
Q—Make up questions using the subtitles (for example, if the subtitle reads "Congress of the United States" ask yourself, "How many members are there? Where is it located? What does it do?")
R—Read to answer your questions
R—Write the answers down
R—Review the answers at the end (and keep all notes to review at a later date when you will be tested on the material)

Long-Term Assignments
Many teenagers with ADHD find themselves working on a major assignment the night before it's due, even though they have known about the assignment for weeks. The only way they seem to be able to accomplish this at the last minute is by throwing themselves into "hyperfocus" and working well into the night. Encourage your teenager to break the project down into manageable parts to be worked on each week during the established time frame. Here is a sample project:

Week One: The student gathers the resource materials she'll need to write the report. Photocopies of articles from magazines and pages from books are made.

Week Two: After reading the materials, she decides which main topics to include in the report and lists them on separate sheets of paper, index cards, or on the computer. Articles relating to each main topic are divided into appropriate categories and placed in a separate file folder according to the number assigned to each topic.

Week Three: Take notes on each topic, listing the notes on index cards using the number assigned to each topic. All number one cards are then paper clipped together or entered on the computer, as are number two cards, and so forth. Notes should always be written in the students own words and in complete sentences. This will make the rough draft relatively simple to pull together and write.

Week Four: Writing the outline is the next step. With the notes numbered by topics, the student determines the order the facts should be presented in, using a formal or simple outline form.

Week Five: Begin writing the rough draft from your index cards (or the computer). Do not stop to look up correct spelling of words, just circle the words you are unsure of and continue writing. You are simply trying to get your facts down in paragraph form on each topic beginning with the number one cards. If writing (rather than using a computer), skip lines so you can insert words or sentences easily. Upon completion of the rough draft, set it aside for a day, then read it again slowly, one line at a time, making corrections in spelling, punctuation, etc.

Week Six: Before writing the final draft, be sure you know how the term paper is to be presented. Where are you to list your name, class, and period? Is the title to be centered or off to the side? What should the margins be? After completing the final draft, once again set it aside for a day or two. Then reread it checking carefully for punctuation, grammar use, etc. When checking for spelling errors read each page from the bottom up. If you are using a computer, make use of spelling and grammar checking tools.

Using an Assignment Notebook

An assignment notebook is essential for all students with ADHD. Older students who have many different teachers and change classes, should use a daily planning calendar to keep track of classes throughout the school year, noting where and what time classes meet, and designated study period times. In this planner they can write down test dates, essay and term paper due dates, and outline plans to study for tests and write papers.

Janet Robinson, RN, PhD, suggests that parents assist students by using a color-coding system on the assignment sheet also. "If there is no assignment for a particular class on a certain day, the student should write 'No Assignment' next to the subject. Parents can give points for entries next to each subject."

Homework

Although homework is definitely the responsibility of the student, most parents will need to monitor their teenager to make sure assignments are being completed. Even older students with ADHD may not be sure what homework they have to do so make sure your teen has an assignment notepad and that she uses it. Reward for assignments that are entered in the assignment pad and homework completed. Accordingly, remove a privilege when there are no entries.

Unclear Assignments
Even with an assignment notepad, your teenager may forget to bring home the books needed to complete homework so you may want to consider purchasing a second set of books. This permits the teenager to highlight or make notes in the margins, something that is necessary for many students with ADHD. If buying another set of books is not affordable, then have her bring all textbooks home each night. Reward her until it becomes a habit.

Parents' Homework Responsibilities
1. To help your teen schedule a regular time for doing homework each evening whether he has actual homework or not. (If he truly doesn't have homework, he can read a book during this time.)
2. To provide an area for doing homework that is as free of distractions as possible.
3. To keep siblings out of the study area (unless they can study together without interrupting each other).
4. To be available to assist, if necessary. This does not mean you do the homework, only that you are available to help him understand what the assignment is and help him get started. You may also need to help him break the assignment down into manageable parts.
5. To allow for scheduled breaks during homework time.
6. To encourage him to take notes during class and record assignments in a notebook.
7. To praise his efforts.
8. To ask to see homework once it has been returned no matter what his age.

Knowing and understanding that homework is not a favorite activity for ADHDers doesn't make it any easier when your teen refuses to do homework, speeds through it passively, forgets his books, or insists that he doesn't have homework. It doesn't really matter what the excuse is because the bottom line is that he must study every night during the time agreed upon for homework.

The Rejectors
The rejectors are the ones who refuse to do any homework. So what do you do? You simply remove all privileges until the homework is done. Once the homework is completed she can make or receive phone calls, visit friends, watch television, etc. It's important that she knows she has a choice. She can do her homework and receive the privileges or she can refuse to do the work and lose them.

Speeders, Insisters, and Forgetters
Speeders sit down and do their homework because they know Mom and Dad will be impressed. They also have more important things to do once the homework is finished. The only thing about speeders is that they usually work too quickly, making

careless mistakes on a paper that looks like it went through the washer and dryer. Speeders, when caught, usually have to redo their homework.

Insisters are the ones who swear they have no homework. Or they tell you they did it all in study hall that day. Parents with insisters should get in touch with teachers to find out what is really happening. Sure some students get their work done at school, but not everyday.

And then there are the forgetters—they forget to bring home their books, they forget to write down their assignments, etc.

The solution for speeders, insisters, and forgetters is the same: A scheduled hour of homework time every evening. In addition, parents should assign homework for insisters and forgetters such as a book report or a math or science assignment. Parents should always assign more than what the teacher would, providing the student the incentive to bring home books and assignment notepads correctly filled in.

PAYING ATTENTION IN CLASS

As your teen encounters more demanding school days and homework sessions, you may want to share these tips, provided by a former high school teacher, with them:

- Sit close to the teacher in lecture-style classes to not only hear better but have fewer distractions
- Take notes and use a tape recorder if possible
- Participate in class or group sessions (this includes asking questions when not understanding something and offering answers when they do)
- Go to class prepared (homework is finished and the student has studied a lesson the night before it is to be presented in class)
- Write a summary of the lecture after class

All of these tips provide the teen with a more active approach to learning as compared to a passive approach, which is usually the case for ADHDers.

CHANGING CLASSES

For those without ADHD it may seem strange to say that teenagers with ADHD will have difficulties changing classes, but they do. The bell rings signaling the end of a class, and the student with ADHD gathers his books and hits the hallway where he is bombarded with stimuli. Finally arriving at his locker to retrieve his books for the next class, he opens the door to find his locker in total chaos, making it nearly impossible to find what he needs to get to his next class on time. At the same time he is distracted by friends whose lockers are near his. Since there are only a few minutes between classes the student with ADHD may be late for the next class but have the right books, be late for the class with the wrong books or no books, or be on time but have the wrong books . . . well, you get the picture.

One young woman with ADHD finally found a solution that worked for her. She carried all of her books for her morning classes in her backpack. At lunchtime she would then go to her locker, drop off the books from her morning classes and pick up her books for the afternoon classes. Although she was still occasionally late for class, she always had the right books with her. She also color-coded book covers, notebooks, etc., making it easier for her to find what she needed in her messy locker.

Some teenagers may need a map showing the location of their locker and the route they must take to each class. Color-code each classroom according to the color used on books and file folders.

IMPROVING TEST-TAKING SKILLS
(from ERIC Digest #101, *Improving Your Test-Taking Skills*)

Here are some valuable tips your teen can use to help prepare for tests. The best way to get ready for a test is to study from the beginning of the course. Study a little bit each day. Preparing for a test gradually allows you to absorb the material, make connections between concepts, and draw conclusions. Studying each subject every night will save the agony of having to cram on the night before a test (typical for ADHDers).

Create your own study aids. Aids such as checklists, flash cards, chapter outlines, and summaries will help the student organize and remember the material better. These aids will help to condense the test material into a manageable size.

Organize a study group. Ask others to arrange a time for a group to study together several nights before the day of the test. If you study with a group, you can combine everyone's resources. By comparing notes you can sometimes determine what may appear on the test. Do not let study groups become social events. Throw a party after the test to celebrate your success.

Before tests or before beginning long-term assignments, you should ask the teacher how she grades, the type of tests she usually gives (essay, multiple choice, etc.), and the most important areas to study.

What Can You Do during the Test?
- Be prepared for taking a test by bringing paper, pencils, and pens with you.
- Read and listen to all directions carefully before starting. One of the most important test-taking skills is the ability to follow directions. Some students with ADHD are so anxious to get the test over with that they skip the directions; this is often a costly mistake. Others take longer to get started than non-ADHD students and often lose valuable time.
- Budget your time. Be sure to allow enough time to answer all parts of the test, not just the hard parts or the parts you know best. Some tests may include a note about how much time you should spend on each section. Use these notes as guidelines to check yourself so that you don't spend too much time on one section.

- Look quickly at the entire examination to see what types of questions are included (multiple choice, matching, true/false, essay, etc.) and, if possible, the number of points for each. This will help you pace yourself.
- Make a special effort to write neatly. Although neatness may not officially count toward your overall grade, a teacher who is faced with a mountain of papers to grade will appreciate a clearly written test. Consciously or unconsciously, neatness has a positive effect on teachers.
- If the test includes both essay and multiple-choice questions, fill out the multiple-choice part first. Answering multiple-choice questions will help you remember the material and make connections between concepts. Multiple-choice questions may also contain information that you can use to answer essay questions.
- If you have extra time, check your answers. If you finish a test before your time is up, don't hand in your test. Use this time to check your answers. Do not frustrate yourself, however, by concentrating on questions that you simply don't know how to answer.
- You may also want to bring a wristwatch and place it on your desk. Some ADHDers have a poor concept of time. A watch can help keep them on target during the test. One young man uses a watch with an alarm. If he knows he has 60 minutes for a test, he sets the alarm for 30 minutes. At the beeping sound, he knows he should be halfway through the test.

How to Take a Multiple-Choice Exam

Here are some strategies for succeeding on multiple-choice tests:

- Make educated guesses. Before you start, ask your teacher how the test is scored. If there is no penalty for guessing, answer every question—even if you have to guess. If you are penalized for guessing, blind guessing will probably hurt your score. If you can eliminate one or two of the choices, then guessing will be more profitable.
- Don't get stuck on any of the questions. Work through multiple-choice tests quickly and carefully. Don't get bogged down on a question that you can't answer or are unsure about. Make a small mark beside the question, and if you have time return to it later.
- Fill in answers on standardized tests carefully. Make sure that the number you are answering corresponds to the number of the question. If you skip a question, be sure to leave the space for that question blank. Make sure you fill in the blanks completely so that the machine that grades the test can easily record your answer.

How to Take an Essay Test
- Read all of the questions on the test before answering any of them. The questions often contain valuable information that may be helpful when you write your answer. Reading all of the questions before starting will help

refresh your memory about the material and will help you make an informed choice if you have to choose from several questions.

- Underline or highlight key verbs in the question. Essay questions usually focus on one or more key verbs. Concentrate on these key verbs; they will give you clues to the type of information that your teacher wants. Here are some key words that often appear on essay exams:
    - compare—examine similarities and differences
    - summarize—briefly give the major points
    - relate—emphasize connections and associations
- Make a brief outline before you start writing. Good organization is important in an essay exam. Take a few minutes in the beginning to collect your thoughts and write a brief outline for your answer. Essays often involve discussing certain key points. Identify these points and put them in your outline. If you run out of time and don't explain all of the points on your outline, write down the points in your outline and add a note saying that you ran out of time. You may get partial credit for your effort.

WHAT ARE THE LEGAL RIGHTS OF CHILDREN WITH ADHD
(From "Attention Deficit Disorder: Adding Up the Facts,"
published by the U.S. Department of Education)

The federal government has established several legal provisions that affect the education of children with ADHD—the Individuals with Disabilities Education Act and Section 504 of the Rehabilitation Act of 1973. Students with ADHD, like students with any other disability, do not automatically qualify for special education and related services under the IDEA without meeting certain conditions.

If a child with ADHD is found not to be eligible for services under Part B of the IDEA, the requirements of Section 504 of the Rehabilitation Act of 1973 may be applicable if he or she meets the Section 504 definition of disability, which is any person who has a physical or mental impairment that substantially limits a major life activity such as learning. Depending on the severity of their condition, children with ADHD may or may not fit the definition of either or both laws—not all children with ADHD are covered.

Although ADHD is not a separate disability category under the IDEA, children with ADHD who require special education and related services can be eligible for services under the "other health impaired" category of Part B of the IDEA when "the ADD is a chronic or acute health problem that results in limited alertness, which adversely affects educational performance." Children with ADHD may also be eligible for services under the "specific learning disability" or "seriously emotionally disturbed" categories of the IDEA when they have those conditions in addition to their ADHD.

These laws require schools to make modification or adaptations for students whose ADHD results in significant educational impairment. Children with ADHD must be placed in a regular classroom to the maximum extent appropriate to their educational needs, with the use of supplementary aids and services if necessary.

While children covered under the IDEA must have an Individual Education Plan (IEP), students covered under Section 504 need a less formal individualized assessment.

WHERE DO I BEGIN IF I BELIEVE MY CHILD NEEDS SPECIAL EDUCATION SERVICES?
(From "Questions Often Asked About Special Education Services," published by NICHY, The National Information Center for Children and Youth with Disabilities, 1993)

Begin by asking questions and developing a better understanding of the Individuals with Disabilities Education Act (IDEA), Public Law 102-119. This law guarantees a free appropriate public education to children with disabilities.

What Is the First Step toward Obtaining Special Education Services?
The first step is to arrange for your child to receive an evaluation. The term "evaluation" refers to the total process of gathering and using information to determine whether a child has a disability and the nature and extent of the special education and related services that the child needs. The public schools are required to conduct this evaluation of your child at no cost to you.

What is an Individualized Education Program?
An Individualized Education Program (IEP) is a written statement of the educational program designed to meet a child's special needs. Your child's IEP should include statements of his strengths and weaknesses and should describe the instructional program developed specifically for him. The IDEA requires that every child receiving special education services have an IEP, that parents be included in the development of this IEP, and that the child's parents are entitled to receive their own copy of the IEP (upon request) in order to keep track of progress and to maintain home records.

What Type of Information Is included in an IEP?
According to the law, an IEP must include the following statements regarding your child:

- His present level of educational performance, which could include information concerning academic achievement, social adaptation, prevocational and vocational skills, sensory and motor skills, self-help skills, and speech and language skills;
- Specific special education and related services to be provided and who will provide them;
- Dates for when the services will begin and how long they will continue;
- Percentage of the school day in which your child will participate in regular education and special education programs;
- Annual goals

- Short-term instructional objectives (individual steps that make up the goals);
- Transition plan, when applicable; and
- Appropriate objective criteria and evaluation procedures to be used to measure your child's progress toward these goals on at least an annual basis.

When Is the IEP Meeting Held and May I Attend?

The law is very clear that parents have the right to participate in the meeting in which their child's IEP is developed. The school staff will try to schedule the IEP meeting at a time that is convenient for parents (and other team members) to attend. However, if no mutually agreeable time can be set, the school may hold the IEP meeting without you. In this event, the school must keep you informed by telephone or mail.

What Should I Do before an IEP Meeting?

The IEP meeting is scheduled for the purpose of developing your child's Individualized Education Program. You can prepare for this meeting by looking realistically at your child's strengths and weaknesses, talking to teachers and therapists, visiting your child's class or other classes that may be appropriate for her, and talking to your child about her feelings about school. It is a good idea to write down what you feel your child will be able to accomplish during the school year. It also helps to make notes about what you would like to say during the meeting.

What Occurs during an IEP Meeting?

The IEP meeting takes place after the specialists have tested your child and recorded the test results. As you listen to the results of the tests (either eligibility tests or measures of progress), make sure that you understand what the tests are meant to measure and how the performance of your child compares to other children the same age. Take notes on what you hear, and ask questions if you do not understand.

During the IEP meeting, you will be asked to share the special things you know about your child, including how your child behaves and gets along with others outside of school. You will also be asked about your child's school experiences and personal life. This will allow the team to discuss and determine the following:

- What educational goals and objectives are appropriate for your child;
- What type of special education your child needs;
- Which related services are necessary to ensure your child benefits from his or her special education;
- What assistive technology devices or services your child needs to benefit from special education; and
- What placement alternatives exist, and which is most appropriate for your child.

As a parent, you should understand why the school proposes certain special education services or related services (such as therapy) for your child, and you should be comfortable with these ideas before listing them in the IEP. If you hear something about your child that is surprising to you or different from the way you perceive your child, you will want to bring this to the attention of the other members of the team. In order to design the most appropriate program for your child, it is important to work closely with the other team members and share your feelings about her educational needs.

Before you sign the IEP, ask any questions you have, so you are sure you understand what is being said. Signing the IEP means that you agree to the services, goals, and other matters listed in the IEP.

It is helpful to remember that the IEP can be changed. If you are unsure about some of the ideas being presented, set a date for evaluating progress and a time to get together again to discuss the results of the evaluation. You may request a review or revision of the IEP at any time.

What If I Disagree with the School about What Is Appropriate for My Child?

It is important to know that before the school system can place your child in a special education program for the first time, you, as parents, must give your written consent. School districts can only override your lack of consent through the use of certain procedures specified in federal or state law.

Even if your child has been receiving special education services for some time, you have the right to disagree with the school's decisions concerning new IEPs or educational placements for him. If you do not agree with what has been proposed in your child's IEP, then you should not sign it. However, in all cases where family and school disagree, it is important for both sides to be able to discuss their concerns and come to a compromise, at least temporarily. It is usually possible to agree on a particular plan of instruction or classroom placement and then establish a time frame for trying it out. At the end of the prearranged time, agree on a time for and the type of evaluation to be conducted to measure progress. Set a time to meet again to discuss the results of the evaluation and decide what to do next.

How Can I Get Services for My Child Increased?

If your child is not making progress with the current schedule, talk to the IEP team about the need for making changes in the IEP. The school personnel will either agree with you and change the IEP, or they will disagree with you.

With any disagreement, you can appeal the decision of the IEP team. Appealing a decision can mean bringing in a third party to mediate your concerns, or it may mean requesting a due process hearing. Your local department of special education can provide you with your state's guidelines for providing services in your state and for appealing decisions. You may also contact NICHY, The National Organization for Children and Youth with Disabilities, or The Council for Exceptional Children. Both organizations can provide you with copies of the these federal laws and offer guidelines outlining parental rights and responsibilities, and the rights of children and youth with disabilities.

What's Next?
(From NICHY's "Transition Summary," no. 7, September 1991)

This section presents suggestions for how students with disabilities can work with their families and school professionals to put together an action plan for transition after high school. The key words here are "plan" and "action." There's a saying that goes "Plan your work, and then work your plan." Planning requires action—information gathering, self-assessment, weighing of alternatives, and decision making. Working the plan also requires action—following through on decisions that have been made, evaluating progress, gathering more information, and making new decisions as necessary.

Leaving secondary school is an eventuality that all students must face. Under IDEA, preparing for this transition has become more than a personal choice. Each student's IEP must now include a statement of the transition services needed by the student, beginning no later than age sixteen. The transition plan must also include, where appropriate, a statement of interagency responsibilities or linkages (or both) before the student leaves the school setting. [Much of the following is excellent advice for all students, not just those with IEPs.]

In Junior High School: Start Transition Planning

- Become involved in career exploration.
- Visit with a school counselor to talk about interests and capabilities.
- Participate in vocational assessment activities.
- Use information about interests and capabilities to make preliminary decisions about possible careers: academic versus vocational or a combination.
- Make use of books, career fairs, and people in the community to find out more about careers of interest.

In High School: Define Career and Vocational Goals

- Work with school staff, family, and agencies in the community to define and refine your transition plan. Make sure that the IEP includes transition plans.
- Identify and take high school courses that are required for entry into college, trade schools, or careers of interest.
- Become involved in early work experiences, such as job tryouts or internships, summer jobs, volunteering, or part-time work.
- Reassess interests and capabilities based on real-world or school experience. Is the career field still of interest? If not, redefine goals.
- Participate in ongoing vocational assessment and identify gaps of knowledge or skills that need to be addressed. Address these gaps. If you have decided to pursue postsecondary education and training prior to employment, consider these suggestions:

- Identify postsecondary institutions (colleges, vocational programs in the community, trade school, etc.) that offer training in any career of interest. Write or call for catalogues, financial aid information, and applications. Visit the institution.
- Identify what accommodations would be helpful to address your special needs. Find out if the educational institution makes, or can make, these accommodations. Many colleges maintain advisors and tutors for individuals with learning disabilities.
- Identify and take any special tests (e.g., PSAT, SAT, MNSQY) necessary for entry into postsecondary institutions of interest. Many special tests can now be taken untimed by youth with ADHD. For information on taking untimed SATs, contact the College Educational Testing Service, 1441 Lower Ferry Rd., Trenton, New Jersey 08618, (609) 771-7137.

PROCEDURAL GUIDELINES FOR SUSPENSION OR EXPULSION
(From *What Works: Schools Without Drugs,*
United States Department of Education, 1992)

Students facing suspension or expulsion from school are entitled under the U.S. Constitution and most state constitutions to commonsense due process protections of notice and an opportunity to be heard. Because the Supreme Court has recognized that a school's ability to maintain order would be impeded if formal procedures were required every time school authorities sought to discipline a student, the Court has held that the nature and formality of the hearing will depend on the severity of the sanction being imposed.

A formal hearing is not required when a school seeks to suspend a student for ten days or less. The Supreme Court has held that due process in that situation requires only the following:

- The school must inform the student, either orally or in writing, of the charges against him and of the evidence to support those charges.
- The school must give the student an opportunity to deny the charges and present his side of the story.
- As a general rule, this notice and rudimentary hearing should precede a suspension. However, a student whose presence poses a continuing danger to persons or property or an ongoing threat of disrupting the academic process may be immediately removed from school. In such a situation, the notice and rudimentary hearing should follow as soon as possible.

The Supreme Court has also stated that more formal procedures may be required for suspensions longer than ten days and for expulsions. Although the Court has not established specific procedures to be followed in those situations,

other federal courts have set the following guidelines for expulsions. These guidelines would apply to suspensions longer than ten days as well:

- The student must be notified in writing of the specific charges against him,
  which, if proven, would justify expulsion.
- The student should be given the names of the witnesses against him or her
  and an oral or written report on the facts to which each witness will testify.
- The student should be given the opportunity to present a defense against
  the charges and to produce witnesses or testimony on his or her behalf.

Many states have laws governing the procedures required for suspensions and
expulsions. Because applicable statutes and judicial rulings vary across the country,
local school districts may enjoy a greater or lesser degree of flexibility in establishing procedures for suspensions and expulsions.

School officials must also be aware of the special procedures that apply to suspension or expulsion of students with *disabilities* under federal law and regulations.

Effects of Criminal Proceedings against a Student

A school may usually pursue disciplinary action against a student regardless of the
status of any outside criminal prosecution. That is, federal law does not require the
school to await the outcome of the criminal prosecution before initiating proceedings to suspend or expel a student or to impose whatever other penalty is appropriate for the violation of the school's rules. In addition, a school is generally free
under federal law to discipline a student when there is evidence that the student has
violated a school rule, even if a juvenile court has acquitted (or convicted) the student or if local authorities have declined to prosecute criminal charges stemming
from the same incident.

Effect of Expulsion

State and local law will determine the effect of expelling a student from school.
Some state laws require the provision of alternative schooling for students below a
certain age. In other areas, expulsion may mean the removal from public schools for
the balance of the school year or even the permanent denial of access to the public
school system.

GUIDELINES FOR PARENTS

Be involved in your teenager's education. Maintain relationships with school guidance counselors and teachers. Educating your teenager is not totally the school's
responsibility—it also includes your active participation as an equal partner. You
have the right to meet and talk with your teen's teachers and know how she is pro-
gressing in every subject she is taking. Know what the laws are for educating teens

with ADHD, continue to read and learn about ADHD, and share information with teachers.

If you recognize that your daughter is having difficulty in school, make an appointment with various teachers for a parent-teacher meeting. Bring your daughter to the meeting. Be prepared to problem-solve along with the teacher. To do this you must first identify the problem or problems. For instance, the problem is that homework is usually completed but it is not being turned in. Together with the teacher brainstorm for ideas that might help your daughter remember to turn in homework.

Then evaluate each idea for effectiveness and choose the one everyone feels most comfortable with, including your teenager. Decide what you will be responsible for, what she is responsible for, and what the teacher will be responsible for. In this scenario, the teacher agrees to make sure that your daughter has written down the assignment in her notebook. You, in turn, agree to make sure the homework is completed and she places the homework in her color-coded folder for this class. The teacher agrees that she will ask your daughter each morning to turn in her homework. Once you have agreed on a plan of action, try it out for a few weeks, and meet or phone the teacher to see how it is working. Remember, your teenager should be involved in meetings where everyone is looking for a solution to a school problem.

More and more teachers are becoming aware of the needs of students with ADHD. However, each school year involves new teachers, new subjects, and new challenges for both you and your teenager. Many teens have ADHD, but parents who are actively involved in the education of their children will provide a greater opportunity for their teens to get through school successfully and meet their potential.

ELEVEN

ADHD AND SUBSTANCE ABUSE

S ubstance abuse among adolescents is about ten times more prevalent than parents realize. Some teens believe they can use drugs or alcohol without their parents knowledge. Why? Because most parents are unaware of the extent of substance abuse among young people, have limited knowledge of drugs, and are unfamiliar with the warning signs of drug use. Because research indicates that 25% to 35% of teens with ADHD will engage in the use of alcohol, drugs, or both, it behooves parents to learn the facts.

William C. Van Ost, MD and Elaine Van Ost, authors of *Warning: A Parent's Guide to In-Time Intervention in Drug and Alcohol Abuse* state that "The kids most likely to get into trouble with drugs are the ones who aren't comfortable about being themselves; who feel like outsiders; who can't seem to tell the difference between what they need and what they'd like to have; who want instant gratification, and who don't listen . . ." These are teens who also have difficulty understanding the cause and effect of their actions. Sound familiar?

Drug use affects all young people. It is not confined to specific geographic areas or certain economic backgrounds. It is a serious problem in elementary, middle school, and high school students. According to the United States Department of Education, the following was true for 1991:

- 30% of high school seniors report that they had five or more drinks on one occasion
- 50% of seniors were occasional users of alcohol
- 80% of high school students had used alcohol
- 24% had used marijuana
- $3^1/2$% had used cocaine
- $1^1/2$% had used crack

131

- 19% reported that they had started smoking by sixth grade, and 11% had used alcohol by that time
- 44% of eighth graders had tried cigarettes
- 75% had tried alcohol
- 2.8% had used marijuana and inhalants by the sixth grade. (In the sixth grade the highest number of youth use marijuana for the first time. First-time use of cocaine and hallucinogens peaks in tenth and eleventh grades.)

HOW DRUG USE DEVELOPS
(from *What Works: School Without Drugs,*
United States Department of Education)

Social influences play a key role in making drug use attractive. The first temptations to use drugs may come in social situations in the form of pressures to act "grown up" by smoking cigarettes or using alcohol or marijuana.

A 1987 *Weekly Reader* survey found that television and movies had the greatest influence on fourth through sixth graders in making drugs and alcohol seem attractive; the second greatest influence was peers. Children in grades four through six think that the most important reason for using alcohol and marijuana is to fit in with others, followed closely by a desire to feel older. [Not only must we teach our youth about drugs and alcohol, but we must also provide them with the necessary skills to resist peer pressure.]

Students who turn to more potent drugs usually do so after first using cigarettes and alcohol and then marijuana. The greater a student's involvement in marijuana, the more likely it is the student will begin to use other drugs in conjunction with marijuana.

Drug use frequently progresses in stages—from occasional use, to regular use, to multiple drug use, and ultimately to total dependency. With each successive state, drug use intensifies, becomes more varied, and results in increasingly debilitating effects. But this progression is not inevitable. Drug use can be stopped at any stage. However, the more deeply involved teens are with drugs, the more difficult it is for them to stop.

EXTENT OF ALCOHOL AND OTHER DRUG USE

The United States has the highest rate of drug use in teenagers in the industrialized world. The United States Department of Education reports that "forty-four percent of high school seniors have tried an illicit drug by the time they graduate."

The United States Department of Education makes three recommendations to parents regarding the use of drugs:

1. Teach standards of right and wrong and demonstrate these standards through personal example. Teens who are brought up to value individual responsibility and self-discipline and to have a clear sense of right and wrong are less likely to try drugs than those who are not. Parents can help instill these values by:

   - Setting a good example by not using drugs themselves.
   - Explaining at an early age that drug use is wrong, harmful, and unlawful, and reinforcing this teaching throughout adolescence. [To tell a teen you don't want him using drugs or alcohol is simply not enough. The strongest points you must relay are that it is against the law and harmful to his health.]
   - Encouraging self-discipline by giving children regular duties and holding them accountable for their actions.
   - Establishing standards of behavior concerning drugs, drinking, dating, curfews, and unsupervised activities, and enforcing them consistently and fairly.
   - Encouraging teens to stand by their convictions when pressured to use drugs.

2. Help them resist peer pressure to use alcohol and other drugs by supervising their activities, knowing who their friends are, and talking to them about their interests and problems. When parents take an active interest in their teen's behavior, they provide the guidance and support children need to resist drugs. Parents can do this in the following ways:

   - Knowing their teen's whereabouts, activities, and friends.
   - Working to maintain and improve family communications by listening to their teens.
   - Being able to discuss drugs knowledgeably. It is far better for teens to obtain their information from their parents than from their peers or on the street.
   - Communicating regularly with their friends' parents and sharing their knowledge about drugs with other parents.
   - Being selective about their teen's viewing of television and movies that portray drug use as glamorous or exciting.

3. Be knowledgeable about drugs and signs of drug use. When symptoms are observed, respond promptly. Parents are in the best position to recognize early signs of drug use in their teens. To inform and involve themselves, parents should take the following steps:

   - Learn about the drug problem in their community and in their teen's school.

- Learn how to recognize signs of drug use.
- Meet with parents of their teen's friends or classmates about the local drug problem. Establish ways of sharing information to determine which teens are using drugs and who is supplying them.

Parents who suspect their teens are using drugs often must deal with their own emotions of anger, resentment, and guilt. Frequently, they deny the evidence and postpone confronting their teens. But the earlier a drug problem is detected and faced, the less difficult it is to overcome. Parents who suspect their teens are using drugs, should take the following steps:

- Devise a plan of action. Consult with school officials and other parents.
- Discuss their suspicions with their teens in a calm, objective manner. Do not confront a teen while she is under the influence of alcohol or other drugs.
- Impose disciplinary measures that help remove the teen from those circumstances in which drug use might occur.
- Seek advice and assistance from drug treatment professionals and from a parent group. [Twelve-step programs are available for young people in every community, but families must remember that drug addiction of any kind impacts the entire family. To effectively help a young person overcome addiction, the whole family must be involved in the process. Remember individuals with ADHD are at a greater risk for addiction. Smoking, drinking, and drug use must be strongly discouraged *before* a problem develops.]

SIGNS OF DRUG USE
(From *What Works: Schools without Drugs,*
United States Department of Education)

Changing patterns of performance, appearance, and behavior may signal use of drugs. The items in the first category listed below provide evidence of drug use; the items in the other categories offer signs that may indicate drug use. Adults should watch for extreme changes in teen's behavior, changes that together form a pattern associated with drug use.

Signs of Drugs and Drug Paraphernalia

- Possession of drug-related paraphernalia such as pipes, rolling papers, small decongestant bottles, eye drops, or small butane torches.
- Possession of drugs or evidence of drugs, such as pills, white powder, small glass vials, or hypodermic needles; peculiar plants or butts, seeds, or leaves in ashtrays or in clothing pockets.
- Odor of drugs, smell of incense or other "cover-up" scents.

Identification with Drug Culture

- Drug-related magazines, slogans on clothing.
- Conversation and jokes that are preoccupied with drugs.
- Hostility in discussing drugs.
- Collection of beer cans.

Signs of Physical Deterioration

- Memory lapses, short attention span, difficulty in concentration.
- Poor physical coordination, slurred or incoherent speech.
- Unhealthy appearance, indifference to hygiene and grooming.
- Bloodshot eyes, dilated pupils.

Dramatic Changes in School Performance

- Marked downturn in student's grades—not just from Cs to Fs but also from As to Bs and Cs; assignments not completed.
- Increased absenteeism or tardiness.

Changes in Behavior

- Chronic dishonesty (lying, stealing, cheating); trouble with the police.
- Changes in friends, evasiveness in talking about new ones.
- Possession of large amounts of money.
- Increasing and inappropriate anger, hostility, irritability, secretiveness.
- Reduced motivation, energy, self-discipline, self-esteem.
- Diminished interest in extracurricular activities and hobbies.

TEENS AND ALCOHOL

Alcohol is the number one drug problem among teens. The easy availability, widespread acceptability, and extensive promotion of alcoholic beverages within our society make alcohol the most widely used and abused drug.

Alcohol use is widespread. By their senior year of high school nearly 90% of students will have tried alcoholic beverages. Despite a legal drinking age of twenty-one, junior and senior high school students drink 35% of all wine coolers sold in the United States. They also drink an estimated 1.1 billion bottles and cans of beer each year.

Drinking has acute effects on the body. The heavy, fast-paced drinking that young people commonly engage in quickly alters judgment, vision, coordination, and speech and often leads to risk-taking behaviors. Teens absorb alcohol into their blood system faster than adults and exhibit greater impairment for longer periods of time.

Alcohol-related highway accidents are the principal cause of death among people ages fifteen through twenty-four. Alcohol use is the primary cause of traffic accidents involving teenage drivers. [Remember adolescents with ADHD are four times more likely to be involved in car accidents than non-ADHD teens].

Early alcohol use is associated with subsequent alcohol dependence and related health problems. Youth who use alcohol at a younger age are more likely to use alcohol heavily and to experience alcohol-related problems affecting their relationships with family and friends by late adolescence. Their school performance is likely to suffer, and they are more likely to be truant. They are also more likely to abuse other drugs and to get in trouble with the law, or, if they are girls, to become pregnant.

BE A PROACTIVE PARENT

Teenagers need and want rules. Without rules, your teen will believe you don't care what she does. Teenagers need help in setting negotiable rules, but you have every right to establish nonnegotiable ones.

Nonnegotiable rules are those that reflect your values and beliefs, so they may differ from one family to the next. If you are unsure what rules should be nonnegotiable check with parents of your teenager's friends. Nonnegotiable rules also depend on your teenager's level of maturity, responsibility, and trust.

Common nonnegotiable rules are usually no drugs, alcohol, or smoking; no friends in the house unless a parent is home; respecting other's property in the home; meeting friends before being permitted to drive off with them; attending school; no destructive acts of property inside or outside the home; establishing curfews; advising parents on where he is and notifying them if there is a change of plans. Teens may exhibit anger when confronted with nonnegotiable rules. Acknowledge that some rules have to be tough, but the rules are set because you love them not because you don't want them to have fun.

When it comes to drugs and alcohol parents must educate and continue to educate their teens. Discuss television commercials for beer and wine and advertisements for hard liquor. We must make our teens aware of the appeal of these ads, and the messages that are being sent. And we must reach them as early as fifth grade if prevention, rather than intervention, is our goal. Children form basic attitudes about such things as drinking and smoking between fifth and the eighth grade. Personal values and behaviors are shaped by parents well before the child reaches the peer-pressure stage.

So, clearly define the rules in your family and establish the consequences well before intervention becomes an issue. Teenagers who come home and have been drinking need an appropriate punishment (grounding, for instance). However, if the teenager was drinking and driving, you may want to revoke his use of the car for a pre-established length of time. Remember to focus on the deeds of the teenager; it is his actions that you do not approve of, not him. Be sure that the rules you set are not based on whether the teenager is a male or female. Too often when boys drink, it is excused. Parents also need to model appropriate behavior when it comes to drinking and using drugs. Do not send mixed messages to your teenager. Teach them how to say no through role playing because they will face peers who will chide them for being afraid to drink.

Teenagers who possess a good sense of self-worth are usually able to say no to drugs and alcohol, although research is unclear about the relationship between drugs and self-esteem. But the teenager who is able to be assertive, and stand up to others and say no is usually the young person who values himself or herself. However, some teens with ADHD may be at a disadvantage.

THE RELATIONSHIP BETWEEN ADHD AND SUBSTANCE ABUSE

ADHD, alcoholism, and conduct disorder have been the subject of several research studies. It is suspected that ADHD and alcoholism may be related because both disorders are equally prevalent and many alcoholics present a childhood history of what appears to be ADHD (impulsivity and disruptive behaviors). However, the connection between ADHD, conduct disorder, and alcoholism has been more difficult to establish because of the "indistinct nature of the ADHD diagnosis," according to an article in *Alcohol Health and Research World*. "Despite . . . difficulties, the . . . connection . . . can be summarized in one word: aggression. Aggression is one symptom . . . of conduct disorder, and the children most at risk for later alcohol and other drug abuse seem to have a history of aggression." Further studies support these conclusions.

Barkley et al. assessed a large sample of children and reassessed them eight years later. Their findings showed that children with ADHD and conduct disorder were more apt to abuse drugs or alcohol than children who had pure ADHD. Therefore, the ADHD alone does not necessarily predict a future of substance abuse.

Despite what some people believe, the use of medication to treat the symptoms of ADHD does not lead to drug abuse in the teenage years. Actually, the opposite is true. Teens with ADHD who take medication are less apt to become involved in the use of drugs or alcohol. If your teenager's ADHD is in the moderate to severe range, she should be taking medication to control the symptoms of the ADHD.

If you discover your teen is involved with drugs or alcohol, do not confront her when she is high or drunk. When you do speak with her be prepared for any number of excuses ("I only tried it once." or "That doesn't belong to me. My friend asked me to hold onto it for him." or "Every one drinks."). Don't fall for these tricks. If your teen attempts to make you feel guilty, skip the guilt trip and tackle the problem! Get professional help immediately. Call your doctor, call a substance abuse treatment center, or call Alcoholics Anonymous, but do something!

TWELVE

SEXUALITY AND DATING

The Alan Guttmacher Institute estimates that over a million adolescent girls become pregnant each year. That's one in every ten girls. Of those girls, approximately 30,000 of them will be under the age of fifteen. One third of these girls will choose an abortion. Some will opt for marriage, some will miscarry, and others will make a plan for adoption. However, of the more than two hundred thousand babies born to unwed mothers each year, most decide to parent the child. Only about 6% will choose adoption.

"Personal factors are important predictors of early sexual activity," says Erika Nolph Ringdahl, MD, University of Missouri Health Sciences Columbia, Missouri. "Teenagers with low self-esteem and low educational goals may feel inadequate and may use sex to gain acceptance." According to Dr. Ringdahl, slightly over 50% of teenagers do not use contraception the first time they engage in sexual intercourse. Twenty percent of these teens will become pregnant almost immeditely. Most teens do not begin using contraception for at least one year after their first sexual experience.

Sexual activity is risky behavior for all teenagers, but particularly for teens with ADHD. Because of immature cognitive abilities, they do not always realize the consequences of their behavior and many lack the ability to plan ahead. Their impulsivity and inability to delay gratification often leads to untimely pregnancies. Because ADHD is almost always inherited, you might conclude that this accounts for the high rate of adopted children with ADHD (the current estimate is 25% to 40% percent of adopted children have ADHD). "If a teenager is not emotionally or cognitively mature enough to realistically estimate the risk of pregnancy, he or she will not see the need to use contraception," says Dr. Ringdahl. She goes on to say that those teenagers who are sexually active but do not become pregnant develop a false sense of security.

An article in *The Journal of the American Medical Association* identifies teenagers who are at the greatest risk of engaging in coitus at an early age; these are teenagers who lack family support and few parental controls, are less religious, begin dating at an early age, lack future educational goals, and are encouraged by peer pressure.

The nonsexual motivations (revolting against parents, looking for love) are the most fundamental reasons for sexual activity. Teenagers who feel loved and accepted, have definite goals, and have the support of their family are least likely to become sexually active. Teenagers with ADHD and conduct disorder are at the greatest risk for precocious sexual activity, STDs, and pregnancy.

If you suspect that your teenager is sexually active and you have not addressed contraception and protection from diseases, do so immediately or ask your family physician to discuss contraception with her. Not only can unplanned pregnancies be avoided but so can sexually transmitted diseases. About three million teenagers a year contract a sexually transmitted disease, and the number of teenage girls who have contracted AIDS has nearly doubled in a five-year period.

Why do teenage girls take such risks? Many of them are looking for love. According to Carol Cassell, PhD, an authority on teenage sexuality and the author of *Straight From the Heart: How to Talk to Your Teenagers About Love and Sex,* adolescent girls believe that their initial sexual encounter will lead to love or marriage plans. Boys tend to see their first experience as a casual but thrilling relationship and a sign of maturity. Girls usually feel guilty afterwards.

Recently, a nationwide survey conducted by the Kinsey Institute indicated that most Americans know little about sexually transmitted diseases and contraception and many are misinformed about the facts. It behooves all parents to learn as much as they can in these areas so appropriate information can be shared with their teens.

TEACHING CHILDREN AND YOUTH ABOUT SEXUALITY

(excerpts from *Sexuality Education for Children and Youth with Disabilities,* published by NICHY)

The vast majority of parents want to be—and, indeed, already are—the primary sex educators of their children (Sex Information and Education Council of the U. S., 1991). Parents communicate their feelings and beliefs about sexuality continuously. Parents send messages to their child about sexuality both verbally and nonverbally, in the interactions they have with their child, in the tasks they give the child to do, and in the expectations they hold for their child. Children absorb what parents say and do not say, and what they do and do not do, and children learn.

Of course, a great deal of education about socialization and sexuality takes place in settings outside the home. The school setting is probably the most important, not only because most students take classes in sexuality education, but also because it is there that children and youth encounter the most extensive opportunities to socialize and mix with their peers. Thus, both parents and the school system assume responsibility for teaching children and youth about appropriate behavior, social skills, and the development of sexuality. Parents are strongly encouraged to get information about what sexuality education is provided by the school system and to work together with the school system to ensure that the sexuality education their child receives is as comprehensive as possible.

Depending on the child, emotional maturity may not develop in some adolescents at the same rate as physical maturity. Parents can help their child or teen to cope with physical and emotional development by anticipating it and talking openly about sexuality and the values and choices surrounding sexual expression. This will help prepare children and youth to deal with their feelings in a healthy and responsible manner. It's important to realize that discussing sexuality will not create sexual feelings in young people. Those feelings are already there, because sexuality is a part of each human being throughout the entire life cycle.

Ages 8 through 11

One of the most important things that parents can do during their children's prepubescent years is to prepare them for the changes that their bodies will soon undergo. No female should have to experience her first menses without knowing what it is; similarly, boys should be told that nocturnal emissions (or "wet dreams" as they are sometimes known) are a normal part of their physical development. To have these experiences without any prior knowledge of them can be very upsetting to a young person, a trauma that can easily be avoided by timely discussions between parent and child. Tell your child that these experiences are a natural part of growing up. Above all, do so before they occur. Warning signs of puberty include a rapid growth spurt, developing breast buds in girls, and sometimes an increase in "acting out" and other emotional behaviors.

In addition to the topics mentioned above, other topics of importance for parents to address with children approaching puberty are:

- Sexuality as part of the total self
- More on reproduction and pregnancy
- The importance of values in decision making
- Communication within the family unit about sexuality
- Masturbation
- Abstinence from sexual intercourse
- Avoiding and reporting sexual abuse
- Sexually transmitted diseases, including HIV/AIDS

According to the National Guidelines Task Force (1991) some topics that may need to be addressed before the age of eight include:

- The similarities and differences between girls and boys
- The elementals of reproduction and pregnancy
- The qualities of good relationships (friendship, love, communication, respect)

- Decisions-making skills, and the fact that all decisions have consequences
- The beginnings of social responsibility, values, and morals
- Avoiding and reporting sexual exploitation

[If these topics were not discussed before the age of eight, they should be addressed between the ages of eight and eleven years.]

Adolescence: 12 years to 18 years

During this period it is important to let your adolescent assume greater responsibility in terms of decision-making. It is also important that adolescents have privacy and, as they demonstrate trustworthiness, increasingly greater degrees of independence. For many teenagers, this is an active social time with many school functions and outings with friends. Many teenagers are dating; statistics show that many become sexually involved. Appropriate sexuality means taking responsibility and knowing that sexual matters have their time and place.

Puberty and adolescence are usually marked by feelings of extreme sensitivity about the body. Let your adolescent voice these concerns, and encourage them to focus on and develop their strengths, not what they perceive as bad points about their physical appearance. Good grooming, diet, and exercise should also be addressed. Without dismissing the feelings as a "phase you are going through," try to help your child understand that some of the feelings are a part of growing up.

There are many other topics that your adolescent will need to know about. Among these are:

- Health care, including health-promoting behaviors such as regular check-ups, and breast and testicular self-exams
- Sexuality as part of the total self
- Communication, dating, love, and intimacy
- The importance of values in guiding one's behavior
- How alcohol and drug use influence decision-making
- Sexual intercourse and other ways to express sexuality
- Birth control and the responsibilities of childbearing
- Reproduction and pregnancy (more detailed information than what has previously been presented)
- Condoms and disease prevention

Many resources are available for sharing information with your teenager. Don't forget that your family physician and school health personnel can be good sources of accurate information and guidance. Remember, young people are receiving information from other sources as well. It may be essential to include the entire family in your resolve to be frank and forthright, for a lot of information comes from siblings. Children may feel more comfortable asking their brothers and sisters questions than directly asking you.

Because sexuality involves so much more than just having sexual intercourse, parents will also need to devote time to talking with their teenager about the values that surround sexuality: intimacy, self-esteem, caring, and respect. Encourage your teenager to be involved in activities with others that provide social outlets, such as going to the community recreation center on weekends, going to sports events or a movie, joining a club or group at school or in the community, or having a friend over after school. These interactions help build social skills, develop a social network for your teenager, and provide him or her with opportunities to channel sexual energies in healthy, socially acceptable directions.

PROTECTION AGAINST SEXUALLY TRANSMITTED DISEASES

The topic of sexually transmitted diseases (STD's) is an extremely important one to discuss with young people. Accurate information about STD's is vital to help young people maintain sexual health and practice health-promoting behaviors. STD's include diseases such as gonorrhea, syphilis, HIV infection (which in advanced stages leads to AIDS), chlamydia, genital warts, and herpes. Most of these diseases can be cured with proper medical care. Exceptions are genital herpes, HIV infection, and AIDS, "although medications are now available which lessen symptoms and slow the development of the disease." (National Guidelines Task Force, 1991, p. 41)

Protecting oneself against sexually transmitted diseases (STD's) is a separate issue from protection against pregnancy. Youth with special needs need to be informed that many methods of birth control do not provide protection against disease. They need to know what *does* offer protection and know how to obtain and use the method. They also need to know that abstinence from sexual intimacy is the surest way to avoid contracting an STD.

It is important to communicate accurate, up-to-date information (rather than use scare tactics) on the following topics:

- What sexually transmitted diseases are and what symptoms are associated with each one
- How each STD is transmitted, including sexual behaviors that place the person at risk of contracting or transmitting the disease
- Myths about how a person can contract particular diseases
- How each STD is treated medically and those STD's that cannot be cured
- Health-promoting behaviors such as regular check-ups, breast and testicular self-exams, and identifying potential problems early

For individuals who have difficulty remembering information, it will be vital for parents and professionals to reteach and re-emphasize the major points about disease prevention.

BETWEEN PARENT AND TEEN

Teenage sex is not inevitable. Parents can be a tremendous source of influence and power in this area—more than they realize—and they can help their teen avoid sexual intercourse. Unfortunately, because many parents do not talk with their teens about sex and the responsibilities that go along with it and many teens are too embarrassed to approach the subject, teenagers are left on their own to handle something they are not emotionally or cognitively prepared to deal with. Parents must accept the responsibility of discussing sex with their teenager because they are in the best position to influence their teen's decision to delay sex until a more appropriate age.

Studies have shown that most girls are talked into having sex. Distressingly, most girls do not know how to say no. An article that appeared in *U.S. News and World Report* in June 1994 reported that a professor of obstetrics and gynecology at Emory University questioned over one thousand adolescent girls as to what they wanted to learn in sex education. "Eighty-four percent answered, 'How to say no without hurting the other person's feelings.'" Parents must teach their daughters that there is nothing wrong in saying no. Hurt feelings subside but untimely pregnancies do not.

Parents can share their own feelings, values, and beliefs about premarital sex. Don't be afraid to say to your teen, "We do not want you to have sex now. You are not old enough or emotionally prepared for it."

Unfortunately, the media sends strong messages to our teenagers that sex is okay before marriage—that it is a sign of maturity. Peer pressure can be extremely strong during these years and many teens are in agreement that everyone is doing it so it must be okay. The fact is that much of this is just talk between peers—teenagers who are trying to make themselves feel important in the eyes of their friends

The same *U.S. News and World Report* article also cited a study showing that a large percentage of young sexually active girls were actually forced to engage in sex. Sixty percent of the girls who had intercourse before age fifteen and 70% of those who had sex before age fourteen said they were forced to have sexual intercourse.

Dating

There is little doubt that dating begins much earlier than it did a few decades ago. Today the initial age of dating is around fourteen for girls and fifteen or sixteen for boys.

It is important for parents of teens with ADHD who want to date to remember that their teen's physical appearance may indicate that they are much more mature than others their age. In reality, they often lag behind peers in areas such as social and interpersonal skills, personal identity issues, accepting responsibility, and decision making. Because of their ADHD, they often make impulsive decisions, not yet realizing or understanding the association between cause and effect. Their ADHD places them at a higher risk of following the crowd. If the crowd is an unacceptable one, their impulsivity may lead to experimenting with drugs, alcohol, or other risky behaviors. Low self-esteem acquired over the years by many failures may lead to early sexual experiences especially if they are looking for love as a way to make themselves feel accepted, important, and wanted.

Because some children begin dating as early as twelve or thirteen, the issue of when to permit your preteen or teenager to date should be discussed well in advance. In other words, don't wait until your daughter is asked out to tell her that she cannot date for another two years. Again, it is always better to address such issues before they become a problem.

If you feel strongly that your teen should not date until she is fifteen or sixteen, discuss this with her as soon as possible. Stress the value of same-sex friendships. Girls who begin dating at an early age are more apt to be dating boys several years older. Studies show that girls between the ages of fifteen and nineteen years are more likely to have sexual intercourse with boys who are three years older than them. Younger adolescent girls who date earlier may also find that they are alienated from their peers who are not yet dating. The young teenager who is dating will be more wrapped up in her boyfriend and have less time for friends, families, and even school work. If you are not opposed to your teen attending chaperoned parties with both boys and girls or going somewhere with a group, then negotiate. You can also open your home to your teenager's friends and encourage group get together's while you supervise unobserved.

The following are some guidelines to keep in mind if your teen is ready to begin dating or is already dating:

1. Establish clear, appropriate guidelines for dating:

   - What nights they are permitted to go out.
   - Who may they date? The ideal person is someone you know but, if you don't, you have the right to meet the date. Make sure you have the name and address of the date. Try to meet the date's parents if possible. Get to know the date without being intrusive. Be suspicious of teens who do not want you to meet their dates or friends, because they may know you would not approve.
   - Set an age limit for who they can date. Girls typically date boys older than them, but a fourteen year old should not be going out with someone who is nineteen.
   - Know where your teen is going and what time she'll be home unless you have given her a curfew. Be sure she knows what places are off limits.
   - Decide what age is appropriate for car dating. Should you restrict car dates to double dating only? Until what age?
   - What are the consequences for breaking the agreed upon rules?

2. Remind your teenager of the rules before each date since they need to hear them more frequently than non-ADHD teens. Some teenagers with ADHD often have poor self-control, poor internal monitoring, are impulsive and

insatiable, and have difficulty delaying gratification. Repeating rules and expectations will help them avoid situations that may lead to unwanted pregnancy, drug abuse, or other problems that can result from peer pressure. Write the rules down and give a copy to your teen.

3. Make sure she has pocket money. She should, at the very least, have money to make a phone call if she needs a ride home.

4. Discuss driving and drinking with your teen. A teenager who calls for a ride home because her date has been drinking should be commended because this shows good judgment.

5. What if you do not like the person she is dating? Although you would like to end a relationship you feel uncomfortable with, think carefully before discouraging the relationship unless you know your teen is involved in an abusive relationship. Forbidding her to date someone may lead her to rebel against you. Parental intervention can actually encourage a relationship that might have ended on its own.

6. Sex, contraception, and AIDS should be discussed long before dating begins. The figures vary greatly, but there is little doubt that the number of teenagers who are sexually active is higher today than ever before. "Be sure to talk to your sons as well as your daughters about sexuality and their responsibility to prevent unwanted pregnancies," suggests Millie Waterman, consultant to the National PTA's Health and Welfare Commission. "Don't give one message to your daughter and another to your son."

A boy must know that no matter how far a girl may let him go with sexual advances, he must stop if the girls says no. If he continues and forces her into intercourse, he must know that this is rape and he may face criminal charges. If your teenage daughter does not want to become sexually involved, she must know how to say no.

All teenagers need to make choices and face problems that they have not encountered before, but for the teenager with ADHD their symptoms will present special difficulties or challenges. Teens who understand their ADHD are one step ahead of those who don't. Don't be afraid to discuss ADHD with your teenager, especially those symptoms that present the greatest obstacles for them. Explain how these symptoms may interfere with their decisions or how diversions can cause problems.

ADDITIONAL THOUGHTS FOR PARENTS

Talk to your teenager about the power of peer pressure. Teenagers must realize that peers may encourage them to smoke, drink, use drugs, and engage in sexual activity. Help them devise a plan to handle the pressures they will face. Teach them how to say no. Let them know that anytime they do not want to do something they feel uncomfortable with, that it is all right for them to say, "I'm not allowed. My parents will not let me."

Assure them that you will always be available to calmly discuss issues and feelings regarding sex. Even though you may not always agree, he must know that he can come to you about anything without being judged for his thoughts and feelings. If he does not receive support from you, he will get it from his peers.

The media paints glamorous pictures of teen sex and drug use, which may look exciting and adultlike. Stress the importance of two people making a commitment to each other out of love, not lust. Be sure that they understand that sexual involvement also means taking responsibility for your actions, including the conception of a baby. Ask her if she became involved in sexual activity with someone today, would she be receiving this type of commitment?

Emphasize that some sexually transmitted diseases, such as herpes and HIV, have no cure. If one of these is contracted, it will last a lifetime and be carried into a marital relationship. HIV, which leads to AIDS, has increased among the teenage population. There is no lifetime with AIDS because the ultimate result is death. Use your influence and power by accepting the responsibility of educating your teen on sexuality and dating.

THIRTEEN

THE SUICIDAL TEEN

Suicide is now the second leading cause of death, after accidents, for teenagers and young adults. The main ingredient in suicide attempts is depression. Problems within the family organization (poor parent-child interactions, family conflicts, marital discord, communication deficits, etc.) are the most significant factors in teenage suicide. Researchers have also found other contributing factors, such as substance abuse, poor peer relationships, social isolation, and internalized anger.

"Children with ADHD are going nuts inside," explains Stella Francis, PhD, director of the Psychoeducational Learning Center in Toledo, Ohio. "Teens with hyperactivity exhibit their anger externally, whereas teenagers without hyperactivity often experience greater turmoil and confusion on the inside. One day they seem fine, then all of a sudden they are trying to die or following some dangerous alternative lifestyle."

Although dysfunctional families make it more difficult for teens to manage stress, all families of teens who attempt suicide must understand that these teens live in a broader context and outside influences (peers, advertising, school, and other adults) can be extremely powerful. Substance abuse may also play a tremendous part in precipitating suicidal behavior. Parents are almost never the sole cause of a child's suicide attempt.

"In functional families, the teenager is usually buffered from outside influences because their fundamental sense of self and well being are maintained," states H. Charles Fishman, MD, in *Treating Troubled Teens: A Family Approach*. Families that do not provide support and consistency can create the unrestrainable despair that distinguishes the depressed teenager in passage to suicide. The teenager with ADHD who faces challenges and pressures from parents, teachers, and peers, and competitiveness in school often feels unloved, confused, and depressed. Add the ingredients together and self-destructive behavior may be the outcome. Research indicates a greater number of suicide attempts in teens with ADHD, especially in those who also have conduct disorder.

Impulsive teenagers with ADHD may react on the spur of the moment to such things as the loss of a loved one, a broken romantic relationship, harsh punishment by parents, the death of a pet, a failed exam, and parental divorce. They frequently react without thinking of the consequences. Teens with ADHD who are contemplating suicide may have an immense absence of hope for the future because of their narrow vision of tomorrow, poor recall of yesterday, lack of optimism, and an overwhelming feeling of unhappiness. These teenagers experience more problems with substance abuse, depression, and behavior problems and have poorer peer relationships, self-esteem, and communication skills. The teenager with ADHD is particularly vulnerable to suicidal impulses that evolve from the culture of immediate gratification, impatience, and an inability to endure opposition. Insufficient medical supervision of teenagers with ADHD and inadequate supportive techniques and strategies in today's fast-paced but weakening social framework can lead to an increase in attempted or completed suicides.

The American Association of Suicidology stresses that there are three clues to an impending suicide: 1) verbal ("I don't want to live" or "I won't be around much longer"); 2) behavioral (a change in academic performance, sleep patterns, or eating habits); 3) situational (loss of a loved one or an important relationship).

WARNING SIGNS

Parents should recognize the danger signs of suicide so they can take the necessary action needed if they suspect their teenager is suicidal. As you read through this section, keep in mind that the warning signs of suicide are closely related to the signs of depression. This depression may be comorbid with ADHD and often develops as the teen experiences more frustration, distress, or repeated failures over a period of time.

1. Previous attempt

The teenager who has attempted suicide in the past is at the greatest risk of attempting it again. Whether attempted suicide is a deliberate but unsuccessful attempt to die or a plan to only hurt oneself or others is not always clear. What is clear is that the teenager who attempts suicide is making a strong plea for help. They want to die because life is unbearable for them, yet at the same time they want to live. (Only a small percentage of teenagers between the ages of thirteen and sixteen view death as an end to life.) Research indicates that 40% of those who attempt suicide will try again in the near future and 10% will succeed. A thought-out attempt at suicide may suggest a psychiatric disorder. If help is not received, more serious attempts are likely to ensue.

2. Suicide threats or a statement of the wish to die

A suicidal threat ("Everyone would be better off if I was dead") should always be taken seriously. The idea that someone who threatens suicide won't really do it is a myth. Often, children and teenagers talk about suicide first, so it is extremely important to address the issue rather than ignore it. It is important that you seek professional help for your teenager immediately if you suspect that he is in danger. Never, never ignore threats of suicide.

3. Personality change or odd behavior

Watch for abrupt behavior changes, such as the teen who is normally quiet unexpectedly becoming loud, talkative, and excitable, or the teenager who has always been outgoing suddenly becoming withdrawn and noncommunicative. Risk-taking activities or little regard for personal safety can also be signals. If you notice a rapid change in behavior or personality that does not subside, talk to the doctor who treats your teen's ADHD. Such changes are possible warning signs, especially if your teen has suffered a recent loss or other significant change in his life.

4. Isolation and depression

A teen who suddenly withdraws from friends and family, does not communicate, and spends much of his time isolated in his room is exhibiting common signs of suicidal intent. However, these are also warning signs of depression. Depression may also be camouflaged by acting-out behaviors (truancy, hostility, running away from home), so professional intervention is recommended. (See chapter 8 for the symtpoms of depression.)

5. Putting affairs in order

The youth who is contemplating suicide may suddenly begin giving away treasured possessions. This is often a sign that the teen is making final arrangements. Immediate intervention is called for, especially if the teenager is displaying other danger signs of suicidal intent.

6. Drug or alcohol abuse

Researchers Michael L. Peck, PhD, and Robert E. Litman, MD, conducted a study on suicidal youth in which they found that nearly one-half of the teens had used drugs or alcohol shortly before completing suicide. Did the substance abuse lead to the suicide? Not necessarily, according to Peck and Litman. "Rather, the same factors that made them unhappy enough to commit suicide probably contributed to their abuse of the drugs." Peck and Litman also reported that approximately 99% of the teenagers they studied believed that their parents did not understand them, and nearly 66% had an inadequate relationship with their families. Mark S. Gold, MD, director of research at Fair Oaks Hospital, says that "alcohol and drugs attract teenagers, especially suicide-prone teens . . . and offer a false sense of control. For some troubled teenagers, drugs provide a risk . . . This risk-taking element of excitement is especially evident in teens with behavioral problems." Dr. Gold stresses that the use of drugs breaks down "inhibitions, facilitating impulsive and thrill-seeking actions which may result in suicide."

7. Running away from home

Teenagers who run away from home are also pleading for help. If they do not receive the help they need, suicide may be the end result. Females who run away are more likely than males to be depressed and attempt suicide.

8. Preoccupation with death

If your teenager seems preoccupied with death or has an obsessive fascination with it, intervention is needed. Often a teacher is the first to notice that something has gone astray. Signals a teacher may observe are often seen in writings or artwork that depict thoughts of dying.

9. Other warning signs

Other warning signs include the recent death of a loved one; a history of conduct disorder, risk-taking activities, or antisocial acts; disruptions within the family unit; a family history of suicide; changes in school attendance; a lack of self-esteem due to learning difficulties; inherited depressive disorders; and changes in eating habits, sleep patterns, and personal hygiene.

ARE SIBLINGS AT RISK?

Although little research has been conducted on the effect a teen with suicidal symptoms has on other siblings, an article appearing in the *Journal of Abnormal Child Psychology* (June 1994) notes that there is "initial evidence of . . . sibling concordance of suicide ideation." Authors Bary M. Wagner and Patricia Cohen believe that there are least three theories that "may explain the degree of sibling concordance. First, genetics . . . studies have documented an elevated degree of suicidal behavior in family members of youth who completed suicide . . . [and] suicide attempters." A second possibility involves a sibling who may imitate suicidal behavior. The suicide of one child "may trigger suicidal [gestures] in a second child, particularly if that child is vulnerable [in temperament or personality, has coping deficits, etc.]. A third possibility is that "negative environmental factors . . . within or outside of the family may influence more than one child in a family in a similar manner."

WHAT TO DO

If your teenager makes a comment about wishing he was dead or how much simpler things would be for everyone if he wasn't around, what should you do? Take the comment seriously and open the lines of communication. Avoid statements like, "Don't you realize how fortunate you are. You have everything, including your whole life in front of you." A remark like this will close the lines of communication immediately.

Instead, calmly ask him how long he has felt this way and if he understands why he feels the way he does. As difficult as this may be, you must ask if he knows how he would end his life and if he has made a plan. Opening the lines of communication will offer relief to your teenager. Remember suicidal teens want to live, but they also desperately want the pain to go away.

Gently and calmly questioning your teen will give you information about how serious the risk is. A detailed plan indicates that the situation is serious and must be acted upon at once. Call your teen's physician, psychologist, or psychiatrist, contact a suicide prevention center, or take him to an emergency room. The teenager who does not have a clear idea or plan of what he would do is usually not in immediate danger, but help should be sought from a professional just the same. Your teenager's life may be saved because of one phone call.

FOURTEEN

OPPOSITIONAL DEFIANT DISORDER AND CONDUCT DISORDER

He's defiant, annoying, spiteful, verbally abusive, hostile, bitter, and argumentative. Your home is a battleground from morning to bedtime. Lately he lies about everything and has been skipping school. You suspect he's using drugs, and you've found several expensive items in his bedroom that don't belong to him. You don't understand what is happening, and you don't like what you see. You're worried that he will carry this oppositional behavior out into the community and eventually get into trouble with the police.

Oppositional defiant disorder (ODD) and conduct disorder (CD) are the other side of ADHD—the dark side that parents fear. Although briefly mentioned in parenting books, these disorders create turmoil and chaos for the teen with ADHD and his family. If parents knew more about the disorders and how they evolved, it's possible that in some cases the development of ODD and CD could be avoided or the symptoms at least decreased. Children are born with ADHD, but this does not necessarily mean that the ADHD will lead to ODD or CD. Oppositional defiant disorder and conduct disorder usually develop gradually through the years partly because of the ADHD and partly because of environmental factors, including the family system.

Many parents don't want to, or can't admit, that they are experiencing oppositional or severe conduct problems with their teen. It's hard to admit that we feel defeated, frustrated, and overwhelmed by our teenager's behavior. To make matters worse, much of the population has never heard of ADHD, or if they have they don't understand the dynamics involved. Some people are actually convinced that if the child or teenager is bad the parents have caused that badness.

So here you are with a teen who not only has ADHD but also some serious behavioral problems. Why our family, you've asked a million times? What have we done to cause these problems? Where can we find help? Is it too late for our child?

"In most cases, it's never too late to help our children," says Brenda Wilder, PhD, from Clinton, Mississippi. "We should never give up on them, even though we understandably get discouraged many times. We must keep trying and seeking ways to help the children with ADD. Our children can be successful and develop their talents and abilities."

Wrestling with these issues is not easy because ADHD is inherited. Many of you may be wrestling with your own shadow. You may see aspects of yourself coming out in your child, and that may hurt even more because you may be reliving some painful experiences through your child. The pain you feel for your child is also about your own inner pain and grief.

"I think at least some of my grief has come out on my ADHD daughter as I see her get hurt and watch her struggle in ways similar to myself," says John Shumate, a Baptist minister in California. "Then I realize it's because I have not dealt with some of my own grief. I need to stop and let that awful feeling identify exactly what I am seeing in her that needs healing in me."

Parenting the teenager with ADHD and ODD or CD is not easy. You're going to cry. You're going to hurt inside. And sometimes you're going to scream and throw up your arms in frustration because there are, unfortunately, no easy solutions to these types of behavior problems. These are tough issues and behaviors to face, and you won't learn about them in general parenting classes. The important thing to remember is that you are not alone. There are other parents who are just as afraid and concerned as you are. Like you, these parents ask themselves daily what they did wrong to have raised such a defiant, hostile child. Inside they are filled with grief and guilt, just as you may be. And they are searching for answers just as you are.

WHAT IS OPPOSITIONAL DEFIANT DISORDER?

Oppositional defiant disorder, as defined by the *Diagnostic and Statistical Manual of Mental Disorders* (a clinical manual that describes behavioral symptoms of all disorders presently identified by the American Psychiatric Association), is a persistent pattern of behaviors that include at least four of the following: often loses temper, argues with adults, refuses to comply with requests or rules, deliberately annoys people, blames others for their own mistakes, is often easily annoyed, angry, and resentful, spiteful, or vindictive. Stephen Katz, a pediatrician in Brick, New Jersey, notes, "According to the *DSM-IV*, these behaviors should not be termed ODD if they are only occasional, transient, typical for age and development, or not severe enough to cause a serious problem."

ODD is usually first manifested in the home and directed at those the child or teenager knows best. It "may be the result of harsh [or inconsistent] parenting methods, or the result of numerous caretakers in the earlier years of the child's development," as stated in the *DSM-IV*. Rarely does the teenager see himself as defiant. He's reacting to what he perceives to be unfair treatment. Parents usually feel like they are caught in a vicious circle of arguments and defiant behavior with no end in sight. ODD is more prevalent in boys before puberty but appears to equal out between boys and girls after puberty. A significant number of teens with ADHD move from the diagnosis of ODD to CD.

"Not surprisingly, ODD is more commonly observed in families where I see marital discord or a parent has a history of ODD, ADHD, or a mood disorder," says Dr. Katz. "ODD is not the same as the behaviors that can result from the impulsivity and inattentiveness seen with ADHD, but the two conditions are often seen together. It can be a very subjective judgment call to distinguish ADHD and ODD, if [it can be distinguished] at all. Sometimes the differences are quite obvious, and sometimes the two conditions are closely intertwined. As a pediatrician, I often feel that ODD is a consequence of failure to fully address the needs of a child with ADHD. That actually isn't accurate, and I have seen children where ODD is clearly part of the intrinsic nature of the child and the family background. However, that attitude keeps me striving to do a better job."

It's important to note here that teenagers without hyperactivity are at a lesser risk of developing ODD or CD because their primary deficits are in focused attention and perceptual processing speed. They are less active and less disruptive than hyperactive children. Whereas, the primary deficit in children with hyperactivity is behavioral disinhibition, which means these children have less self-control and greater impulsivity, producing an added risk for developing aggressive or oppositional behavior.

"ODD is a potential at any time for an ADHD kid, developing very early in the preschooler or developing in adolescence," states George Lynn, MS, CMHC. "A lot depends on how their energy is handled at home and in school." Proactive parents who understand the dynamics involved between hyperactivity, oppositional behaviors, and conduct problems (defiance and hostility), those who have consistent parenting skills and lots of patience, are going to handle the energy of these children much differently than the parents who are reactive."

According to Lynn, "Oppositional defiant disorder is a byproduct of the symptomology of ADHD. ODD is a reaction to the environment and the child's intent to control the internal chaos he's experiencing. Because of the continual barrage of criticism these kids receive, they've developed a sense of what I call touchiness." They are quick to anger, have difficulty controlling their feelings and emotions due to the internal chaos and will lash out at those around them. Struggles between the teen and the parent easily develop. (This is a perfect example of why medications are needed.)

Because the child is constantly bombarded by his internal chaos, he often meets parental requests and demands head-on. He can't handle anything more, so he builds a wall around himself that says, "Leave me alone. I can't handle anything more now. I have so much chaos around me that when I say no, I mean no. I can't evaluate whether it is right or wrong. I can't wait and reason with you. Because I feel totally overwhelmed by my own internal chaos I must draw rigid boundaries around myself." Remember the internal world of the ADHDer is chaotic, which means it is constantly changing and shifting.

Not realizing or understanding the depths of this inner chaos, parents push harder. The harder they push, the more the teen resists and the more his behavior is negatively reinforced. Children quickly learn that screaming, arguing, and defiance gets results from Mom and Dad. As a result, parent and teen tend to bring out the worst in each other. It becomes a vicious cycle that is difficult to break without professional intervention and medication.

Once in a cycle, the roles are defined. One pushes, and the other pulls. Each time the teenager blows up and the parent reacts negatively, the teen gains another inch of control. This control is power, and it gradually develops into oppositional defiant disorder.

"ODD can be set up by the school also," cautions Lynn. "I'm working with a boy who is very oppositional in school. He's trying to deny that he is different. He hates being labeled ADHD. The principal and teacher know nothing about ADHD. To his teacher ADHD means defective (meaning you are screwed up and because of that we are going to come down hard on you). So this boy is trying to scramble away from that ADHD label as quickly as possible. His oppositionality is a defensive strategy against the attack from the outside and the chaos he generally feels from the inside."

What can parents do when they experience the defiance? Lynn suggests the following:

- Listen to the messages the teenager is sending. Listen as he explains his sense of internal chaos because that is what he is trying to control. For example, if you make a request and he says, "Back off. Leave me alone. I can't stand listening to you any more," he may be telling you, albeit rudely, that he is knee deep in stimuli right now and can't handle anything more.
- Look at the specific stressors that he encounters in different situations that set off the negativity and defiance. Stress exacerbates the ADHD, so the stresses need to be reduced.
- Give the teen the opportunity to decompress and restore some order to his life. The pressure can be turned down through exercise or sports. Getting him involved in something he enjoys gives him the opportunity to release this pressure valve on a regular basis and helps build self-esteem.
- Look at what is firing up that cycle of oppositionality and avoid getting stuck in it. If he baits you, try to keep a sense of humor; a matter-of-fact attitude. Tell yourself, "No, I'm not going to get into a confrontation with you," and then don't become involved.
- Give a sense of control over situations by offering choices as much as possible. Once he achieves a sense of control in some areas, he often is ready to negotiate.
- Back off rather then continue in the cycle.
- Present a united front with your spouse. If you are a single parent, find a same-sex mentor for your child. Be sure you build a support system around yourself.
- Provide a consistent, structured environment. This structured environment is a must for all teenagers with ADHD, not just for those with ODD or CD.

- Control your anger at all times. You are one of your teenager's most important role models. When he loses control or lashes out, he needs you to stay calm.
- Negotiate rules, consequences, and rewards with your teenager.
- Do everything possible to restructure the home environment to lessen the stress for everyone, but especially for the teenager with severe behavior problems.

For instance, let's say you ask your teen to do something and he says he doesn't want to do it. If you order him to do it, the wall will immediately go up. Because these teens need to have some sense of control, Lynn suggests offering choices and, if necessary, moving on to negotiation. Here is an example:

Mom:	"I understand that you don't want to do it now because you are watching television, so would you rather do it in five minutes or fifteen minutes?"
Teenager:	"I don't want to do it at all."
Mom:	"I understand that, but I need this done. So let's look at what you are going to do and when." ("At this point you may run into a stone wall," cautions Lynn, "if this happens, withdraw.")
Mom:	"I withdraw then. I'm not going to talk with you further about this now. But I want you to know that this is important to me so be aware that you are not going to get the things that you want from me [use of the car, telephone, money] until we discuss this and find a solution."

"Kids with ADD and hyperactivity are struggling to feel alive," explains Lynn. "The hyperactivity is a prognostic indicator of problems to watch for. These kids are motivated by a flood of stimulation and they lack the ability to experience stimulation the way other kids do. Because of this, they leap at high-stimulation activities, have more trouble on the oppositionality side because they have more internal chaos, and are more driven to give themselves a sense of feeling alive while sinking in a sea of stimulation. They will cause more problems and get into more oppositional loops with parents, teachers, siblings, and peers, than other kids." Early childhood temperament (impulsivity, hyperactivity, aggression, anger, and persistence) often sets the stage for an uncertain future if professional intervention is not sought.

The hyperactivity seen as bouncing from one area to another or climbing up bookshelves in childhood may become the fuel for breaking windows and stealing. The impulsivity may lead to making inappropriate decisions. Poor social skills may lead to deviant and antisocial behaviors. Remember though, underneath this tough facade is a teen who is truly hurting inside. He perceives his world much differently than other children due to his cognitive distortions and internal chaos. He needs a tremendous amount of love, patience, and caring. He also needs to know there is hope, because without it he will stop loving others.

CONDUCT DISORDER

While some children with ADHD may break rules, these rules do not usually infringe on the rights of others. Teens with comorbid conduct disorder, however, do infringe upon the basic rights of others (they may physically harm others or destroy property, for example). They have little empathy or compassion for others' feelings or well-being. They lack remorse as they blame the world around them for their challenges and behaviors. Those who are aggressive often misperceive the intentions of others, thus their interactions with parents, peers, and teachers tend to be hostile and defiant because of their lack of insight. Although they appear to be tough kids, they suffer from low self-esteem.

Associated features of CD include recklessness, irritability, low frustration tolerance, and temper outbursts. Three or more of these symptoms lasting at least six months could signal conduct disorder and intervention should be sought:

- deliberate fire setting with the intent to destroy property
- deliberate destruction of the property of another
- stealing without confronting the victim
- stealing while confronting a victim
- the use of a weapon on more than one occasion (in a fight, for instance)
- forcing sexual activity on others
- physical cruelty to animals or people
- breaking into someone else's car, house, or building
- truancy before the age of 13
- running away from home at least twice (or once without returning for a length of time)
- often lies to avoid obligations or to obtain favors

Conduct disorder is divided into two subtypes according to the *Diagnostic and Statistical Manual of Mental Disorders (DSM-IV)*: Childhood-Onset type and Adolescent-Onset type. Childhood-Onset type is characterized by at least one symptom of conduct disorder before the age of ten. These children are usually male, frequently display physical aggressive behaviors towards others, have poor peer relationships, and may have exhibited signs of, or were diagnosed with, ODD in early childhood. Childhood-Onset CD is more likely to lead to antisocial personality disorder or persistent conduct disorder in the adult years.

Teenagers diagnosed with the Adolescent-Onset type do not present any characteristics of conduct disorder before the age of ten. They are less likely to exhibit aggressive behaviors, and are at a decreased risk of developing Antisocial Personality Disorder or to have persistent conduct disorder. Peer relationships are more normal than those diagnosed with Childhood-Onset type.

WHAT DO WE KNOW ABOUT ADHD AND CONDUCT DISORDER?

We know that teens with ADHD are less apt to get into serious trouble than those who have ADHD with comorbid conduct disorder. Children with pure ADHD are at no greater risk for rebellious activities, substance abuse, antisocial personality, etc., than normal children. We know that not all children with ADHD/ODD later develop conduct disorder, although a significant number do. We also know that aggression plays a large role in the development of conduct disorder. So children who display aggressive behavior with ADHD/ODD are at greater risk for comorbid CD.

We also know several other things about teens with ADHD/CD:

- They are at greater risk for developing antisocial personality in adulthood.
- They are at higher risk for using and abusing drugs or alcohol.
- They are at increased risk for more traffic violations and car accidents.
- They often have mothers who are depressed and lack consistency when disciplining their children.
- Their symptoms of conduct disorder are exacerbated (if not engendered) by family environment.
- They are at an increased risk of suicide in adolescence.
- They often have one or more learning disabilities particularly in the areas of reading and language that hinders their ability to verbalize their feelings so they express their frustration and anger by acting out.
- There is a greater occurrence of suspensions and expulsions from school.
- They are at risk for precocious sexual activity.

WHAT TO DO FIRST

At the first sign of extreme inappropriate behavior, parents should immediately do the following:

- seek counseling for the family, the teenager, or both with a competent therapist, preferably a psychiatrist who understands ADHD and how it affects family dynamics
- make sure that all members of the family who have ADHD are being treated with proper medications at therapeutic doses
- reduce marital conflict through counseling
- consider the physical changes that have occurred due to puberty and question whether the teen's medications should be increased or changed
- begin making changes in parenting approaches with the help of a therapist or enroll in a parent training program for difficult teenagers
- join a coalition of parents whose children are also exhibiting acting-out behaviors for assistance and moral support (TOUGHLOVE, or Children and

Adults with Attention Deficit Disorder (CHADD) are examples of such coalitions of parents)

- locate an adult that the teenager respects and likes and enlist his help as a mentor
- become more involved in the teen's activities and spend special time with the teen each day (do not criticize or nag but do show interest, support, and encouragement)
- praise the teen whenever you catch him displaying appropriate behaviors such as doing chores, speaking respectfully to adults, taking responsibility for his actions, etc.
- teach the child how to solve his problems in more healthy and appropriate ways (you will, no doubt, need professional help with this)

Conduct disorder is considered one of the most expensive mental health problems in the United States. According to an article in *The Brown University Child and Teen Behavior Letter,* January 1993, a new form of therapy shows promising results. Under the supervision of specially trained therapists, parents are trained to teach their children how to interact with others. While the therapy requires a long-term commitment from parents, researchers say the results are encouraging. Fifty percent of the teens who participated in the therapy with their parents had no serious behavior problems one year later. In those teenagers whose parents were not involved, almost all were engaged in inappropriate behaviors.

REDUCING THE RISKS

Can we as parents reduce the risk factors for developing ODD and CD? I believe we can. Is it too late to help the teenager who has ODD or CD with ADHD? In most cases it is not, as long as parents are willing to make a commitment to their teens, seek professional intervention, and, if needed, enforce some tough bottom-line solutions to problematic behaviors. Making a commitment means making changes in the way we parent, restructuring the home environment so the chaos and stress are greatly reduced, making sure our teenager is taking medications for the ADHD, and taking the steps we must to break the cycle of severe behavior problems. Teenagers with ADHD with symptoms in the moderate to severe range, including those with ODD and CD, should be taking medications and should be closely monitored by a physician. As you read through the following questions, look carefully and honestly at yourself and your home environment.

Are Your Expectations Realistic?
All parents have idealistic expectations for their children. The problem with these expectations is that they are etched in our minds and hearts. They are based on preconceived ideas of what we expect our child will be. There is a tremendous difference between idealistic expectations and realistic expectations. Parents with realistic expec-

tations accept the teen with ADHD for himself, no matter what his strengths or weaknesses. The teen is loved unconditionally for the unique person he is. High expectations are often difficult to let go of and are terribly unfair to our children. They set them up for failure as they strive to meet approval and fail in your eyes—resulting in lowered self-esteem that can lead to depression. Ultimately, the teen stops trying to gain approval and expresses his frustrations either by withdrawing or through rebellious acts. His I-don't-care attitude is obvious. Unfortunately, when the teen reaches the point of not caring, he has lost a relevant incentive for adhering to society's rules.

Make sure your expectations for your teen are realistic. Be sure you understand adolescent development and how each developmental stage affects a teenager with ADHD. Teens whose parents and teachers expect them to meet age-related responsibilities and develop a feeling of competence but cannot will suffer low self-esteem, depression, and often anger. This depression and anger may be displayed in the form of aggressive or antisocial behavior. Always take into consideration his special needs. Do not expect more than he is capable of giving or achieving.

Is Your Parenting Style Loving but Firm and Consistent?

The way you parent your teen will have a profound effect on her behavior. Discipline strategies that are extremely harsh or inconsistent lead to rebellious behaviors. On the other hand, teenagers who are able to negotiate rules and boundaries with their parents are more apt to abide by the rules because they have had a say in them.

The teen with ADHD must know what the limits are. If rules and boundaries are not defined, she does not know what is expected of her. If rewards and consequences are not immediate and consistent (sometimes she receives a consequence for a specific misbehavior, the next time the same misbehavior is overlooked), the teenager becomes confused and tries to find her limits in different situations through negative behavior.

"My fifteen-year-old daughter has ADHD without hyperactivity and may also have ODD," says Rob Gray, MD, from Tulsa, Oklahoma. "It is hard to differentiate between normal teenage 'individuation' as the psychiatrists call it and true pathologic defiance. In our family, my wife and I and our daughter have all been too hung up on power and control, so our daughter's ODD is as much a parental problem as her problem. The more I learn about appropriate discipline, logical/natural consequences, etc., and apply consistently what I learn, the better our daughter does."

Without established rules and boundaries and consistent discipline, a hostile, defiant teenager—especially one who is not taking medications for the ADHD symptoms—can rapidly develop severe behavior problems. Take a good look at your parenting style and make as many changes as you must. Change your responses, control your anger, and reach out for help. Your teen's future is at stake.

Are You Monitoring Your Teenager?

Teens with ODD and CD must be monitored closely. They do not get into serious trouble when they are supervised, but they can when unsupervised. A survey of four thousand ninth graders found that youth left alone at home after school (or at someone else's house) had an increased incidence of smoking, drinking, drug use, depression, poorer grades, and risk-taking behaviors.

Know where your teen is at all times and who she is with. Monitoring may mean driving by where they say they will be or calling to check on them. If they are going to a party, for instance, call the friend's parents and make sure they will be home to supervise. Offer to help as a chaperone.

Encourage your teens to bring friends to your house when you are home. Establish in-house rules: no drinking, no drugs, no smoking, no closed bedroom doors, etc. Make sure all friends know the rules before they enter the house. Make it clear that if a party is being held in your home, anyone who leaves the house may not come back in. It's easy to sneak outside to smoke a joint or have a beer or two or bring them back into the house.

Are There Problems in Your Marriage?
Marital problems must be addressed. If you and your spouse are always arguing, walking out on each other, or threatening divorce, you must seek professional help immediately. Turn to your church or synagogue, call a psychologist or psychiatrist, but do something. Your teen cannot be exposed to this disharmony. It is simply too much for her to handle with the inner chaos she is already experiencing. If the home environment is not a place where she feels safe, she will act out. If your spouse will not go to counseling, go by yourself. Don't wait to see if marriage problems will subside on their own. You may waste precious time. These children need stability, structure, harmony in the home and a safe place to return each day.

Do You Understand Their Anger?
Managing anger is a major challenge for many individuals with ADHD. Anger develops in response to frustration over the inability to achieve what they know they should be able to do but have so much difficulty accomplishing. Anger also develops in response to the sense of loss of control they feel in their lives. Under this frustration often lurks feelings of helplessness, hopelessness, and fright. Many teens with ADHD wear their emotions on their sleeves. They take every remark and criticism personally and then build on it until it is out of proportion. The hurt can be unbearable, so they build a wall around themselves. When pushed, they lash out in anger as a way of protecting themselves. Anger is bound to occur, but it will build up and become more and more difficult to handle if left on its own. It can also become destructive. Angry teenagers must be taught how to express their feelings in appropriate ways.

Anger is either expressed internally, causing physical problems (ulcers, headaches, high blood pressure, etc.), depression, or both, or it is expressed externally. Research indicates that over 40% of the teens diagnosed with ADHD have problems with anger control. Teens without hyperactivity tend to express their anger internally, whereas teens with hyperactivity tend to display their anger externally. When it is expressed externally, it may be in the form of verbal or physical aggression or acting-out behaviors. Initially, it is directed at the parents in the home, then tumbles out into the classroom or the community. Left on its own, the anger builds and can eventually become explosive. Teens who cannot express their anger appropriately must be taught how to do this. Otherwise, the anger builds up and is released through antisocial behaviors in the community or violent behavior in the home. Help your teen vent anger by talking to someone who understands this anger, through exercising, or spending time alone. Also, make sure that your teen is taking the proper medications for ADHD and any other comorbid condition. (This is sometimes easier said than done. If necessary, set up a contract with your teenager for taking medications.)

Adolescent psychiatric hospitals are full of angry teens, some of whom have ADHD. Behavioral care units have time-out or isolation rooms. Teens use punching bags, hit pillows, write about their feelings in journals, and shred newspaper. Staff and other team members work diligently to teach angry teens appropriate ways to express their feelings.

Some teens have more difficulty than others expressing their anger, regardless of the quality of parenting they have received. Those with certain neurological problems will have more problems handling anger—especially if they have a history of perceptual or learning disabilities.

When confronted with an angry teenager, you must meet her at her level of handling her anger. Recognize the anger because it is real. Tell her it is okay to be angry, but it is not okay to act the anger out in a destructive manner that could hurt others or even herself. Permit her to say what she needs to, even if the language is not appropriate. Do not forbid the expression of anger or overreact to it. Train her to express her feelings through verbalizations or other appropriate forms of expression.

Do You Understand Peer Pressure?

Research studies have shown that teen's relationships with their parents have an impact on peer pressure. Those with strong parental relationships are more likely to choose friends who have similar values. In early adolescence it is imperative for parents to keep tabs on their teens since they are naturally drawn to others who are most like themselves. Be sure you know who your teenager's friends are and what impact they have on her.

Can You Cope with a Difficult Teen?

The ability to cope with a difficult teen's behavior is greatly diminished if parents have difficulties in any of the following areas:

- have ADHD themselves, either undiagnosed or untreated, that gets in the way
- have an unsatisfactory marital relationship (or divorced)
- receive no support from their own parents who could assist but choose not to
- are isolated and alienated from friends and relatives due to the teen's behavior

- lack the time for leisure activities and social pursuits needed to cope with the stress
- have communication and problem-solving skills deficits
- have psychological problems
- face daily depression
- have a substance abuse problem
- have job-related pressures or are unemployed
- have financial difficulties
- have an aging parent or relative living in the home
- have other children in the home with ADHD
- have too many commitments outside the home that takes time away from the family and does not permit the parent to monitor the teenager's activities
- overreact to misbehaviors
- feel threatened by the teenager and lose their cool

Parents who are psychologically or physically disabled, depressed, substance abusers, and so forth, are often unable to provide the structure and consistency needed by the teen. Some parents are so overwhelmed by the hostile, defiant teenager that they may physically or emotionally abuse the teen. Others may have a low tolerance for stress and screaming is the way they deal with problematic behavior. Still others may find that their own needs supersede those of their teenager and are less likely to monitor activities. Substance abusing parents are usually unavailable emotionally and physically for the teen. The impact on the teenager may result in defiance or noncompliance with the rules—signals for attention and support needed by the teen but unavailable from the parent.

Almost 65% of teens with ADHD will meet the criteria for ODD. Of that 65%, approximately 45% percent will eventually meet the criteria for conduct disorder. It is worth noting that parents who are hostile and aggressive themselves may not recognize these traits as unusual in their teens.

The point that needs to be stressed here is that parents who have difficulties and challenges of their own cannot begin to help their teenager until they receive help with their own problems. The intent of this chapter is certainly not to imply that parents are by any means the sole cause of their teen's ODD or CD, because they are not. However, parents can play a role in the development of these disorders. Similarly, it is important to remember that the teen's symptoms interfere in all areas of her life. Such challenges include but are not limited to the following:

- academic problems in school
- repeated failures in the home
- poor interrelationships with family members
- poor peer relationships due to intrusive behavior, immaturity, and social-skill deficits that may lead to socially unacceptable friends or a lack of friends
- an overreaction to situations

- depression, anxiety, or other psychiatric disorders
- poor self-esteem
- low frustration tolerance
- untreated ADHD or irregular use (or no use) of medication when indicated
- lack of professional intervention (educational adjustments in the classroom, psychotherapy, behavior modifications, social-skills training, etc.)

Arthur Robin, PhD, of the Children's Hospital of Michigan, says inattention difficulties make it difficult for the teen with ADHD to attend while attempting to resolve family conflicts, to honor agreements, to follow through on chores and homework assignments, and to handle responsibilities within the home. Parents, on the other hand, often have difficulty differentiating between defiance and inattention. Impulsivity fuels conflicts between the teen and parent, making it difficult for the teen with ADHD to control herself. This only prolongs the confrontation. A low frustration level, an inability to weigh the consequences, and a hot temper, lead to explosive outbursts, frequent arguments, and physical confrontations, according to Dr. Robin. All of these factors place additional stress on family relationships.

Parenting a difficult teenager with ADHD is a serious challenge—one that should not be taken lightly because their future is at risk. Unfortunately, there is little doubt that teens who are born with difficult temperaments, ADHD, and show oppositional and aggressive behaviors at an early age are at greater risk of developing conduct disorder.

Parents who are struggling with a hostile, defiant teenager need to be aware of the factors that play a relevant role in the development of ODD and CD. They must assess themselves, their teen, and the structure of the family, and then work toward finding the necessary solutions to establishing harmony within the family organization.

When a teenager with severe behavior problems does not respond to the parenting strategies outlined here, it may be that the teenager is too far along the path to delinquency, according to James Windell, a practicing psychotherapist and clinical psychologist and the author of *8 Weeks to a Well-Behaved Child*.

Once rebellious activities emerge that parents cannot handle on their own, professional intervention must be sought. It is important to remember that the teen who is exhibiting severe behavior problems is actually making a plea for help. Unfortunately, despite all of our best intentions and efforts, some teenagers develop behaviors that are less than desirable even when the family is basically healthy. The troubled teen with ADHD in a healthy family has the best opportunity to receive help because parents are able to recognize a problem and are willing to work on a solution. Others are not so fortunate.

FIFTEEN

BREAKING THE CYCLE

Rebellious activities such as running away from home and stealing are usually not the first signs that trouble is brewing. Parents of difficult teenagers will tell you that they have ongoing problems with their children for years. In the home they may have faced defiance, hostility, explosive episodes, destruction of property, and noncompliance. In school the child may have been defiant, disruptive in the classroom, and truant. There has been an accumulation of problems over the years, usually beginning as oppositional behavior during the preschool years. If the conduct problems were not addressed effectively at that time, despite repeated attempts to rectify them, you have no doubt watched the troubling behavior escalate through the years.

Acting-out, rebellious teens with ADHD may have been diagnosed at a young age due to severe hyperactivity, impulsivity, and defiance, and placed on medication before they entered school. Some parents have reported taking their child from one doctor to another during childhood in an attempt to seek help with behavior control problems. Often the child and the parents have been in psychotherapy off and on for years. Some parents reached out for help for years knowing their child was headed down the wrong path. These are loving parents who care about their children and are willing to do anything to help them. Although many parents sought help before puberty, the most frequent complaint is that no one really listened or took their concerns seriously and that it wasn't until the child got into serious trouble that their pleas for help were finally heard.

Signs that severe problems are developing usually begin to surface in middle childhood, often between six and eight years of age according to Russell Barkley, PhD, an authority on ADHD. Around this age 30% to 50% of children with ADHD will exhibit some signs of conduct problems. Indications of serious behavior problems in elementary school children include stealing, chronic lying, disrespectful behavior toward authority figures, aggressive behaviors, destruction of property, an I-don't-care attitude, and threats of suicide.

Hostile and defiant teens are difficult to live with. They are often angry and depressed and rarely smile or laugh and appear enraged at the world. Parents often describe these teens as out of it, hyperactive, impulsive, and in need of instant gratification. Adult requests are usually met with noncompliance. Since these teens are often not threatened by authority figures and have a disdain for rules, they frequently engage in rebellious activities and often exhibit violent behavior. Rather than trying to deal with problems or feelings in a constructive manner, they rid themselves of these feelings by acting out. In an attempt to cope with their feelings and frustrations, they may run away from home, stop attending school, display violent behavior in the home, commit petty crimes, or turn to drugs, alcohol, or even suicide. They know of no other way to deal with their frustration and feelings of helplessness.

Most parents who are committed to restructuring the family organization, reassessing their parenting methods, revising their expectations, addressing their own problems (as well as stress and pressure in their lives), and making some tough decisions involving the teen's behavior are usually able to regain parental control. There are no easy solutions for tough problems. Bottom-line solutions are tough actions to deliver, but they may be the only solutions that will break the path of self-destructive behavior the teenager is following.

RUNNING AWAY FROM HOME OR RUNNING TO SOMETHING?

More than one million American teens a year run away from home. These teens are between the ages of twelve and seventeen and half are Caucasian females often younger than fourteen.

Teens who run, do so on purpose. Factors that may prompt the teenager to leave home include chaos in the family structure, poor communication and deficits in problem solving, cognitive distortions, overly protective or controlling parents, unrealistic parental expectations, a lack of limits and consequences, and inconsistent parenting methods. Now add in the symptoms of ADHD and the fact that other family members may have ADHD (or a psychiatric condition), and you end up with many home-based problems.

It is not unusual for teenagers to storm out of the house in a fit of anger and return home a few hours later or the next morning after going to a friend's house. Parents should not be overly concerned with an isolated incident but should be aware that the teenager is signaling attention to a problem within the family organization. When she returns home, in a nonthreatening manner, try to find out what motivated her to run. Ask her to explain exactly what she is running away from. Discuss ways that all family members can work together to improve the situation at home. Despite what some parents may feel, most children who run away do care about their parents. They just feel trapped in the family system.

Most teens return home within a few days, and others (a little under a half million) will return home and leave again and again. Other teens may leave and never return home. Running away is the ultimate breaking away from a family structure that has broken down according to H. Charles Fishman, MD, author of *Treating Troubled Teens.*

What Can Parents Do?

If your teen runs away from home more than once over a few months, counseling is indicated for your teen, your family, or both. The object of such therapy, says Dr. Fishman, ". . . is to keep the parents in their executive position . . . enabling them to present options for the child. The goal is to establish a family system in which the child does not have to run away from home, but can walk away at the appropriate time."

The therapist you choose should be knowledgeable about ADHD and the role it plays in family organization, structure, and relationships. Although there are many mental health professionals, finding the right one for your family is not always easy. Your best sources of information are recommendations you receive from other parents whose children are displaying the same or similar type behaviors. A local CHADD chapter, a support group of parents of children with ADHD, can often provide many good referrals. A school psychologist or guidance counselor may also be sources of referrals. A network such as TOUGHLOVE can also provide helpful information.

Most professionals choose to meet the parents first before meeting with the teenager. As parents, this gives you the opportunity to also interview the therapist. Listen carefully and trust your instincts. Just because your teenager is having problems does not mean your ability to parent is flawed. A good therapist knows this. Finding a good mental health professional for your family is a matter of a good fit. Not all therapists will be a good match for your family.

According to Arthur Robin, PhD, Chief of Psychology at Children's Hospital of Michigan, therapy sessions should address such things as how ADHD interferes with the family structure, teenage independence issues, school problems, peer relationships, the marital relationship, parenting skills, parental expectations, communication and problem-solving skills, and the use of medication if indicated.

A good therapist will also explore the possibility that one or both parents may have ADHD. The therapist will outline goals and strategies for regaining parental control in the home, help the parents establish a bottom line if the teen continues to act out despite their efforts, and address the fears that the parents and teen have (parents fear what action the teen will take if they enforce rules and the teen fears the parental action for breaking the rules). Counseling should include separate sessions with the parents, and individual sessions with the teenager. Sessions with the teenager should address medications; redirecting anger to more acceptable behaviors; coping with depression, anxiety, and low self-esteem; improving academic efficiency; and developing appropriate social skills.

Dr. Fishman also points out that the outlook for lasting changes within the family of a runaway is based on the parents' ability to be both firm and flexible while allowing the teen to be free and make choices. The family must learn to make concessions and find a middle ground that all are comfortable with while establishing rules against specific behaviors.

"Parents must express consistent but flexible attitudes and expectations while emphasizing personal responsibility," says Victor M. Uribe, author of *Therapies that Offer Hope for Hyperactive Children* (*Pediatrics for Parents*, February 1994). He goes on to say that "equally important, parents [must learn] to curb their anger and impatience . . . showing love and support . . . to work through his problems."

The authors of *ToughLove Solutions,* Phyllis York, David York, and Ted Wachtel, stress that not all teens who run away are escaping from difficult home situations. Some teens who run away are actually running to something. The authors refer to these teens as "run-tos" because they are running away to have fun. During the time they are away from the home, they can usually be found at a friend's house.

Parents of a run-to will do just about anything to keep the teen from running away again. The bottom line is that most run-tos seek the stimulation of partying and having a good time. "Most are into drugs and partying, cannot manage their lives at home, school, or work . . . make impulsive decisions, or simply want their own way," say the authors of *ToughLove Solutions*. TOUGHLOVE advocates for a strong coalition with other families involved in TOUGHLOVE groups to decrease the acting-out behaviors of teens.

Members of TOUGHLOVE work with each other's families by brainstorming for possible solutions that will help both the family and the runaway teenager. For instance, a member of TOUGHLOVE may offer to take in a runaway teen from another family until he agrees to meet the conditions established by the parents for re-entry into the home (perhaps a drug rehab program or weekly counseling sessions). The teen must then prove then that she is working on returning to her home and express a willingness to compromise and negotiate. Allowing her to return home without a strong commitment to change does not work. The result will always be the same—another cycle of manipulative conduct.

Parents must determine a bottom line (a residential treatment center, boarding or military school, psychiatric hospital, a move into a foster family, calling the police, etc.). The teen is informed of what will happen the next time she runs, and parents must follow through and deliver the consequences. Parents should also look into the possibility that their teen may be suffering from depression, anxiety, or another psychiatric disorder comorbid with the ADHD. An evaluation or re-evaluation should be requested and medications checked for serious behavior problems being displayed by your teenager.

WHY DO TEENAGERS RUN AWAY FROM HOME?

Most often they leave because of turmoil in the home. Essentially these teens feel that their families are not providing the fundamental encouragement, affection, nurturing, caring, and support they desperately need. Most often, according to Dr. Fishman, parents are facing a "mid-life crisis . . . increasing the vulnerability of the family system . . . [that] frequently stimulates behavior problems for children."

How the Teen Feels

Many teens with ADHD are extremely sensitive individuals—they tend to overly personalize remarks or criticism directed toward them. Their low self-esteem often makes them feel unloved and unlovable. From early childhood they have taken all of the unfavorable things that have happened personally. Often, they are taught not to cry or not to get angry so they eventually shut down. When teens shut down inside because they feel rejected or unloved, they are vulnerable and may run away to escape the chaos of the home or turn to drugs or alcohol. Other teens may display extreme anger or exhibit violent behavior in the home.

VIOLENT BEHAVIOR IN THE HOME

There may be several reasons a teenager with ADHD displays aggressive, violent behavior in the home: undiagnosed and untreated comorbid psychiatric disorders, perceived unfair treatment, inconsistent rules and consequences, little attention and support from parents, cognitive distortions, deficits in communication, and anger resulting from frustration. These factors have a tremendous impact on teenagers with ADHD from the development of oppositional defiant disorder to conduct disorder to truancy to even suicide.

Aggressive behavior is usually an attempt to hurt someone or destroy property. There is no excuse for violent behavior. It is not acceptable and should not be tolerated. A teen who is violent in the home is attempting to exercise control over his parents.

"When a teenager becomes violent in the home, for instance, and pulls out a weapon (knife, hammer, etc.), parents have to make a tough decision," says Stella Francis, PhD, director of the Psychoeducational Development Center in Toledo, Ohio. "If an adult pulled out a weapon, the police would be called in. Parents must do the same. They have to be willing to be tough enough and follow through so the teenager experiences logical consequences. Hopefully because of the lumps that they will encounter, the teenager will begin to come around to the point where they can say to themselves, 'I really do need to do something about my behavior.' This is a very serious situation and must be dealt with accordingly." If your child or teen is threatening you, immediately call 911 and tell them that your teenager is mentally ill and threatening to kill himself or you.

On the other hand, Dr. Francis says, "A teenager with ADHD who behaves this violently may need to have medications changed, or they may need a combination of medications. These children also should be in individual counseling as well as family counseling. Hospitalization may be necessary in extreme cases."

What Can Parents Do?

You can begin by tracking the behavior and the events leading up to the explosive behavior, including what each spouse did to increase or decrease the problem. Save these notes as you may need them later, especially if you need to go to court to seek legal protection from your teen. Put your ego aside because time is valuable. Find a good psychiatrist knowledgeable and trained to understand the mind of an individual with ADHD. A child psychiatrist can not only provide therapy but can also monitor medications. If you have uncertainties about a particular therapist, try to appraise them impartially but expeditiously.

"Truly spectacular rages may mean that there's something more going on," says Dale Hammerschmidt, MD, associate professor of medicine at the University of Minnesota and the senior editor of the *Journal of Laboratory and Clinical Medicine*. "There may be a more complex neurobehavioral disorder than ADHD present, or there may be an additional problem overlayered. Increasingly recognized is something called an 'episodic explosive disorder' in which kids have neurologically-based rages that are almost seizure-like in their suddenness. Such sudden rages may improve on antiseizure medications like Tegretol—even though the EEG and related tests may fail to show clear evidence of a seizure disorder. The idea here is that there may be seizure-like electrical abnormalities in the brain that are on too 'micro' a scale to be picked up by electrodes on the skin. Or it may be that the seizure medicines help for reasons that aren't part of their antiseizure activity. A child [or teenager] with rages that seem to be more than just tantrums should have a comprehensive evaluation [to find out] what's going on."

TRUANCY

Truancy is an absence from school without parental permission. Truant teenagers are usually failing in school. Truant teens with ADHD are at higher risk for using drugs and for delinquent behavior because they usually hang out with other estranged teens, many of whom may be involved in antisocial activities.

If your teen has skipped school more than once over a few months time, he is approaching serious truant behavior that must be dealt with now. Involve the school and do not cover for your teen by calling him in sick (attending or not attending school is the student's responsibility). Some parents may choose to homeschool, which obviously takes a firm commitment on the parent's part. "There are also other options to explore, such as an alternative program like a job training program, preemployment programs, or tutoring," says Dr. Francis. "Parents may have to become creative to find what will work for their son or daughter."

Parents who are dealing with a truant teenager should set strict consequences such as taking away the use of the car and withholding spending money until they have attended school everyday for several months. Teenagers who complain of physical problems (headache, stomachache) or social difficulties at school (they have no friends or others make fun of them) may be depressed. Depression and other emotional problems warrant medical intervention.

Hyperactive teens are three times more likely to have been suspended from school or held back a grade and eight times more likely to be expelled from school or drop out. As many as 17% of teens with ADHD will be classified as truant.

FAMILIES, CRIME, AND JUVENILE DELINQUENCY

"Research published by the National Institute of Justice solidly demonstrates that parents of delinquent children often lack involvement with their children, provide poor supervision, and administer inadequate or erratic discipline," says Anthony Hallett, director of research and information systems at the Ielase Institute. "Almost all symptoms of ADHD can be found as underlying factors in criminal behavior. An unpredictable temper or wide mood swings are almost always found in crimes of violence. The combination of poor academic performance, poor attention practices, the allure of excitement, and the disdain for rules and boundaries all contribute to behavior problems. The inability to meet adult expectations may result in the teen trying to prove himself, leading to illegal activities. Families of delinquent youths appear to have one common characteristic: parental power has deteriorated. The structure of the family has weakened or collapsed often due to such situations as a lack of a father figure or a father who is rarely around to help in the care of the child; parents who are not in agreement as to how to manage the teenager; parental psychopathology in the family; or communication problems between the parent and the teenager."

Setting limits and boundaries and following through with consequences is extremely difficult for some parents because they often fear alienation from their teen, they are unable to present a united front, or their own ADHD gets in their way.

Research by Scott W. Henggeler and associates shows that families of delinquent teenagers who participated in family therapy had a relevant reduction especially in the area of conduct problems. Marital relationships improved, mother-teen interactions improved, and the teen became more involved in the family. Prior to family therapy, delinquents were either detached from the family or engaged in conflict with the parents.

According to H. Charles Fishman, MD, you must zero in on the cause of the disintegration of the "emerging self" in the delinquent teenager, and how it can be repaired. Fishman says that the key to eliminating the delinquent behavior in a teenager is to find a situation where a more capable self can appear (sports, volunteer work, etc.) so when the teen tests delinquent behaviors, he has a reference for "being good." If this context can be found, the teen is not as likely to be completely drawn into delinquent behaviors.

BREAKING AND ENTERING, SHOPLIFTING, STEALING

Without a doubt these are serious illegal activities. Since you cannot be with your teenager every minute of every day, you may not be able to stop these behaviors. However, these activities do infringe on the rights of others, and teens must suffer the consequences of their actions. If you are fortunate (yes, I mean fortunate) the police will step in and deliver those consequences. While you may be tempted to rescue your teen, you must remember that he is responsible for his actions. ADHD cannot, and should not, be used as an excuse. Rescuing teens in trouble only tells them that if they do it again, Mom and Dad will help them out. An encounter with the police may be the only thing that will put an end to his activities. It's certainly better for the teen to be retained in Juvenile Hall than face a prison sentence as an adult. Teenagers involved in such activities must know that antisocial behaviors have consequences, and those consequences must be enforced. They must also know that stealing requires restitution, whether it is monetary or otherwise.

THE SPOKEN UNTRUTH

Lying! Most of us deplore lies but our teens grow up exposed to them, especially if they watch television. "Teach your children to be critical thinkers, to see the false-hoods around them . . . reality vs. nonreality; truth vs. nontruth." says George Lynn, MA. All teens need to be critical thinkers, but this is especially true for teens with ADHD.

Sometimes teens lie because they hear their parents lie (you ask them to tell a phone caller or visitor that you are not home, or you say one thing but really mean something else). Sometimes teens lie because they fear the reaction they will receive from parents. Watch how you phrase questions. Don't put your teen in the position where he feels the need to lie. "Discuss with the teenager what is going on with them, why the need to lie," says Stella Francis, PhD. "If a parent reacts negatively, kids are more apt to lie. Obviously a parent needs to change his or her behavior in such cases."

There is a distinction between purposeful lying and telling something the way we perceive it. This is a problem for some individuals with ADHD. What your teenager says may be totally different from what you witnessed or heard, but it does not necessarily mean that she is lying for the purpose of lying. Because the brain of the ADHDer is wired differently, information is processed differently, sometimes erroneously. For example, ADHDers may miss clues in their surroundings that then leads them to fill in the gaps when relaying information to others. We may know for fact that something did not happen exactly the way we're being told, and it's easy to assume that our teen is deliberately lying. When we realize that this lying is often the result of the ADHD, it's important for parents to help their teens by educating them about their lying. If the pattern in not broken, lying can easily become a habit.

FIRE SETTING

Playing with matches is normal for some teens. Despite repeated warnings, their curiosity gets the best of them. But sometimes the behavior does get out of hand. "Setting fires is normal, but the impulsiveness of ADHD may make the activity hap-pen in places and at times that are more dangerous than the usual kid's exploration of fire," says Dale Hammerschmidt, MD. "I worry, however, when severe impulsive-ness persists when the teen is receiving adequate medication treatment. In some instances, fire setting could be a compulsion rather than just poor impulse control, and thus could be a tip-off that the child has a more complex neurobehavioral disorder than 'just' ADHD. For instance, obsessive-compulsive disorder or Tourette's syndrome may have real compulsions, some of which may be destructive, and may also have ADHD features.

"Two pretty obvious bottom-lines include 1) the child needs a complete evaluation of his current status, both diagnostic assignment and medication strategy, and 2) you must get all firestarting materials out of the house. If you smoke, you've just received an indisputable sign from the Almighty that it's time to quit."

BOTTOM-LINE SOLUTIONS

Bottom-line solutions are tough decisions for parents to make. Sometimes, despite all efforts, hospitalization may be required to break the cycle. It is important to remember, however, that hospitalization, twenty-four-hour-a-day residential treatment care, or intensive day treatment programs are only temporary solutions; the teen still has to learn how to live and function appropriately in the outside world. The advantage of this type of treatment strategy is that the entire family has the opportunity to be removed from the stress in the home on a short-term basis, the cycle between the teenager and the parents is temporarily broken, and the teenager has the opportunity to learn appropriate responses for handling aggressive and rebellious behaviors and anger. Eventually, in most cases, the teen must return to the home setting. If the home environment remains unchanged, the cycle will only continue. While most teenagers with ADHD do not display the types of behaviors described here, the minority that do are in desperate need of help.

AFTERWORD

Shortly after completing *The ADHD Parenting Handbook: Practical Advice for Parents from Parents,* I discovered the ADD Forum on CompuServe. Reading posted messages to and from parents of teenagers with ADHD day after day as they wrote of trying times, the idea for this book gradually developed. From these messages I also discovered the other side of ADHD—the side many parents are unaware of until it is staring them in the face—the acting-out behavioral problems that parents of some teens encounter with great fear.

While certainly not all teens with ADHD engage in rebellious acts, some do, and this needs to be addressed. And so began my adventure through medical literature. I was shocked to learn how much information was available but had not been adequately addressed in other ADHD parenting books.

As the book progressed, I realized how many parents (myself included) did not know or understand the complex nature of ADHD, including the comorbidities that often accompany it. Although I began writing this book thinking that it would be illuminating and Pollyannaish from beginning to end (much like my first book, which is full of concrete advice for parenting younger children), it lead to hardcore problems parents faced that needed bottom-line solutions. It was then that I became fearful—worrying that parents really wouldn't want to read about these tough issues—but I was assured repeatedly by many professionals, including George Lynn, that even if my readers would rather not know about this side of ADHD, they simply had to have the information presented to them.

I have emphasized repeatedly the importance of the family, how they react and respond to the teen with ADHD, and the impact they have on the teen. But my main goal was to impart the message that with proper amounts of support, encouragement, guidance, and a lot of unconditional love from parents (and medication

179

treatment and psychotherapy, when indicated) most teens with ADHD have an excellent chance at succeeding and shining in adulthood.

The point I wish to reiterate is that many of these children simply cannot get through childhood and adolescence without interventions, whether at home or at school, and that responsibility belongs to you, dear parents. You are your teen's best advocate. You are their role models, their light, their strength. Your home must be a safe haven that they can return to daily for an emotional refill.

For most of us, parenting teenagers with ADHD is challenging and often frustrating—I know. But I sincerely believe we can make a difference. So I wish you much success as you continue on your parenting journey, and I implore you to reach out to others, both parents and professionals, to help you guide your teen along the road to adulthood. Whatever you do, don't give up on your teenager.

I am interested in hearing your comments and suggestions. Please feel free to contact me through my publisher by mail: Colleen Alexander-Roberts, Taylor Publishing Company, 1550 West Mockingbird Lane, Dallas, TX 75235. For those of you who have access to CompuServe, you can reach me on the ADD Forum where I am a daily visitor. The ADD Forum is an online support community for parents, adults with ADD, and professionals. Its membership of nearly fifty thousand makes it the largest online ADD support group available. My address on CompuServe is 74347,3231.

RECOMMENDED READING

Barkley, Russell. *Attention Deficit Hyperactivity Disorder.* (New York: Guilford Press, 1990).

Fowler, Rick and Jerilyn Fowler. *"Honey Are You Listening?": How Attention Deficit Disorder Could Be Affecting Your Marriage.* (Nashville, TN: Thomas Nelson, Inc., 1995).

Friel, John and Linda Friel. *Adult Children: The Secrets of Dysfunctional Families.* (Deerfield Beach, FL: Health Communications, Inc., 1988).

Fowler, Mary Cahill. *Maybe You Know My Kid: A Parent's Guide to Identifying, Understanding and Helping Your Child with Attention Deficit Disorder.* (New York: Birch Lane Press, 1990).

Hallowell, Edward M. and John Ratey. *Driven to Distraction: Recognizing and Coping with Attention Deficit Disorder from Childhood through Adulthood.* (New York: Pantheon Books, 1994).

_____ *Answers to Distraction.* (New York: Pantheon Books, 1994).

Hartmann, Thom. *Attention Deficit Disorder: A Different Perception.* (Grass Valley, CA: Underwood Books, 1993).

Hartmann, Thom. *ADD Success Stories: Maps, Guidebooks, and Travelogues for Hunters in this Farmer's World.* (Grass Valley, CA: Underwood Books, 1995).

Quinn, Patricia O. *ADD and the College Student: A Guide for High School and College Students with Attention Deficit Disorder.* (New York: Magination Press, 1994).

Weinhaus, Evonne and Karen Friedman. *Stop Struggling with Your Teen.* (New York: Penguin Books, 1988).

Weiss, Lynn. *Attention Deficit Disorder in Adults: Practical Help for Sufferers and Their Spouses.* (Dallas, TX: Taylor Publishing Co., 1992).

BIBLIOGRAPHY

Alexander, James F. "Defensive and Supportive Communication in Normal and Deviant Families" *Journal of Consulting and Clinical Psychology,* (1973) vol. 14, 223–231.

Alexander-Roberts, Colleen. *The ADHD Parenting Handbook: Practical Advice for Parents from Parents.* Dallas, TX: Taylor Publishing Company, 1994.

American Psychiatric Association: *Diagnosis and Statistical Manual of Mental Disorders,* 4th Edition, Washington, D.C., American Psychiatric Association, 1994.

Anastopoulos, Arthur D., et al. "Parent Training for Attention-Deficit: Its Impact on Parent Functioning." *Journal of Abnormal Child Psychology,* (Oct 1993) vol. 21 no. 5, 581 (16).

Anderson, Carolyn A., Stephen P. Hinshaw, and Cassandra Simmel. "Mother-child Interactions in ADHD and Comparison Boys: Relationship with Overt and Covert Externalizing Behavior, (Attention-deficit hyperactivity disorder)." *Journal of Abnormal Child Psychology,* (April 1994) vol. 22, no. 2, 247(19).

Arbetter, Sandra R. "The Many Faces of Anger." *Current Health 2,* (Jan. 1990) vol. 16, no. 5, 4(6).

"Attention Deficit Disorder: Adding Up the Facts." Published by the Division of Innovation and Development, Office of Special Education and Rehabilitative Services, U.S. Department of Education.

"Attention Deficit Disorder: What Teachers Should Know." Published by the Division of Innovation and Development, Office of Special Education and Rehabilitative Services, U.S. Department of Education.

August, G. and B.D. Garfinkel. "Behavioral and Cognitive Subtypes of ADHD." *Journal of the American Academy of Child and Adolescent Psychiatry,* (1989) vol. 28, 739–748.

Barkley, Russell, et al. "The Adolescent Outcome of Hyperactive Children Diagnosed by Research Criteria: An 8-year prospective follow-up study." *Journal of the American Academy of Child and Adolescent Psychiatry,* (1990) vol. 29, 546–557.

Barkley, Russell. *Attention Deficit Disorder: A Handbook for Diagnosis and Treatment.* New York: Guilford Press, 1990.

"Before It's Too Late: What to Do When Someone You Know Attempts Suicide." Pamphlet: American Association of Suicidology, (July 1, 1991) 1(8).

Bell, Alison. "10 Easy Ways to Make Friends." *Teen Magazine,* (April 1994) vol. 38, no. 4, 48(3).

Bell, Tammy L. "Dysfunctional Parenting Styles." *Addiction and Recovery,* (Jan.–Feb. 1992) vol. 12, no. 1, 12(3).

Berk, Bernice R. "The Dating Game." *Good Housekeeping,* (Sept 1993) vol. 217, no. 3, 192.

Blouin, A.G., M.A. Bornstein, and R.L. Trites. "Teenager Alcohol Abuse Among Hyperactive Children: A Five Year Follow-Up Study." *Journal of Pediatric Psychology,* (1978) vol. 3, 188–194.

Botwick, Libby. "Playing Hookey is Serious Stuff." *Pediatrics for Parents.* (May 1988) vol. 9 no. 5, 8 (1).

Boyd, Ronald T.C. "Improving Your Test-Taking Skills." ERIC Digest Number 101.

Brent, David A., et al. "The Presence and Accessibility of Firearms in the Homes of Adolescent Suicides" *Journal of the American Medical Association,* (1991) vol. 266, no. 21, 2989.

Brown, Ronald T., et al. "Depression in Attention Deficit-Disordered and Normal Children and Their Parents." *Child Psychiatry and Human Development.* (1988) vol. 18, 119–132.

Brown, Thomas. "The Many Faces of ADDs: Basic Types and Comorbidities." Presentation at Sixth Annual CHADD Conference, Oct. 1994.

Bukstein, Oscar G., David A. Brent, and Yifrah Kaminer. "Comorbidity of Substance and Other Psychiatric Disorders in the Adolescent." *American Journal of Psychiatry,* (Sept. 1989) vol. 146, no. 9, 1131(11).

Canter, Lee and Lee Hausner. *Homework Without Tears.* New York: HarperPerennial, 1993.

Cantwell, D.P. "Psychiatric Illness in the Families of Hyperactive Children." *Archives of General Psychiatry.* (1985) vol. 42, 937–947.

"Children with Disabilities: Understanding Sibling Issues." *NICHY News Digest,* (1988). National Information Center for Children and Youth with Disabilities.

Cook, E.H., et al. "Association of Attention-Deficit Disorder and the Dopamine Transporter Gene." *American Journal of Human Genetics.* 1995, 56:993–998.

Cotton, Nancy S. "Discounting Adolescent Angst as Natural Could be Dangerous for Suicidal Teens" *The Brown University Child and Adolescent Behavior Letter* (June 1994) vol. 10, no. 6.

Crumley, Frank E. "Substance Abuse and Adolescent Suicidal Behavior." *JAMA, The Journal of the American Medical Association,* (June 13, 1990) vol. 363, no. 22, 3051(6).

Cutright, Melitta. "Dating: Teen Dating in the 90's." *Redbook,* (March 1991) vol. 176, no. 5, 18(3).

de Wilde, Erik J., et al. "The Relationship Between Adolescent Suicidal Behavior and Life Events in Childhood and Adolescence." *American Journal of Psychiatry,* (Jan. 1992) 1149, no. 1, 45(7).

Deal, James E., Charles F. Halverson, and Karen S. Wampler. "Parental Agreement on Child-rearing Orientations: Relations to Parental, Marital, Family, and Child Characteristics." *Child Development,* (1989), vol.60, 1025–1034.

DeSisto, Michael. *Decoding Your Teenager: How to Understand Each Other During the Turbulent Years.* New York: William Morrow, 1991.

Dodge, Kenneth A. "Nature Versus Nurture in Childhood Conduct Disorder: It is time to ask a different question." *Developmental Psychology,* (1990) vol. 26, no. 5, 698(4).

"Driving-related Risks and Outcomes of Attention Deficit Hyperactivity Disorder in Adolescents and Young Adults: a 3–5 year follow-up survey." *Pediatrics,* (August 1993) vol. 92, no. 2, 212(7).

Durand, V. Mark. *Severe Behavior Problems: A Functional Communications Training Approach.* New York: Guilford Press, 1990.

Ehrman, Jan. "Auto Accident Injuries, Greater for Young Adults with Attention Deficit Disorder." *NIH Healthline,* (Oct./Nov. 1993).

Elkind, D. "Clashes Over Clothes." *Parents' Magazine,* (Sept. 1993) vol. 66, no. 9, 199(1).

_____. "Power Struggles." *Parents' Magazine,* (Oct. 1989) vol. 164, no. 10, 239(1).

_____. "Resist Children's Pressure to Permit Early Dating." *The Brown University Child and Adolescent Behavior Letter,* (Aug. 1993) vol. 9, no. 8, S1(2).

Erlandson, Kelly Madigan. "Guiding Teens' Behavior" *Total Health,* (Feb. 1993) vol. 15, no. l, 56(4).

Evans, Steven. "Helping Asolescents Succeed at School," *Ch.A.D.D.E.R.,* (October 1993).

"Families, Crime, and Juvenile Delinquency." U.S. Department of Justice, National Institute of Justice, Crime File.

Farone, Stephen, et al. "A Family-genetic Study of Girls with DSM-III Attention Deficit Disorder." *American Journal of Psychiatry,* (1991) vol. 148, no. 1, p. 112(6).

Fishman, H. Charles. *Treating Troubled Adolescents: A Family Approach.* New York: Basic Books, 1988.

Gold, Mark S. "Adolescent Suicide and Drugs: Most Prevention Programs Falsely Stress that Suicide can Happen to Anyone." *Addiction and Recovery,* (March/April 1991) vol. 11, no. 2, 15(1).

Goldstein, Sam. "ADHD in the Adolescent Years." *The Ch.A.D.D.E.R. Box.* (June 1993), 1, (7–8).

Goldstein, Sam and Michael Goldstein. *Hyperactivity: Why Won't My Child Pay Attention?* New York: John Wiley and Sons, 1992.

Grace, Nancy C., Mary L. Kelley, and Alyson P. McCain. "Attribution Processes in Mother-Adolescent Conflict." *Journal of Abnormal Child Psychology.* (April 1993) vol. 12, no. 2, 199(13).

Guevremont, David. "Social Skills and Peer Training." *Attention Deficit Hyperactivity Disorder: A Handbook for Diagnosis and Treatment,* Russell Barkley. New York: Guilford Press, 1990.

Hartmann, Thom. *Attention Deficit Disorder: A Different Perception.* Grass Valley, CA: Underwood Books, 1993.

Hallowell, Edward and John J. Ratey. *Answers to Distraction: Attention Disorder in Children and Adults.* New York: Patheon, 1994.

_____. *Driven to Distraction: Attention Disorder in Children and Adults.* New York: Pantheon, 1994.

"Helping Teenagers Face Money Limits." *USA Today* (Magazine) (1993) vol. 122, no. 2578, 8(1).

"Helping Teens Through Adolescence." *Health News,* (June 1994) vol. 12, no. 3(4).

"Help Your Child Improve in Test-Taking." Published by the U.S. Department of Education, Office of Educational Research and Improvement (April 1993).

Henry, Bill, et al. "The Importance of Conduct Problems and Depressive Symptoms in Predicting Adolescent Substance Abuse." *Journal of Abnormal Child Psychology.* (Oct 1993) vol. 21, no. 5, 469(12).

Hinshaw, S.P. "Stimulant Medication and the Treatment of Aggression in Children with Attention Deficits." *Journal of Clinical Child Psychology,* (1991) vol. 20, 301.

_____, et al. "Aggression, Prosocial, and Nonsocial Behavior in Hyperactive Boys: Dose Effect of Methylphenidate in Naturalistic Settings." *Journal of Consulting and Clinical Psychology,* (1989) vol. 57, 636–643.

Holmes, C.T. and K.M. Matthews. "The Effects of Nonpromotion on Elementary and Junior High School Pupils: A Meta-analysis Review of Educational Research." *Review of Educational Research,* vol. 54, 225–236.

Holmes, C.T. "Grade Level Retention Effects: A Meta-analysis of Research Studies." In L.A. Shepard and M.L. Smith (Eds.) *Flunking Grades: Research and Policies on Retention.* London: The Falmer Press, 1989.

Hoy, E., et al. "The Hyperactive Child at Adolescence: Cognitive, Emotional, and Social Functioning." *Journal of Abnormal Child Psychology.* (1978) vol. 6, 311–324.

Ingersoll, Barbara and Sam Goldstein. *Attention Deficit Disorder and Learning Disabilities: Realities, Myths, and Controversial Treatments.* New York: Doubleday, 1993.

Johnson, Valerie and Robert J. Pandina. "Effects of Family Environment on Adolescent Substance Use, Delinquency and Coping Styles." *American Journal of Drug and Alcohol Abuse,* (March 1991) vol. 17, no. 1, 71(18).

Kerkhof, A. J. and F.M. "Suicide and Attempted (Causes of and Treatment for Suicide)." *World Health,* (Mar./Apr. 1994) vol. 47, no. 2, 18(3).

Kernberg, Paulina F. and Saralee E. Chazan. *Children with Conduct Disorder.* New York: Basic Books, 1991.

Klein, Jonathan D., et al. "Adolescents' Risky Behavior and Media Use." *Pediatrics,* (July 1993) vol. 92, no. 1, 24(8).

Leo, John. "Learning to Say No." *U.S. News and World Report,* (June 20, 1994) vol. 116, no. 24, 24(1).

Levy, Janice C. and Eva Y. Deykin. "Suicidality, Depression, and Substance Abuse in Adolescence." *American Journal of Psychiatry,* (Nov. 1989) vol. 146, no. 11, 1462(6).

Lytton, Hugh. "Child and Parent Effects in Boys with Conduct Disorder: A Reinterpretation." *Developmental Psychology,* (Sept. 1990) vol. 26, no. 5, 683(15).

McAnarney, Elizabeth R. and William R. Hendel. "Adolescent Pregnancy and Its Consequences." *JAMA, The Journal of the American Medical Association,* (July 7, 1988) vol. 262, no. 1, 74(4).

McKinney, James D., Marjorie Montague, and Anne M. Hocutt. "Educational Assessment of Students with Attention Deficit Disorder." *Exceptional Children,* (Oct–Nov 1993) vol. 60, no. 2, 125(7).

McLesky, James and Kenneth L. Grizzle. "Grade Retention Rates Among Students with Learning Disabilities." *Exceptional Children,* (1992) vol. 58, no. 6, 548(7).

Marriage, K., et al. "Relationship Between Depression and Conduct Disorder in Children and Adolescents." *Journal of the American Academy of Child Psychiatry* (1986) vol. 25, no. 5, 687.

Martin, Christopher, S., et al. "Aggressivity, Inattention, Hyperactivity, and Impulsivity in Boys at High and Low Risk for Substance Abuse." *Journal of Abnormal Child Psychology,* (April 1994) vol. 22, no. 2, 177(27).

Millstein, S., et al. "Promoting the Healthy Development of Adolescents." *JAMA, The Journal of the American Medical Association,* (March 17, 1993) vol. 269, no. 11, 143(3).

Morrison, J.L. "Adult Psychiatric Disorders in Parents of Hyperactive Children." American Journal of Psychiatry, (1980) vol. 137, 825–827.

Nelsen, Jane, Lynn Lott, and H. Stephen Glenn. *Positive Discipline A to Z: 1001 Solutions to Everyday Parenting Problems.* Rocklin, CA: Prima Publishing, 1993.

O'Leary, K. Daniel and Steven Beach. "Marital Therapy: A Viable Treatment for Depression and Marital Discord." *American Journal of Psychiatry.* (Feb. 1990) vol. 147, no. 2, 183(4).

"101 Ways to Help Children with ADD Learn: Tips from Successful Teachers." Published by the Division of Innovation and Development Office of Special Education and Rehabilitative Services, U.S. Department of Education.

Orbach, Israel. "Familial and Intrapsychi Splits in Suidical Adolescents." *American Journal of Psychotherapy,* (July 1989) vol. 43, no. 3, 356(12).

Payer, Lynn, et al. "Quicker Fixer Uppers." *American Health: Fitness of Body and Mind,* (1991) vol. 10, no. 8, 43(8).

Poplin, M. "The Reductionistic Fallacy in Learning Disabilities: Replicating the Past by Reducing the Present." *Journal of Learning Disabilities,* vol. 21, 389–400.

Phelen, Thomas W. *All About Attention Deficit Disorders: A Comprehensive Guide.* Glen Ellyn, IL: Child Management, Inc., 1992.

Pihl, Robert O. and Jordon B. Peterson. "Attention-deficit Hyperactive Disorder, Childhood Conduct Disorder, and Alcoholism." *Alcohol Health and Research World,* (Winter 1991) vol. 15, no. 1, 25(7).

Plizka, Steven R. "Attention-deficit Hyperactivity Disorder: A Clinical Review." *American Family Physician,* (1991) vol. 43, no. 4, 1267(9).

"The Potentially Suicidal Student in the School Setting." *Pediatrics,* (Sept. 1990) vol. 86, no. 3, 481(3).

Price, J.M. and K.A. Dodge. "Reactive Proactive Aggression in Childhood Relations to Peer Status and Social Context Dimensions." *Journal of Abnormal Child Psychology,* vol. 17, 455.

"Questions Often Asked About Special Education Services." Published by NICHY, The National Information Center for Children and Youth with Disabilities, 1993.

Rey, Joseph M. "Oppositional Defiant Disorder." *American Journal of Psychiatry,* (Dec. 1993) vol. 150, 12, 1769(10).

Ringdahl, Erika Nolph. "The Role of the Family Physician in Preventing Teenage Pregnancy." *American Family Physician,* (May 1992) vol. 45, no. 5, 2215(6).

Robin, Arthur. "Training Families with ADHD Adolescents." *Attention Deficit Hyperactivity Disorder,* Russell Barkley. New York: Guilford Press, 1990.

Robin, Arthur and Sharon L. Foster. *Negotiating Parent-Adolescent Conflict.* New York: Guilford Press, 1989.

Roizen, Nancy J., et al. "Adaptive Functioning in Children with Attention-Deficit Hyperactivity Disorder." *Archives of Pediatrics and Adolescent Medicine,* (1994) vol. 148, 1137–1141.

Rosen, Margery D. "Teens and Money." *Ladies Home Journal,* (Sept. 1991) vol. 108, no. 9, 138.

Rotheram-Borus, Mary J. "Suidial behavior and Risk Factors Among Runaway Youth." *American Journal of Psychiatry,* (1993) vol. 150, no. 1, 103(5).

Rowe, David C. *The Limits of Family Influence: Genes, Experience, and Behavior.* New York: Guilford Press, 1994.

Samalin, Nancy. "The Right Way to Discipline: Get Your Point Across without Saying a Single Word." *Parents' Magazine,* (July 1994) vol. 69, no. 7, 48(3).

"Sexuality Education for Children and Youth with Disabilities." *NICHY News Digest,* (1992) vol. 1, no. 3 National Information Center for Children and Youth with Disabilities.

Shore, William B. "The Family Physician's Role in Keeping Parents Involved in their Adolescents' Lives." *American Family Physician,* (Feb. 1, 1994) vol. 49, no. 2, 327(2).

Silver, Larry B. *The Misunderstood Child.* New York: McGraw-Hill, 1984.

Schroepfer, Lisa. "Flunking Fails As a Solution: Repeating a Grade can Actually Hurt a Student Who's in Trouble at School." *American Health: Fitness of Body and Mind,* (1990) vol. 9, no. 9, 84(1).

Shamoo, Tonia K. and Philip G. Patros. *Helping Your Child Cope with Depression and Suicidal Thoughts.* New York: Lexington Books, 1990.

Stein, Mark A., et al. "Adaptive Skill Dysfunction and ADD/ADHD." *Journal of Child Psychology and Psychiatry,* (in press) (1995), vol. 36, no. 4, 665–670.

Steinberg, L. and A. Levine. *You and Your Adolescent: A Parent's Guide for Ages 10–20.* New York: HarperCollins, 1990.

Stiffman, Arlene Rubin. "Suicide Attempts in Runaway Youths." *Suicide and Life-Threatening Behavior,* (Summer 1989) vol. 19, no. 2, 147(13).

Strayhorn, Joseph M. *The Competent Child,* New York: Guilford Press, 1988.

"Suicide in Young People." Pamphlet by: American Association of Suicidology, (Jan. 1991) 1(9).

"Teaching Children and Youth About Sexuality." *NICHY News Digest* (1992) vol. 1, no. 3. National Information Center for Children and Youth with Disabilities.

"Transition Services in the IEP." Published by NICHY, National Information Center for Children and Youth with Disabilities, (1993) vol. 3, no.1.

"Treatment for Conduct Disorder Needs Long-term Parental Role." *The Brown University Child and Adolescent Behavior Letter,* (Jan. 1993) vol. 9, no. 1, 4(1).

Uribe, Victor M. "Therapies that offer Hope for Hyperactive Children." *Pediatrics for Parents,* (Feb. 1994) 2(2).

Van Ost, William C. and Elaine Van Ost. *Warning: A Parent's Guide to In-Time Intervention in Drug and Alcohol Abuse.* New York: Warner Books, 1988.

Varela F. "On Observing Natural Systems." *Co-evolution Quarterly*, (1966) vol. 10, 26–31.

Wagner, Barry M. and Patricia Cohen. "Adolescent Siblings' Differences in Suicidal Symptoms: the role of the parent-child relationships." *Journal of Abnormal Child Psychology*, (June 1994).

Webster-Stratton, C. and M. Hammond. "Maternal Depression and its Relationship to Life Stress, Perceptions of Child Behavior Problems, Parenting Behaviors, and Child Conduct Problems." *Journal of Abnormal Child Psychology*, (1988) vol. 16, 299–315.

Weiss, G. and L. T. Hechtman. *Hyperactive Children Grown Up*. New York: Guilford Press, 1986.

Wendell, James. *8 Weeks to a Well-Behaved Child*. New York: Macmillian Publishing, 1994.

What Works: Schools Without Drugs. Booklet, United States Department of Education, 1992.

"Which Family Factors are Related to Crime?" U.S. Department of Justice, National Institute of Justice, Crime File.

York, Phyllis, David York, and Ted Wachtel. *ToughLove Solutions*. New York: Bantam Books, 1985.

"You Can Help Your Adolescent in the Search for Identity." *The Brown University Child and Adolescent Behavior Letter*, (March 1994) vol. 10, no. 3, S1(1).

Zentall, Sydney S. "Research on the Educational Implications of Attention Deficit Hyperactivity Disorder." *Exceptional Children*, (Oct.–Nov. 1993) vol. 60, no. 2, 143(11).

Zylke, J.W. "Characterizing Healthy Adolescent Development: Distinguishing it From Possible Disturbances." *JAMA, The Journal of the American Medical Association*, (Aug. 18, 1989) vol. 262, no. 7, 880(2).

INDEX

A

Abortion, 139

ADD Forum, 107, 179, 180

Addiction, 16, 134

Adoption, 149

Adrenaline, 26

Advantageous qualities, 8, 35, 45, 53, 109

Advertising, 136

Advice, 76

Aggression
  alcoholism and, 137
  conduct disorder and, 160, 161
  hyperactivity and, 157
  inappropriate, 85
  parental, 166
  paternal, 104
  unrealistic expectations and, 163
  violent, 173–74

AIDS (disease), 140, 146, 147

Alan Guttmacher Institute, 139

Alarm timepieces, 82, 121

Alcohol use, 24
  conduct disorder and, 137
  driving and, 136, 146
  juvenile, 131, 132, 135–36

maternal, 99
  suicide and, 151

Allergies, 24–25

Allowances, 61–62, 73

American Association of Suicidology, 150

American Psychiatric Association, 10, 156

Americans with Disabilities Act, 1

Amphetamines, 16, 22

Anger
  expression of, 164–65
  family dynamics and, 98
  in family meetings, 68
  nonnegotiable rules and, 136
  ODD and, 157
  parental management of, 55, 108, 159
  unrealistic expectations and, 163
  word choice and, 78

Antidepressants, 19–20, 99

Antipsychotic drugs, 20

Antisocial Personality Disorder, 160–61

Anxiety, 19, 76, 172

Anxiety disorders, 94, 93–94, 95

Arrhythmias, 23

Assessment, 17, 123
Assignment notebooks, 117
Attention deficit disorder, 2, 6, 100
Attention problems, 31–32, 167
Automobile accidents, 136
Automobile use
    cost-response arrangement for, 73
    curfew rules and, 66
    dating and, 145
    drinking and, 136, 146
    negotiated rules for, 57–59
    study habits and, 115
    "unfair" use of, 46

B
B vitamins, 24
Barkley, Russell A., 29, 98, 99, 104,
    137, 169
Bedrooms, 83
Behavioral changes, 135, 151
Behavioral problems, 5, 94
    in early adolescence, 43
    identity development and, 40
    marital discord and, 79
    peer relationships and, 42
    truancy and, 174
    in young children, 169–70
Behavioral rules, 49–50
    for dating, 145–46
    drug problems and, 134
    establishment of, 56–57
    fears associated with, 171
    follow-through in, 80, 81
    negotiable, 51–52, 57–60, 62, 67–68,
        159
    nonnegotiable, 136
    oppositional behavior and, 163–64
    overprotection and, 79–80
    personal values and, 133
    relaxation of, 65–67
    sex difference and, 137
Behavioral therapy, 23
Berk, Bernice R., 41
Biofeedback, 27–28

Bipolar disorder, 20, 93
Birth control, 139, 140, 143, 146
Blood pressure, 20, 23, 27
Borrowing, 83
Bowman, Janie, 114
Boys, 5–6, 8
    dating by, 145
    drinking by, 137
    in early adolescence, 43
    ODD in, 157
    premarital sexuality and, 140, 146
    runaway, 152
Brain
    cell wall function in, 24
    electrical abnormalities in, 174
    endorphins and, 26, 27
    information processing in, 176
    laughter and, 106
    limbic/cortical balance in, 7
    metabolic abnormality of, 4
Breathing, 107
Brown, Thomas E., 3

C
Cady, Louis B., 4, 99, 104, 110
Caffeine, 25
Cardiac arrhythmias, 23
Cardiovascular system, 27
Career choices, 109, 126
Cassell, Carol, 140
Catapres, 20
Causation, 4–5
Cerebral cortex, 7
Child psychiatrists, 100, 174
Children and Adults with Attention
        Deficit Disorders
    (organization), 11, 100, 104, 107,
        162, 171
Choices, 70
Choline, 24
Chores, 59–60, 61, 63, 80–81
Citric acid, 25
Clonidine, 20
Coaches, 60

Cognitive skills, 43, 104, 139
Cohen, Patricia, 152
College Educational Testing Service, 127
Color codes, 117, 120
Commercials, 136
Communication, 55, 97, 105, 105–6, 152–53
Comorbidities, vi, 30, 91–95
 diagnosis of, 3
 genetic studies and, 5
 running away and, 172
Compliments, 66, 71, 73
Compromises, 68
Compulsions, 96, 177
CompuServe (on-line service), 107, 179, 180
Computer software, 114
Conduct disorder, 5, 10, 94, 155–68
 alcoholism and, 137
 family dynamics and, 98
 risks associated with, 91–92
 substance abuse and, 95
 suicide and, 150
Confrontations
 escape technique and, 77
 family dynamics and, 98, 167
 parental response to, 52, 81, 158
 reduction of, 63
 selection of, 54
 word choice and, 78
Contraception, 139, 140, 143, 146
Contracts, 71–73
Cost response, 73
Council for Exceptional Children, 125
Counseling, xi, 23–24, 171, 174
Creativity, xii, 2, 8
Crews, Bill, 54
Criminal behavior, vi, 83, 94, 103, 175–76
Criminal proceedings, 128
Criticism, 54–55, 56
Cross-generational coalitions, 78–79
Curfews, 62, 66

D
Daily calendars, 117
Daily evaluation, 107
Daily reminders, 106
Dangerous behavior, 31, 135, 151
Dating, 144
Death, 149, 152
Decision-making, 52
Decongestants, 25
Depression
 anger and, 165
 chronic, 92–93
 maternal, 5–6, 99, 161
 medication and, 14, 16, 19
 parental, 100
 running away and, 172
 suicide and, 149, 150, 151, 152
 truancy and, 175
 unrealistic expectations and, 163
 withdrawal and, 43, 86
Despair, 149, 150
Developmental stages, 42–44
Dexedrine, 21–22
Diagnosis, 3–4, 10–11
Discipline, 65–85, 127–28
Dominating parenting, 50
Dopamine, 5
Drop-outs, 110
Drug abuse, 16, 83, 131–35, 151
Drug Enforcement Agency, 18
Due process protections, 127–28
Durand, V. Mark, 77

E
Early adolescence, 42
Edison, Thomas Alva, 10
Elementary school children, 169–70
Elkind, David, 49, 50
Elliott, Paul, 2, 110
Emotional development, 141
Employment, 67
Endorphins, 26, 27
Environmental influences, 149, 152, 155, 157, 159

Ephedrine, 24, 25
Episodic explosive disorder, 174
Escape technique, 77
Essay tests, 121–22
Exercise, 26–27, 107, 158
Expectations, 53
Expulsion (schools), 127–28
Extended families, 101
Extracurricular activities, 60, 87
Eye contact, 87

F
Failure, 54, 56, 74, 77, 107
Families
    addictions and, 134
    behavioral impacts on, 56
    decision-making in, 52
    delinquency and, 175
    dynamics of, 97–108
    dysfunctional, 45, 94, 149, 171, 173
    extended, 101
    histories of, 91
    hospitalization and, 177
    meetings of, 68–69
    ODD and, 157
    oppositional behavior and, 155,
        167–68
    parental traps and, 78–80
    teen sexuality and, 140, 142
    trips by, 52–53, 85
    united front in, 55
Fathers, 103–4
Fatigue, 16
Fatty acids, 24
Federal courts, 128
Federal laws, 1, 122, 125, 128
Feingold Diet, 25
Filtered rebound, 22
Fire setting, 177
Fishman, H. Charles, 149, 171, 172,
    175–76
Food additives, 24–25
"Forgetters," 118–19
Forgiveness, 56
Foster, Sharon L., 78–79, 80

Francis, Stella, 149, 173, 174, 176
Franklin, Benjamin, 10
Frontal lobes, 4

G
Genetic factors, 4–5, 91
Girls, 5–6, 8
    dating by, 145
    in early adolescence, 43
    ODD in, 157
    pregnant, 137, 139
    premarital sexuality and, 140, 144,
        146
    runaway, 153, 170
Global control, 24, 28
Gold, Mark S., 151
Goldstein, Sam, 3
Grandmother's rule, 73
Grandparents, 101
Gray, Rob, 163
Grounding, 69–70
Growth retardation, 16
Guanfacine, 20
Guevremont, David, 86

H
Haiti, 110
HALL Program, 114
Hallowell, Edward, 5
Hammerschmidt, Dale, 174, 177
Handwriting, 95, 121
Hartmann, Thom, vii, xii, 8, 10
Hemingway, Ernest, 10
Henggeler, Scott W., 175
Herbal preparations, 24, 26
High blood pressure, 20, 23, 27
High-risk behavior, 31, 135, 151
High school, 126, 131, 135
HIV infection, 147
Hoffman, Heinrich, 3
Holmes, C.T., 110
Homeschooling, 113–14, 174
Homework, 32, 115–19, 129
Hopelessness, 149, 150
Hospitalization, 165, 174, 177

Household chores, 59–60, 61, 63, 80–81
Humor, 14, 106
Hunter theory, xii, 8
Hyperactivity, 33
    anger and, 165
    emotional expression and, 149
    fatty acids and, 24
    oppositional behavior and, 157, 159
    schooling and, 175
    symptoms of, 11
Hypertension, 20, 23, 27

I
"I" statements, 73–74
Identity formation, xiii, 39–47
Impulsivity, 11, 31, 144–45, 150, 157
Incompetence, 55
Individualized Educational Programs,
        111, 113, 122–25, 126
Individuals with Disabilities Education
        Act, 1, 122, 123
Individuation, xiii, 39–47
Information sources, 106–7
"Insisters," 118–19
Insomnia, 18–19, 20, 33
Instant gratification, 32–33
Intelligence, 2, 30
    A mode brain function and, 26
    low, 20
    school achievement and, 95, 110
    treatment goals and, 13, 14
Invisible disabilities, 42

J
Jaffer, Susan, 114
Jobs, 67
Judgment, vi
Junior high school, 126
Juvenile courts, 128
Juvenile delinquency, 175–76

K
Katz, Stephen, 156–57
Kinsey Institute, 139

L
Landau, Carol, 6
Language disorders, 43, 97, 161
Late adolescence, 44
Laundry, 83
Learning disabilities, 5, 13, 95, 122, 161
Lecturing, 76–77
Legal rights, 122–23, 127–28
Leniency, 50–51
Listening skills, 87
Lithium, 20
Litman, Robert E., 151
Locke, John, 3
Logical consequences, 74
Lott, Lynn, 51
Love, 38, 54
    firm parenting and, 51
    ODD and, 160
    premarital sexuality and, 140
    realistic expectations and, 163
Lying, 176–77
Lynn, George T., 179
    on ADHD, 7–8
    on negotiation, 159
    on ODD, 157, 158
    on organizational skills, 33–34
    on parental stress, 98, 107–8
    on social isolation, 102

M
Ma-Huang, 24, 26
Manipulation strategies, 75
Marijuana, 132
Marital conflict, 5
    child gender and, 6
    differential parenting response and,
        104
    oppositional behavior and, 157, 164
    teen rebellion and, 79, 102–3
Mass media, 132, 133, 144, 147
Matthews, K. M., 110
Medical tests, 17
Medications, vi, xi, xii, 17–23
    adult use of, 6
    anger and, 165

biofeedback and, 28
exercise and, 27
family dynamics and, 103, 105
grandparent challenges to, 101
indications for, 17
limitations of, 4, 15
nonprescription, 25–26
overdoses of, 25
performance fluctuation and, 34
psychotherapy obviated by, 23
resistance to, 14, 163
self-administered, 99–100
side effects of, 18, 20, 21, 23, 24
social skills and, 89
study habits and, 115
substance abuse and, 16, 137
violence and, 174
Menstruation, 141
Mental disorders, 5, 11, 91, 150
Mental health professionals, 100, 171,
    174
Metabolic abnormalities, 4
Middle adolescence, 43–44
Midlife crises, 103, 173
Mineral supplements, 24
Mistakes, 54, 56, 74, 77, 107
Mitral valve prolapse, 23, 27
Monitoring, 164
Monoamine oxidase inhibitors, 20
Mood disorders, 92–93
Moral values, 132–33, 141, 143, 144
Mothers, 5–6, 98, 99, 103–4, 161
Multiple-choice tests, 121

N
Nagging, 76–77
National Guidelines Task Force, 141–42,
    143
National Institute of Justice, 175
National Organization for Children and
    Youth with Disabilities, 125
Natural phenomena, 8
Nausea, 14
Neglect, 50

Negotiation, 51–52, 57–60, 62, 67–68,
    159
Nelsen, Jane, 51
Nelson, Carla, 113–14
Neurobiological malfunction, 5, 165,
    174, 177
Niacin, 24
Nicotine, 25
Night terrors, 20
Nocturnal emissions, 141
Noncompliance, 55, 68, 99, 166
Notetaking, 115
Notewriting, 70–71
Nutritional supplements, 24

O
Obsessive-compulsive disorder, 94, 95,
    177
Oil of evening primrose, 24
Oppositional defiant disorder, 5, 10, 94,
    98, 155–68
Organizational skills, 33–34, 104

P
Panic disorder, 93–94
Part-time jobs, 67
Pasch, Bruce A., 4, 35
Patience, 53
Peck, Michael L., 151
Peer relationships, 33, 85–89
    conduct disorder and, 161
    in early adolescence, 42–43
    extracurricular activities and, 60
    grounding and, 70
    identity development and, 41
    in middle adolescence, 43
    misbehavior and, 42
    parental relationships and, 165
    resistance to, 146–47
    sexuality and, 143, 144
    substance abuse and, 132, 133
    undesirable, 89, 144–45
Perfectionism, 107
Personal appearance, 40

Personal organization, 33–34, 104
Personal rights, 160
Personal safety, 151
Personal values, 132–33, 141, 143, 144
Personality change, 151
PET scanners, xi
Phelan, Thomas, 8
Physical development, 42, 141, 143, 144
Physical examinations, 17
Physical exercise, 26–27, 107, 158
Physical problems, 135, 165
Picking up, 84
Plizka, Steven R., 4
Positive qualities, 8, 35, 45, 53, 109
Positive reinforcements, 66, 71, 73
Possessions, 151
Postsecondary education, 127
Potassium, 20
Pregnancy, 136, 139
Prevalence, 8
Privacy, 40, 83
Privilege removal, 74
Proactive parenting, 136–37, 157
Problem-solving skills, 55, 103
Procrastination, 32
Protectiveness, 39, 79–80
Pseudoephedrine, 24
Psychiatric disorders, 5, 11, 91, 150
Psychiatric hospitals, 165
Psychological tests, 17
Psychotherapy, xi, 23

R
Rape, 144, 146
Ratey, John, 5
Reading, 115–16, 161
Realistic expectations, 108, 163
Rehabilitation Act, 1, 122
"Rejectors," 118
Responsibility, 32, 41, 65–66, 81–82
Retention (schools), 110
Richwood Pharmaceutical Company, 21
Rights, 122–23, 127–28, 160

Ringdahl, Erika Nolph, 139
Risk factors, 162
Risky behavior, 31, 135, 151
Ritalin, 16, 22–23, 85
Robin, Arthur L., 78–79, 80, 167, 171
Robinson, Janet, 111–12, 117
Role modeling, 55
Runaways, 152, 170–73

S
School assignments, 32, 115–19, 129
School performance
    drinking and, 136
    drug use and, 135
    extra credit work and, 111
    extracurricular activities and, 60
    fatty acids and, 24
    medication and, 14
School phobia, 93
School tests, 110, 115, 120–22, 124, 127
Schooling, 99–129
    absence from, 174–75
    attention problems and, 31
    family dynamics and, 99
    lateness to, 74, 82–83
    learning disabilities and, 95
    medication and, 22
    ODD and, 159
    organizational skills and, 33
    sexuality education and, 140–41
Selective Serotonin Re-uptake Inhibitors, 19
Self care, 106
Self-destructive behavior, 92
Self-esteem, 30
    conduct disorder and, 160
    grounding and, 70
    invisible disabilities and, 42
    nurture of, 45, 46
    peer comparison and, 41–42
    premarital sexuality and, 145
    running away and, 173
    social isolation and, 88
    special interests and, 67

substance abuse and, 137
unrealistic expectations and, 163
Self-medication, 99–100
Self-monitoring, 31, 34–35, 157
Self-paced instruction, 114
Self-talk, 108
Selye, Hans, 105
Separation-individuation, xiii, 39–47
Serenity prayer, 106
Sex Information and Education Council
  of the U.S., 140
Sexuality, 139–47
Siblings, 102, 142, 152
Sierra Leone, 110
Sleep aids, 99
Sleep disorders, 18–19, 20, 33
Smith Kline Beecham (firm), 21
Snyder, Mark, 32, 76, 91, 101, 103, 106
Social attention, 77
Social isolation, 43, 85–86, 102, 151
Special education, 122, 123–26
"Speeders," 118
SQ3R Method, 116
Squire, Mary, 97, 112–13
State constitutions, 127
State laws, 125–28
Stealing, 83
Stein, Mark A., 4–5
Stepfamilies, 79
Stimulants, 16, 18
  cardiovascular function and, 27
  counterindicated, 19
  in nonprescription drugs, 25–26
  relative effectiveness of, 20
  school performance and, 110
  social relationships and, 85
  Vitamin B6 and, 24
Stimulation needs, 34
Stress
  depression and, 99
  family dynamics and, 97, 99, 177
  low tolerance for, 166
  management of, 105–8

ODD and, 158
siblings and, 102
Study skills, 15, 115–19
Substance abuse, 95, 131–37
  medication and, 16, 137
  parental, 100, 166
  suicide and, 149, 151
Sudafed, 24
Suicide, vi, 149–53
Suspension (schools), 127–28
Symptoms, 30–35

T
Tachycardia, 23
Tardiness, 74, 82–83
Teachers
  death preoccupation and, 152
  expectations of, 109
  homeschooling and, 114
  letters to, 111–13
  meetings with, 128, 129
  proximity to, 119
Tegretaol, 174
Telephone privileges, 59, 70, 84, 115
Tenex, 20
Testosterone, 105
Textbooks, 116, 117–18, 119–20
Therapy, 3, 13–28
Thought life, 46, 77, 106
Tics, 16, 20, 95
Time
  awareness of, 13–14, 34, 104, 121
  management of, 24, 60, 117, 120
Timepieces, 82, 116, 121
Tobacco use, 24, 25, 132
TOUGHLOVE (organization), 162, 171,
  172
Tourette's syndrome, 16, 20, 95, 177
Transition planning, 126–27
Triangulation, 79
Tricyclic antidepressants, 19, 20
Truancy, 174–75
Tutoring, 111

Twelve-step programs, 134

U
University of Chicago, 4–5
Uribe, Victor M., 172
U.S. Constitution, 127
U.S. Department of Education, 131,
  132–33
U.S. Drug Enforcement Agency, 18
U.S. National Institute of Justice, 175
U.S. Supreme Court, 127–29

V
Van Ost, Elaine and William C., 131
Video tapes, 114
Violent behavior, 173–75
Vision tests, 17

Vitamin supplements, 24, 25
Vocational goals, 109, 126

W
Wachtel, Ted, 172
Wagner, Barry M., 152
Waterman, Millie, 146
Wilder, Brenda, 156
Windell, James, 54, 167
Wright, Pamela Darr, 30
Written assignments, 116–17
Written contracts, 71–73
Written notes, 70–71
Wymer, Heidi, 42–43

Y
York, David and Phyllis, 172